THE WISDOM OF THE

LOTUS SUTRA

A DISCUSSION

VOLUME IV

EXAMINING CHAPTER 16:
THE LIFE SPAN OF THE THUS COME ONE

Daisaku Ikeda

Katsuji Saito • Takanori Endo • Haruo Suda

World Tribune
Press

Published by
World Tribune Press
606 Wilshire Blvd.
Santa Monica, CA 90401

© 2011, 2002 by the Soka Gakkai

ISBN 978-0915678-72-3

Design by Gopa & Ted2
Cover image © Photodisc

10 9 8 7 6 5 4

Library of Congress Cataloging-in-Publication Data

The Wisdom of the Lotus Sutra : a discussion : /
   Daisaku Ikeda... [et al].
     p. cm.
     Includes index.
     ISBN: 0-915678-72-1 (v. 4 : alk.paper)

     1. Tripitaka. Sutrapitaka.
Saddharmapundarikasutra — Criticism.
interpretation, etc. I. Ikeda, Daisaku.

BQ2057.W57 2000   294.3'85—dc21
                     00-011670

Table of Contents

PART III: "THE LIFE SPAN
OF THE THUS COME ONE": *The Eternity of Life*

Editor's Note

This book is a series of discussions among SGI President Daisaku Ikeda, Soka Gakkai Study Department Chief Katsuji Saito and vice chiefs Takanori Endo and Haruo Suda. It was first serialized in English starting with the April 1995 issue of *Seikyo Times* (now *Living Buddhism*).

The following abbreviations appear in some citations:

✦ GZ, page number(s) refers to the *Gosho zenshu*, the Japanese-language compilation of letters, treatises, essays and oral teachings of Nichiren Daishonin.

✦ LSOC, page number(s) refers to *The Lotus Sutra and Its Opening and Closing Sutras*, translated by Burton Watson (Tokyo: Soka Gakkai, 2009).

✦ OTT, page number(s) refers to *The Record of the Orally Transmitted Teachings*, translated by Burton Watson (Tokyo: Soka Gakkai, 2004).

✦ WND-1, page number(s) refers to *The Writings of Nichiren Daishonin*, vol. 1 (WND-1) (Tokyo, Soka Gakkai, 1999) and vol. 2 (WND-2) (Tokyo: Soka Gakkai, 2006).

PART I

*"The Life Span of the
Thus Come One" Chapter:*

TO LEARN ABOUT DEATH IS
TO LEARN HOW TO LIVE

1 An Irrepressible Zest for Life— the Spirit of the "Life Span" Chapter

Katsuji Saito: Recently, much attention has been focused on training that prepares people for the inevitability of death. Participants in these workshops and seminars engage in various exercises, for example, role-playing in which they are told they only have six months to live. They are then asked to decide how they would spend those final six months. Another exercise might be to have people rank the three most important things to them in life. What these techniques seem to suggest is that thinking about death involves a refocusing on life.

Takanori Endo: It seems that in Europe and the United States, these seminars are also included in the curriculum of many schools. I understand there is even a program for elementary school students.

In Japan, too, given the unprecedented "graying" of society, it seems that more attention is being paid nowadays to issues of aging and death. All the same, I think that far too few people reflect on death as an issue that involves them personally.

Daisaku Ikeda: In life, nothing is more certain than the fact that one will some day die. Everything else is indefinite and subject to change; death alone is a fact of eternal certainty.

And yet, people try to turn away from this most certain of all things. While it may be true that, as the Japanese saying goes, "You cannot gaze directly at the sun or at death," the lives of those who lack a sound understanding of life and death are like rootless grass. It is certain that without a perspective on death, one cannot lead a stable and sure-footed life.

Haruo Suda: I think that to avert one's eyes from death is comparable to averting one's eyes from his or her true self. Incidentally, I notice that young people these days seem to be increasingly interested in learning about their past lives. One psychiatrist theorizes that this is because today's youth, finding it difficult to ground their identity in their present self, are seeking to discover roots in the past.[1]

Ikeda: That may be so. Superficially, such a tendency might seem like nothing more than a passing fad. But on a deeper level, it may well signify that people yearn for a firmer foundation on which to base their lives.

One of the more salient characteristics of modern civilization has been treating death as taboo and not to be discussed. The current boom in seminars and workshops about death the world over suggests that this tendency is rapidly changing. People today earnestly seek a clear-sighted understanding of life and death. I sense a passionate desire to learn about the mystery of life.

A Buddhist Movement To Learn About Life and Death

Suda: I feel we have truly begun making our way down the runway toward the twenty-first century, the century of life.

Ikeda: From the standpoint of helping people learn about life and death, I think we can say that the SGI study movement is on society's cutting edge.

Saito: Yes. Through our study movement, both young and old are continually deepening their understanding of the Buddhist view of life and death. For instance, I heard about an eighty-year-old grandmother who took the essay exam in Japan recently for the rank of professor in the Soka Gakkai. The theme she chose for her essay was life and death.

I understand that afterward she remarked: "Never in my life have I studied so hard. In the process of learning about the Buddhist view of life as transcending the three existences—past, present and future—the prospect of dying no longer frightens me." The fact that members are acquiring such insight through participating in study activities is remarkable.

A LIFE OF PRIDE IN HAVING WON

Ikeda: That's right. This is true learning. Buddhist study in the SGI is by no means limited to simply memorizing philosophical principles.

We must also learn from the way people die. People who have died, whoever they may be, are our "seniors in life" by virtue of preceding us in death. This is true even if the deceased was younger than we are, even if he or she was a child.

Endo: I am reminded of an episode involving a nine-year-old boy who died of leukemia. It is described by Elisabeth Kübler-Ross, who is well known for her work counseling the terminally ill and investigating near-death experiences.[2]

Jeffy, the boy in question, had been in and out of hospitals since age three. By the time of his last visit, he was extremely weak, and Dr. Ross realized that he had only a few weeks left to live. Jeffy announced with a sense of great urgency that he wanted to go home "today." Dr. Ross talked with his parents, who were worried and reluctant to comply with their son's wishes. She finally persuaded the parents and accompanied them home.

When they arrived in the garage, Jeffy got out of the car and said to his father, "Take my bicycle down from the wall." It was a brand-new bicycle that his father had bought for him three years earlier, but that he had never been able to ride. It was Jeffy's dream once in his life to ride around his neighborhood on his bicycle.

Jeffy could barely stand on his feet. He had his father put training wheels on the bicycle and then said to Dr. Ross, "You are here to hold my mom back." She writes:

> Therefore I held mom back, and her husband held me back. We held each other back and learned the hard way how painful and difficult it sometimes is in the face of a very vulnerable, terminally ill child to allow him the victory and the risk to fall and hurt and bleed. And he then drove off on his solo journey on the bicycle around the neighborhood.

Suda: Did he make it back unhurt?

Endo: Yes. She writes: "He came back, the proudest man you have ever seen. He was beaming, smiling from one ear to the other. He looked like somebody who had won the gold medal in the Olympics."

One week later Jeffy died. A week after that, Jeffy's younger brother Dougy, whose birthday it was, related how after the bicycling episode Jeffy, without their parents' knowledge, had given him the bicycle for a birthday present. "Jeff had told Dougy that he wanted the pleasure of personally giving him his most beloved bicycle. But he could not wait another two weeks until it was Dougy's birthday, because by then he would be dead." He thus was taking care of his "unfinished business."

Dr. Ross continues: "The parents had a lot of grief, but no grief work, no fear, no guilt, no shame . . . They had the memory of this ride around the block and that beaming face of Jeffy."

According to Dr. Ross, everyone has a purpose. "In all my work with patients, I learned that whether they are chronic schizophrenics, severely retarded children, or dying patients, each one has a purpose. Each one cannot only learn and be helped by you, but can actually become your teacher."[3]

Ikeda: What a moving episode! That young boy died victoriously.

I think it was Yoshida Shoin[4] who said: "A person who dies at ten experiences the four seasons of spring, summer, fall and winter in ten years. A person who dies at twenty has the four seasons in twenty years. Those who die at thirty, fifty or a hundred also each experience the four seasons in their years."[5]

Shoin was thoroughly committed to his beliefs. Though he was executed at the age of twenty-nine, because he based himself on this view of life and death, he was not daunted in the least by the prospect of death. In a sense, the key issue is whether we die having achieved what we need to achieve; whether we die with pride in having won.

To learn about death is to learn how to live. Once on a philosophy exam, the French philosopher Alain[6] postulated the following situation, "A young woman is about to jump off the parapet of the Boïeldieu Bridge," and directed his students to explain what they would say to keep her from jumping.[7] If you were to come upon someone seriously debating whether to live or die, what would you say? Therein lies true philosophy. It might seem that this question pertains to an extreme and special situation, but in fact that is not the case. The question of how one ought to live as a human being is a fundamental issue that has been asked throughout time, in all places and by all people.

DEATH HAS TO BE CONSIDERED A PERSONAL ISSUE

Suda: That's right. A psychiatrist describes how he asked a youth who had attempted suicide, "Why did you try to commit suicide?" Turning the doctor's words around, the youth immediately shot back, "Why are you living?" leaving him at a loss for a response. "I was really stumped," he says, describing his reaction.

"Dying and living were opposites; they were like the two sides of a coin. If you cannot clearly articulate the significance of your own way of life and existence, you cannot tell another person, 'You must not die.'"[8]

Saito: It is certainly difficult to consider life and death as personal issues. No matter how eloquent someone may be in philosophizing about life or explaining theories of life and death, it will all count for nothing if deep down the person views such matters as pertaining only to others.

One physician explains that it took the death of his own child before he was able to come to grips with the meaning of life. He writes that formerly, when he cured a patient of illness, he was drunk with pride as a doctor: "I was mortified to realize, only after the death of my own child, how shallow my attitude had been. Instead of seeing it as happening to someone else, I began to see it as my own death." [9]

Endo: That's a heart-rending confession.

Ikeda: The experience of losing a loved one impels us toward a deeper understanding of life. Josei Toda, the second Soka Gakkai president, would talk about the profound sadness he felt at the death of his daughter. She had died some years before he took faith. He recounted how he had cried the night through holding her cold body in his arms:

> The day my daughter died was the saddest day in my life... I thought to myself, "What if my wife were to die?" That brought me to tears. And then my wife did indeed die. Later I wondered what I would do if my mother died. I was, of course, very fond of my mother. Pursuing things still further, I shuddered at the thought of my own death.
>
> While in prison during the war, I devoted some time

to reading the Lotus Sutra, and one day I suddenly understood. I had finally found the answer. It took me more than twenty years to solve the question of death. I had wept all night long over my daughter's death, and I dreaded my wife's death and the thought that I, too, would die. It's because I could finally answer this riddle that I became the president of the Soka Gakkai.[10]

For human beings, to fear death is natural. Even President Toda struggled with the prospect of death. It's impossible for people to have no fear of death or to be entirely indifferent to whether they live or die without struggling to develop such a resolute state of life.

Everyone fears and is saddened by death. That is natural. But by struggling to overcome the pain and sadness that accompanies death, we become more aware of the dignity of life and develop the spirit to share the sufferings of others as our own.

Endo: I understand what you're saying very well. I myself was in that position. Twelve years ago, my eldest son, who was then four years old, contracted bronchopneumonia and suddenly died. At the time, it was all I could do to contain my grief. I was in a daze.

But thanks to the repeated encouragement that I received from you, President Ikeda, and others, I could directly face the reality of my son's death. I feel boundless gratitude for the support everyone showed me.

From then on, with your words to me, "This will definitely have meaning for your life," ever in mind, I began chanting much more earnestly. I read Nichiren Daishonin's writings and hungrily studied your guidance. In everything, I found fresh meaning. Everything touched me with new impact. I felt as though my life had been cleansed.

I keenly feel that without having gone through the ordeal of losing my son, I probably would not have developed the deep conviction I now have in faith. And I'm afraid I would have remained shallow in my ability to understand people's hearts or the profundity of life. I might add that I am personally confident that my child has been reborn.

Ikeda: I also feel certain that is the case. Buddhism teaches the principle of the oneness of parent and child. You are giving many people hope by discussing the Lotus Sutra and sharing your personal perspective on the eternity of life. Through these efforts, your son is alive. You and your son are one. Whether he is in the phase of life or the phase of death, your son, because of the oneness of parent and child, fully shares the benefit of your efforts.

Life is long, and it is not all clear skies. There are rainy days and days of fierce wind. But no matter what happens, as long as we maintain our faith, in the end everything that happens will turn into benefit. President Toda would say: "As long as you have faith, everything will be your benefit. On the other hand, if you lose faith and have doubts, everything will be punishment."[11]

We have to live out our lives with firm belief in the eternity of life. Through our victory in this life, we show proof of life's eternity. This is the teaching of the Lotus Sutra and of the "Life Span" chapter. No matter what happens, we have to continue living, we have to survive; this is the spirit of the "Life Span" chapter.

Saito: The "Life Span" chapter teaches life's eternity not simply as words or as a philosophical concept but as a reality we can directly experience. This is its essence.

WE CAN MANIFEST THE ETERNAL LIFE OF THE UNIVERSE

Ikeda: It is important to live with great vitality. The "Life Span" chapter reveals the boundlessness of life, which is eternal and as vast as the universe. And the practice of the "Life Span" chapter is to manifest that immense life in the reality of our own lives. The unabbreviated title of the chapter means "fathom the life span of the Thus Come One." The practice, in other words, is to cause the great and eternal life force of the Buddha to well forth in one's own being.

The "eternal life" described in the "Life Span" chapter is the life of the universe, endowed with infinite vitality, wisdom and compassion, that sustains all living beings. The "Life Span" chapter clarifies that this life is Shakyamuni's true identity and the true aspect of all Buddhas. This is consistent with President Toda's realization that the Buddha is life.

This eternal life is also the Mystic Law, the Thus Come One, the essential nature of the Law and the true aspect. It is the fundamental law of the universe that pervades all phenomena in the Ten Worlds and the three thousand realms. The Daishonin identified this eternal life as Nam-myoho-renge-kyo.

Life and death are the mysterious functions, the innate rhythm, of this eternal life of the universe. Viewed solely in terms of the phenomena of life and death, life is impermanent. These "sufferings of life and death" and "sufferings of impermanence" are the wellspring of all human suffering. Shakyamuni worked exhaustively to teach people this.

This is certainly not just some old wives' tale. The sufferings of life and death lie at the foundation of all the sufferings of modern society. The "Life Span" chapter's teaching of "eternal life" is the good medicine to cure these sufferings of life and death.

Saito: Yes. Nichiren Daishonin states that the essential teaching for solving the sufferings of life and death is to be found only in the "Life Span" chapter (see WND-2, 985).

Ikeda: I think many people have studied the "Life Span" chapter many times already. For that matter, we all recite it each day. But to confirm the basics, why don't we begin by going over the outline of the chapter?

The Teaching of Shakyamuni's Enlightenment in the Remote Past Overturns All Earlier Teachings

Suda: OK. The "Emerging from the Earth" chapter describes the appearance of countless splendid bodhisattvas from within the earth. Bodhisattva Maitreya asks Shakyamuni to explain just when and where he instructed these myriad bodhisattvas. In response, Shakyamuni begins expounding the "Life Span" chapter.

Endo: Just a few decades had passed since Shakyamuni attained enlightenment beneath the bodhi tree. Thus it would have been impossible for him, in such a short time, to have instructed such a vast number of bodhisattvas to the point of their being practically on a par with the Buddha himself in level of attainment. This is the substance of Maitreya's question.

Ikeda: Seeing the wonderful appearance of these disciples, Maitreya must have wondered: "Just what kind of being is my mentor? He must be a person of far greater attainment than I had previously imagined."

Saito: Shakyamuni's response takes the form of his revelation at the outset of the "Life Span" chapter that he in fact attained enlightenment in the remote past. In the pre-Lotus Sutra teachings and the first half (or theoretical teaching) of the Lotus Sutra, Shakyamuni had taught that he first attained enlightenment during his lifetime in India. But here he completely overturns this teaching, revealing that "it has been immeasurable, boundless... kalpas since I in fact attained Buddhahood."

Ikeda: In other words, Shakyamuni did not become a Buddha for the first time in his present existence. Rather, he had been a Buddha all along.

Endo: Everyone must have been very surprised.

Suda: Some may well have reacted with alarm, thinking: "What? Have I been deceived all this time?"

Saito: Shakyamuni discards his provisional status as the Buddha who attained enlightenment for the first time in his present existence and reveals his true identity as the Buddha enlightened since the remote past. This is called "casting off the transient and revealing the true." I think it might be a good idea for us to go over the meaning of this concept in depth on another occasion.

Ikeda: I agree. It is a very profound doctrine. Also, it relates to the matter of time without beginning. I propose we discuss it later in light of the overall flow of the "Life Span" chapter.

Suda: Numberless major world system dust particle kalpas is a metaphor used to indicate the extremely distant time in the past when Shakyamuni attained Buddhahood. It is described as follows:

> Suppose a person were to take five hundred, a thousand, ten thousand, a million nayuta asamkhya major world systems and grind them to dust. Then, moving eastward, each time he passes five hundred, a thousand, ten thousand, a million nayuta asamkhya worlds he drops a particle of dust. (LSOC, 266)

We might imagine the person to be traveling in a rocket ship or something. In any event, he continues in this manner until he has dropped every particle of dust.

Endo: *Nayuta* and *asamkhya* are ancient Indian numerical units; they are both enormous numbers of ten to numerous tens of powers. According to one source, a *nayuta* is equal to the number one followed by eleven zeros (a hundred billion), and an *asamkhya* is equal to one followed by fifty-one zeros.

The major world systems indicate the universe as conceived in the worldview of the day. The number of lands passed in the manner that you described is utterly beyond calculation; one cannot even imagine such an enormous number.

Suda: That's right. But we're not done yet. Surprisingly, it says that if all the worlds that have been passed so far, whether they received a particle or not, are then ground to dust, and that each of these particles of dust represents one aeon. An aeon is an extremely long period of time; according to one explanation, it is equal to about sixteen million years.

The time since Shakyamuni attained enlightenment is said to surpass even the utterly incalculable period of time represented by all these particles of dust, by "a hundred, a thousand, ten thousand, a million nayuta asamkhya" kalpas (LSOC, 266). This total period of time since his enlightenment is termed "numberless major world system dust particle kalpas."

Endo: It truly boggles the mind.

Suda: Shakyamuni's enlightenment at such a remote time is called his "actual attainment in the remote past."

Saito: Since he explains that he actually attained enlightenment at that particular time in the remote past, we get the sense that there was a point of beginning. On one level, therefore, numberless major world system dust particle kalpas may be thought of as representing a fixed period of time, albeit a very long one. In substance, however, it seems that Shakyamuni is trying to describe an infinite period.

Ikeda: He's trying to express the idea of the eternal.

The Eternal Buddha Exists Here and Now

Suda: This teaching of his enlightenment in the remote past alone would have been enough to, as the saying goes, "startle the heavens and shake the earth." But Shakyamuni follows this up by making a declaration that overturns the prevailing common wisdom. Namely, he explains that ever since he attained Buddhahood in that remote past, he has been constantly in this saha world expounding the Law and instructing people.

Endo: In the pre-Lotus Sutra teachings, he had explained that the saha world was an impure land defiled with earthly desires and that the Buddha dwells in a pure land located elsewhere. The Pure Land of Perfect Bliss in the west or the Emerald Land to the east are well-known examples.

But in the "Life Span" chapter, he says that this saha world *is* the pure land where the Buddha, enlightened since the remote past, dwells eternally. A pure land is also called a Land of Tranquil Light. The principle that the saha world is itself the Land of Tranquil Light is another landmark teaching of the "Life Span" chapter.

Saito: The Great Teacher T'ien-t'ai of China calls this the "mystic principle of the True Land."

Suda: More mysterious still, Shakyamuni explains that he has been teaching people not only in this world but in countless other lands.

Endo: We can imagine the Buddha enlightened since the remote past as in some sense pervading the entire universe.

Ikeda: That's right. He can be thought of as a Buddha who dwells anywhere in the entire universe and who may appear anywhere to lead beings to enlightenment. For precisely that reason, we can say that the saha world—the place we live here and now—is the pure land where the Buddha, enlightened since the remote past, dwells eternally.

Suda: The mysterious preaching continues. Shakyamuni, as the Buddha enlightened since the remote past, explains that the discussions he held in the past where he mentioned other Buddhas with various names living at different times had been merely expedient means that he employed to lead people to enlightenment.

Endo: Shakyamuni explains that those Buddhas were all provisional Buddhas.

Suda: Provisional Buddha means a Buddha who exists as the shadow of the true Buddha. If the true Buddha is like the moon in the sky, a provisional Buddha is like the moon's reflection in a pond.

Saito: The Shakyamuni who is understood as having attained enlightenment for the first time during his lifetime in India is also such a provisional Buddha.

Ikeda: The purpose of the "Life Span" chapter is to explain that all living beings, not just Shakyamuni, have in fact been Buddhas since the remote past and to cause people to become aware of this. Its purpose is to open people's eyes to the great and eternal life of the universe. Nichiren Daishonin's revelation of the implicit teaching of the Lotus Sutra [Nam-myoho-renge-kyo] makes it possible on a practical level for people to do so.

President Toda said: "The ultimate purpose of practicing Nichiren Buddhism is to awaken to the eternity of life. It is to realize with one's entire being that life is eternal. When we do so, we experience absolute happiness. This happiness continues eternally; it can never be destroyed. We practice faith in order to establish such a state of happiness."[12]

The important thing is that we realize this with our entire being. And the only way to do that is through faith; by polishing and deepening our faith. President Toda would often say, "To understand something intellectually is easy; but to grasp it through faith is entirely different."[13] This is certainly true of the eternity of life.

ENLIGHTENMENT IN THE LATTER DAY MEANS FAITH IN THE GOHONZON

Suda: For that matter, regarding President Toda's enlightenment while in prison, there have been inquiries from readers wondering whether they can have the same experience.

Ikeda: For many people, the word *enlightenment* seems to have associations with mystical powers, such as the ability to remember past lives or to see into the future. But that is certainly not the case. Those who casually speak of enlightenment in such terms are definitely frauds.

President Toda remarked: "What is enlightenment in the Latter Day of the Law? It is to believe wholeheartedly in the Gohonzon."[14] To not doubt the Gohonzon no matter what happens, to believe earnestly—this is enlightenment in the Latter Day. Faith in the Gohonzon itself equals enlightenment.

To illustrate, there might be someone who agonizes over his home situation. The person lives in anguish, feeling that he is the most miserable person in the world. He feels resentment toward others and complains constantly. As a result of opening his eyes to faith and learning about Buddhism, however, he comes to understand that the causes of his misery are within his own life. He then strives to carry out his human revolution. As his faith deepens and his state of life expands, he can splendidly overcome his sufferings.

Through this experience, the person grasps the truth that when one's frame of mind or spirit changes, everything changes. This is the case of embodying the principle of three thousand realms in a single moment of life. Isn't this an instance of brilliant enlightenment?

Suda: Members who have had such experiences are numerous. Indeed, they could well be described as countless.

Ikeda: Of course, President Toda possessed a wonderful state of life uniquely his own. But it was inseparable from his absolute, unparalleled confidence in the Gohonzon; no one could match his strength of conviction. His state of life was that of great confidence itself.

THE TRUE NATURE OF LIFE AND DEATH

Endo: Shakyamuni explains that the Buddha enlightened since the remote past can appear in various forms and guide people to enlightenment because he "perceives the true aspect of the threefold world exactly as it is" (LSOC, 267).

Saito: Threefold world means the actual world where beings who have not eradicated illusion dwell.

Ikeda: The phrase "The Thus Come One perceives the true aspect of the threefold world exactly as it is" refers to the wisdom of the Buddha to discern the true aspect of all things. Because he possesses this wisdom, the Buddha can freely expound teachings in accord with people's capacity.

What, then, is the true nature of life and death as seen with the eye of the Buddha? This is described in the next passage.

Saito: Yes. Shakyamuni says, "There is no ebb or flow of birth and death, and there is no existing in this world and later entering extinction" (LSOC, 267). In the threefold world, there is neither birth nor death, there is neither withdrawing from this world nor appearing in it. Accordingly, there is no distinction between those currently in the world and those who have died.

Suda: It seems to me that this clarifies the eternal existence of life.

From a common sense standpoint, we can only think of birth as appearing in the world and of death as withdrawing from it. But from the Buddha's perspective, birth and death are only alternating phases of life, which is itself eternal.

Ikeda: That's right. But the statement, "There is no...birth and death," emphasizes the eternal aspect of life. Then again, if we were only to think of life from that angle, we may fall into abstraction. After all, life and death are realities of existence. To ignore them, therefore, is to engage in theoretical speculation.

Nichiren Daishonin goes one step further in saying, "Passing through the round of births and deaths, one makes one's way on the Land of the Dharma nature, or enlightenment, that is inherent within oneself (OTT, 50). Based on the Mystic Law, we perceive life and death as dramas played upon the stage of our eternal life, that is, "the Land of the Dharma nature or enlightenment, that is inherent within oneself." When we realize that we are in some sense enacting a drama, our existence becomes a source of inexhaustible joy. Life and death are not fraught with suffering; they are filled with joy. This is how we realize the ultimate state of life in which "life is joyful and death is joyful, too."

The Mystic Law is the great beneficial medicine for overcoming the sufferings of life and death. The "Life Span" chapter says, "This is a highly effective medicine" (LSOC, 269).

The SGI members who day in and day out unsparingly use their minds and their bodies for the sake of the Law and for their friends are truly advancing along the path of eternal victory.

Saito: How noble it is to live out one's life based on faith in the Mystic Law! How truly fortunate we are!

A Drama in Which Both Life
And Death Are Joyful

Suda: I heard about the experience of the grandmother-in-law of an acquaintance of mine. Her name was Chiyo Nakatani, and she died in 1993 at age seventy-six. She was survived by eight children and their spouses, grandchildren and great-grandchildren. In all, thirty-seven family members were there chanting daimoku for her when she died. Everyone in the family is active at the ward, headquarters, chapter or district levels of the organization. When they get together, it's like a chapter general meeting.

Endo: Did she have any living siblings or relatives of her own generation?

Suda: No. Her parents and siblings died when she was young, and because she had moved away from her native village, it seems she had been without a living relative.

During and after the war, she lost two husbands and a number of her children. In 1956, while struggling to raise those children who survived, she joined the Soka Gakkai. She reportedly developed strong confidence in faith as a result of overcoming cancer.

The husband of one of her granddaughters is an acquaintance of mine. Everyone in the family would say that she was like a mountain. She carried through with unswerving faith, not flinching in the least no matter how fiercely the storms of destiny might blow.

If her children would complain about how difficult their lives were, she would tell them: "If your stomach were full, you might not be able to practice faith correctly. Isn't it because you have a lot of difficulties that you can earnestly exert yourself in activities? You should be appreciative."

She brought the family business to a certain level of prosperity and provided a home for her children in the Shirogane area of Tokyo's Minato Ward. She reportedly remained active as a district-level leader during her later years, taking particular joy in propagation activities.

She was always citing passages from Nichiren Daishonin's writings. One of her favorite passages goes: "This body of ours in the end will become nothing more than the soil of the hills and fields. Therefore, it is useless to begrudge your life, for though you may wish to, you cannot cling to it forever. Even people who live a long time rarely live beyond the age of one hundred. And all the events of a lifetime are like the dream one dreams in a brief nap" (WND-1, 760).

"I Received My Long Life From the Gohonzon"

Endo: I have also heard the experience of Yuki Katsura of Tokyo's Suginami Ward. When Mrs. Katsura died last October, reportedly more than 360 people attended her funeral, including members of the local senior citizens group and many shopkeepers. For the funeral of an eighty-four-year-old woman who lived in a block housing complex and had no particular status in society, this was unusual. It became quite a topic of conversation.

Although she was tough enough to single-handedly raise four daughters, it seems that Mrs. Katsura had been born two months prematurely and that as an adult she had a very slight build, weighing less than eighty-eight pounds. Toward the end of her life, she weighed only sixty-one pounds. Nonetheless, she remained extremely energetic and cheerful.

Mrs. Katsura would often say: "It really shouldn't have been possible for me to live this long. I received my long life from the Gohonzon." Ten years ago her doctor thought that she might have cancer. Throughout the time she was hospitalized, she chanted resolute daimoku, saying: "I entrust everything to the Gohonzon. If I have a mission, I will recover without fail."

After her discharge, she remained active with the local senior citizens' group and took great pleasure in helping others. She did not seem the least fatigued or worn down by her active life.

Suda: She must have been well trusted in the community.

Endo: She also worked tirelessly as a district leader, and it seems that each month she would get at least one new person to start taking the *Seikyo Shimbun* newspaper or other publications.

On the day she died, she had been planning to go out somewhere with her four children for the first time in a long time. The previous day she had gone to the beauty shop. On the morning of the appointed day, her family came to her room to find that she had died peacefully.

She had apparently been kneeling on her bed and had fallen forward. Her daughters found her lying there peacefully with her eyes closed. Her skin was lustrous. The physician who came out to the house reportedly remarked that he hoped to die as peacefully himself.

Although the funeral did not take place until nearly a week later, her face still had a pink hue and she seemed to have grown younger by the day. In relating their impressions, it was reported that even many nonmembers were so impressed by her appearance that they could only attribute it to her faith.

DEVELOP THE STATE OF BUDDHAHOOD DURING THIS LIFETIME

Ikeda: I heard reports about both Mrs. Nakatani and Mrs. Katsura. Such people are pillars of the Soka Gakkai. They are true practitioners of the Lotus Sutra. They are most worthy of respect. Their lives are models for all.

There are countless such people in the SGI. The passage you cited a moment ago, "Even people who live a long time rarely live beyond the age of one hundred," is really true. President Toda would often remark, "One hundred years from now everyone here will be dead."

This world is like a dream one dreams in a brief nap. From the standpoint of eternity, there is hardly any difference between a "long" and a "short" life. Therefore, it's not whether our lives are long or short but how we live that is important. It is what we accomplish, the degree to which we develop our state of life, the number of people we help become happy—this is what matters.

Those who firmly establish the state of Buddhahood in their lives will enjoy this state of life eternally. This is what attaining Buddhahood in this lifetime means.

Saito: In other words, even if this lifetime is short, we can still use it to establish a state of happiness and fulfillment that continues over eternity.

Ikeda: That's right. That's a fundamental Buddhist principle. At the same time, I always pray that SGI members will enjoy excellent health and longevity.

The "Life Span" chapter says: "Let us live out our lives!" (LSOC, 269). Life span is a matter of life force. Receiving boundless vitality from the Gohonzon, we can live vigorously to the end. This is the "Life Span" chapter's profound teaching of rejuvenation.

Saito: Certainly, many people in the SGI have extended their lives. I know of a woman who had once been sickly and weak, and who, before joining the Soka Gakkai, had been told by a physician that she would not live long. As a result of taking faith, however, she became healthy and is now, at more than one hundred years of age, still vigorously participating in discussion meetings. Meanwhile, the doctor who told her this has long since died.

Ikeda: Through faith, with each passing year our hearts become increasingly youthful. We advance vigorously and filled with a sense of boundless hope for the future. This is true health. This is true longevity. Those who dedicate their lives to kosen-rufu can definitely achieve such a state. That is why we practice faith.

A MESSAGE FOR PEOPLE OF THE FUTURE

Endo: We have gotten as far as the explanation that the Buddha enlightened since the remote past has been constantly dwelling in this world. Shakyamuni next clarifies that the Buddha will be continually in the world throughout the future, too. He says, "Originally I practiced the bodhisattva way, and the life span that I acquired then has yet to come to an end but will last twice the number of years that have already passed" (LSOC, 268).[15]

Saito: This is a message to the future. From the standpoint of "saving living beings," the true intention of the "Life Span" chapter lies not so much with the past as with the future. The Daishonin says that the "Life Span" chapter was expounded exclusively for the people in the world after Shakyamuni's passing and, above all, for the people of the Latter Day.

I believe the significance of its teaching about the past lies in the elucidation of the original cause of Shakyamuni's enlightenment.

Ikeda: That may be so, but from another perspective, it is precisely because the "Life Span" chapter reveals the origin of the Buddha's life (the cause) that it can lead the people of the future who are experiencing the sufferings of birth and death to enlightenment (the effect). The passage just cited, "Originally I practiced the bodhisattva way," suggests this most fundamental of origins.

Saito: In other words, the "original cause of enlightenment" lies in Shakyamuni's attainment of Buddhahood in the remote past. And when we pursue this original cause, we arrive at the Buddhist Law implicit in the sutra as was revealed by Nichiren Daishonin.

Suda: In "The Opening of the Eyes," the Daishonin says, "The doctrine of three thousand realms in a single moment of life is found in only one place, hidden in the depths of the "Life Span" chapter of the essential teaching of the Lotus Sutra" (WND-1, 224). Over the years, various arguments have been made about precisely which passage of the "Life Span" chapter contains this teaching. High Priest Nichikan clearly states that it is contained in the passage, "Originally I practiced the bodhisattva way."

Ikeda: That's right. T'ien-t'ai expresses the marvelous state of life of the Buddha awakened to the eternity of life in terms of "three thousand realms in a single moment of life." And the soul of this doctrine lies in the "Life Span" chapter.

But the "Life Span" chapter reveals the eternity of life through the marvelous appearance that Shakyamuni assumes after attaining Buddhahood (i.e., the true effect). This is called the "mystic principle of true effect." But the real issue is what ordinary people can do to awaken to life's eternity. Nichiren Buddhism of the true cause explains this. I expect that later on we will have the opportunity to delve into this point more deeply.

Toward the "Century of the Human Revolution"

Suda: Incidentally, if the Buddha dwells eternally in this world in both the present and the future and is never extinct, then the question arises of why he enters nirvana.

The Lotus Sutra explains: "If they [people] see that the Thus Come One is constantly in the world and never enters extinction, they will grow arrogant and selfish, or become discouraged and neglectful. They will fail to realize how difficult it is to encounter the Buddha and will not approach him with a respectful and reverent mind" (LSOC, 268). Therefore, the Buddha explains that he enters extinction as an expedient means. This is the meaning of "as an expedient means I appear to enter nirvana" (LSOC, 271).

Saito: I expect we will take up this point again later on. In short, the "Life Span" chapter is the soul of all sutras. The "Life Span" chapter provides answers to the questions: "What is Buddhism?" and "What does Buddhism teach?"

Ikeda: Yes. Nichiren Daishonin states, "If, among all the numerous sutras, this "Life Span" chapter should be lacking, it would be as though there were no sun or moon in the sky, no supreme ruler in the nation, no gems in the mountains and rivers, and no spirit in human beings" (WND-1, 256). To study the "Life Span" chapter is to study the very essence of Buddhism. It is to deepen one's understanding of the essence of life and of the true nature of the self.

If we fail to understand this, then no matter what we might do our lives would be fundamentally shrouded in darkness. Our lives would be filled with illusion and suffering. We would live in a world of darkness truly "as though there were no sun and moon in the sky." The "Life Span" chapter causes the "sun of hope" to rise in our lives. This process is called the human revolution.

Suda: I see.

Elisabeth Kübler-Ross, whom we talked about at the beginning, also writes:

> If you want to heal the world it is terribly important to understand that you cannot heal the world without first healing thyself… it is very important that you heal the world soon, before it is too late: you have to understand that you cannot heal the world without healing yourself first.[16]

Ikeda: That's exactly right. To change the world, we first have to change ourselves. And the fundamental thing that we as members of the human community need to change is our view of existence, our view of life and death, our view of the self. The "Life Span" chapter of the Lotus Sutra offers fundamental guidelines concerning this issue of life and death.

Generally speaking, belief in something eternal makes people more humane. I think it was Kanzo Uchimura who said, "I think that nothing exalts a person more than having a sound view of the afterlife."[17]

It seems to me that if we suppose this lifetime to be the be-all and end-all of existence, then we cannot lead a truly profound life. Unless we understand the eternity of life, our lives will be fundamentally uncertain.

It is like trying to swim in shallow water. In the summer, babies will play in a plastic swimming pool. For babies, that may be sufficient. But when people become elementary-school aged and know of the existence of real pools, they will no longer be satisfied with tiny plastic pools. Further, when they become aware of the joy of swimming in the ocean, even a large modern pool that makes artificial waves will prove unsatisfactory. The same is true in life. When we open our eyes to the ocean of life that stretches out within our being, we can lead an existence of great and profound fulfillment.

People are now increasingly paying attention to the issue of life and death, and focusing on the human being. This is a hallmark of the twenty-first century. The "century of life" will be a "century of the human revolution." It will be a century when we see an unprecedented blossoming of civilization based on the principle of the eternity of life found in the "Life Span" chapter.

NOTES

1. Susumu Oda, *Seishinkai ga akasu—Sei to shi kokoro no shinso* (Life and Death, and the Heart's Inner Reaches Elucidated by a Psychiatrist) (Tokyo: Hamano Shuppan, 1997), pp. 44–58.

2. The following is excerpted from: Elisabeth Kübler-Ross, *Death Is of Vital Importance: On Life, Death and Life After Death*, ed. Göran Grip (Barrytown, NY: Station Hill Press, 1995), pp. 56–60.

3. Ibid., p. 6.

4. Yoshida Shoin (1830–59): A Japanese scholar, teacher and writer, he and his followers played a key role in toppling the Tokugawa regime and ushering in the Meiji era.

5. Yoshida Shoin, *Ryukonroku* (Record of an Enduring Soul).

6. Alain: Pen name of Emile-Auguste Chartier (1868–1951).

7. André Maurois, *Memoirs* (1885–1967), trans. Denver Lindley (New York: Harper and Row, Publishers, 1970), p. 35.

8. Kenshiro Ohara, *Sei to shi no kokoromoyo* (Patterns of the Heart in Life and Death) (Tokyo: Iwanami Shinsho, 1991), p. 100.

9. Hiroomi Kawano, *Gan no ningengaku* (A Study of Humanism in the Face of Cancer) (Tokyo: Kobundo, 1984), pp. 290–91.

10. Josei Toda, *Toda Josei zenshu* (Collected Writings of Josei Toda) (Tokyo: Seikyo Shimbunsha, 1982), vol. 2, pp. 174–75.

11. Daisaku Ikeda, *Ningen kakumei* (The Human Revolution) (Tokyo: Seikyo Shimbunsha, 1967), vol. 3, p. 291.

12. Ibid., p. 106.

13. Ibid., p. 290.

14. *Toda Josei zenshu* (Tokyo: Seikyo Shimbunsha, 1983), vol. 3, p. 415.

15. The phrase "the number of years that have already passed" refers to the period of major world system dust particle *kalpas*.

16. *Death Is of Vital Importance*, pp. 117–22.

17. Kanzo Uchimura, *Kirisutokyo mondo* (Dialogue on Christianity) (Tokyo: Kadokawa Bunko, 1905), p. 21.

2 The Supreme Dignity of the Human Being

Ikeda: The essence of Buddhism lies in developing oneself through one's own determination and tenacious effort—not by depending on anyone or anything else. We need to have the spirit to stand on our own initiative without relying on anyone. We don't need others' sympathy or sentimentality. We have to stand up and advance, even if there is no one to encourage us.

We resolutely and cheerfully take responsibility to change ourselves, our surroundings, society and the land where we live. That is the principle of three thousand realms in a single moment of life. What Buddhism teaches is not abstract theory; it is not a weak-kneed way of life constantly clinging to something for support. At the same time, neither is it to be confused with the egoism to arrogantly suppose, "I alone am correct and respectworthy."

To believe in the great life force within oneself is at once to believe in the great life force existing within all people. Buddhism teaches that we should treasure the lives of others just as highly as we treasure our own.

Saito: The SGI has spread throughout the world because we have put this essential Buddhist teaching into practice. The fact that there are people in 177 countries and territories [now 192] practicing the essence of the Lotus Sutra, it seems to me, surely stands out in the history of Buddhism as a stupendous achievement.

Ikeda: Nichiren Daishonin, along with Tsunesaburo Makiguchi and Josei Toda, the first and second Soka Gakkai presidents, is surely rejoicing at what we have achieved.

Endo: What is the wellspring of energy behind this unprecedented flourishing of Buddhism? As your remarks regarding President Makiguchi and President Toda just now suggest, Mr. Ikeda, I am convinced it is because of the existence in the SGI of the spirit of oneness of mentor and disciple directed toward the realization of kosen-rufu.

Saito: I feel the same. Conversely, I think that we can trace any decline in Buddhism to the absence of this all-important spirit.

WHY DID BUDDHISM DIE OUT IN INDIA?

Ikeda: That's an important point. The oneness of mentor and disciple is in fact the essence of both the Lotus Sutra and the "Life Span" chapter. I try to explain the sutra from a variety of angles in different contexts depending upon the occasion. This is a good time, I think, to introduce the view of Buddhism held by Jawaharlal Nehru, India's first prime minister. He once discussed the question of why Buddhism died out in India with the French author André Malraux.

I, too, once held a dialogue with Mr. Malraux.[1] I will never forget how his eyes shone. He had a certain aura about him; a great spirit of inquiry that seemed to radiate from his entire being. He was an incredibly curious man always seeking a deeper understanding of life. Mr. Malraux had a keen interest in Buddhism, and he suggested the possibility that a new civilization might someday be born that would have its roots in Buddhism.

I once talked about the discussion between Nehru and Malraux in a speech I gave in Germany.[2] At one point in their conversation, Nehru remarked: "The genius of the Buddha has to do with the fact that he is a man. The originator of one of the most profound systems of thought in the history of humanity, an inflexible spirit and the most noble compassion. An accuser, vis-à-vis the teeming multitude of the gods."[3]

Suda: Mention of his stance vis-à-vis the gods calls to mind how Nichiren Daishonin severely rebuked and remonstrated with Bodhisattva Hachiman.[4]

Ikeda: It was the wonderful character of the Buddha that won over people's hearts. After Shakyamuni's death, however, as Nehru deftly observed, "He became deified, he merged with that multitude, which closed round him,"[5] in effect eclipsing his human side.

Saito: It is certainly true that at present there are very few adherents of Buddhism in India. Of course, Shakyamuni generally is revered—but as one of many gods within the Hindu pantheon. The problem is that as soon as Shakyamuni was deified, the path he had revealed for human beings to attain enlightenment disappeared.

Ikeda: Yes. Fundamentally, Buddhism is a teaching about how to live, a teaching transmitted from mentor to disciple. The relationship of mentor and disciple is formed when there are people who desire to follow the correct path in life and who seek a mentor and when the mentor responds to their spirit. But if the Buddha as the mentor ceases to be a human being and becomes a "god," then, practically speaking, the path of mentor and disciple cannot exist.

Suda: By following the same path as the mentor, one can attain the same state of life as the mentor. That is the premise on which the path of mentor and disciple is based. If the mentor is thought to be a "god," then the followers, put off by the seemingly insurmountable gap between themselves and the mentor, cannot muster the aspiration that would otherwise drive them to advance along the same path.

Saito: In Hinayana Buddhism, which emerged relatively early after Shakyamuni's death, the people gradually viewed Shakyamuni as a deity. Consequently they felt that it was enough if they could just strive to attain the enlightenment of persons of learning, or voice-hearers (i.e., the stage of arhat[6]).

In Mahayana Buddhism, other than the Lotus Sutra, which was systematized at a later time as a countermovement to Hinayana, a large number of Buddhas are introduced besides Shakyamuni. These include, for example, Amida,[7] Mahavairochana[8] and Vairochana.[9] But there is an unbridgeable gap between these Buddhas and actual people. They are presented largely as beings to whom people can entrust their hopes for salvation, not as potential mentors.

Thus, the path of mentor and disciple exists neither in the Hinayana nor in the provisional Mahayana teachings.

Ikeda: When "Shakyamuni the human being" was forgotten, Buddhism ceased to be a teaching about how to live the best possible life. The path of mentor and disciple disappeared. Consequently, Buddhism declined and became authoritarian.

Endo: Nichiren Shoshu under the leadership of Nikken, which represents the latest and, possibly, the most egregious case of authoritarianism and abuses by a Buddhist clergy, certainly gives no indication of presenting a teaching concerned with how people should live. They are merely using Buddhism as a shield of authority to hide their own decadence. Such a situation surely represents the destruction of the Law.

Saito: Nichiren Daishonin and Shakyamuni went out among the people to propagate the Law widely while struggling to overcome all kinds of difficulties and attacks—collectively called the three obstacles and four devils. When followers fail to continue along the same path as the mentor, the very life of Buddhism is extinguished. One cannot fail to be impressed by Nehru's wisdom in discerning that Buddhism died out in India when Shakyamuni ceased to be viewed as a human being.

SHAKYAMUNI COMPLETELY REVERSES HIS EARLIER TEACHING

Ikeda: Let's get back to the "Life Span" chapter. The Lotus Sutra's message of "return to Shakyamuni the human being!" is nowhere expressed more clearly than in the principle of casting off the transient and revealing the true found in the "Life Span" chapter. I propose that we consider this in some detail.

Suda: How does casting off the transient and revealing the true imply returning to Shakyamuni the human being? I should think that Shakyamuni's revelation that he has been enlightened since the remote past, rather than making him more human and accessible, would on the surface seem to suggest that he is a great Buddha far removed from ordinary people.

Endo: Since ancient times, people have, in fact, tended to interpret the Buddha of the remote past of the Lotus Sutra as some supreme deity. But such an interpretation certainly does not represent the essence of the Lotus Sutra.

Ikeda: Let's begin by confirming the meaning of casting off the transient and revealing the true. I think a review will be valuable even for those well versed in Buddhist study.

Endo: OK. In the "Life Span" chapter, Shakyamuni says:

In all the worlds the heavenly and human beings and asuras all believe that the present Shakyamuni Buddha, after leaving the palace of the Shakyas, seated himself in the place of enlightenment not far from the city of Gaya and there attained supreme perfect enlightenment. But good men, it has been immeasurable, boundless hundreds, thousands, ten thousands, millions of nayutas of kalpas since I in fact attained Buddhahood. (LSOC, 265–66)

Suda: People thought Shakyamuni had renounced the world at nineteen and attained Buddhahood at the age of thirty while seated beneath a tree near the city of Gaya. While there is some variation among different accounts as to Shakyamuni's age when the main events in his life occurred, they all share in common the view that Shakyamuni attained enlightenment for the first time during the lifetime he lived in India. That is the standard view.

This same view of when Shakyamuni attained enlightenment can also be found in the provisional teachings expounded prior to the Lotus Sutra and in the theoretical teaching (or first half) of the Lotus Sutra.

Endo: In the "Life Span" chapter this view is completely overturned. Here, Shakyamuni reveals that, on the contrary, he has been enlightened since the remote past. In contrast to the view that Shakyamuni attained enlightenment for the first time during his existence in India, he in fact attained Buddhahood long before. This original enlightenment is called "actual attainment in the remote past." Shakyamuni, who attained enlightenment in the remote past, is called the "true Buddha of the remote past," in the sense that he reveals his true identity in the remote past. "True," here, includes the meanings of true identity, true origin or true entity.

By contrast, the Shakyamuni who attained enlightenment for the first time in India is a "transient Buddha" that the true Buddha of the remote past manifested in response to people's capacity and aspirations in order to lead them to happiness. A transient Buddha is to a true Buddha what a shadow is to a body; it is a provisional aspect.

Saito: A transient Buddha is also termed a "provisional Buddha." The relation between the true Buddha and a transient or provisional Buddha is often likened to the relation between the "moon in the sky" and the "moon in a pond"; that is, the difference between the moon and its reflection.

Suda: The designation of the first fourteen chapters of the Lotus Sutra as the theoretical (literally, "provisional") teaching and of the latter fourteen chapters as the essential (literally, "true") teaching is also based on this distinction between the provisional Buddha and the true Buddha.

Ikeda: Regarding the difference between the essential and the theoretical teachings, Nichiren Daishonin says, "One is as different from the other as fire is from water or heaven from earth" (WND-1, 1112). He also stresses that the difference between the essential and theoretical teachings is far greater even than that between the pre–Lotus Sutra teachings and the theoretical teaching of the Lotus Sutra. That's because the essential teaching contains this doctrine of casting off the transient and revealing the true.

SHAKYAMUNI'S LAST WORDS TO HIS DISCIPLES— BASE YOURSELF ON THE LAW

Saito: This raises the question of just how Shakyamuni's casting off of his transient status and the consequent revelation of his true identity as the Buddha enlightened since the remote past translates into a message to "return to Shakyamuni the human being."

Ikeda: Why don't we try to pursue this methodically? In the first place, Shakyamuni's purpose in expounding his teachings lay in opening the eyes of all people to the eternal Law to which he himself had awakened. Shakyamuni further taught that even after his death people should make this Law their mentor.

Suda: Yes. Ananda, who had constantly waited in service upon the Buddha, at one point asks Shakyamuni, "On what should we rely in our practice after you have passed away?" Shakyamuni replies: "Ananda, you should make yourself an island and depend on yourself. Without depending on others, you should make the Law an island and your foundation."[10]

Endo: This dictum is variously phrased as "Depend on yourself, depend on the Law," or "Illuminate the torch of the self, illuminate the torch of the Law."

Ikeda: Yes. The important thing here is the relation of the Law and the Buddha. "Law" has a variety of meanings, including that of "teaching." But, in conclusion, what Shakyamuni refers to as the Law, or Dharma, is in fact no different from the life of the eternal Buddha. We can think of the Law as the property of the Law, or Dharma body, of the eternal Buddha.

This may seem like a bit of a leap, but Shakyamuni's awakening to the eternal Law can be seen as equivalent to his perceiving the eternal Buddha within himself. From the standpoint of the Lotus Sutra, the teaching to "make the Law your foundation" is essentially a directive to make the eternal Buddha one's mentor. More important, Shakyamuni himself attained enlightenment with that eternal Buddha as his mentor.

Endo: "Depend on yourself," here, of course, does not mean to simply rely on the self. One knows best of all just how undependable the self is.

Ikeda: In effect he is saying, "One should become the master of one's mind" (WND-I, 390). For us, this means thoroughly devoting ourselves to faith. The point is to make this self—the self of faith—our foundation.

Saito: There are certainly various ways of looking at the relationship of the Person and the Law. In the writing "On Attaining Buddhahood," Nichiren Daishonin says, "If you think the Law is outside yourself, you are embracing not the Mystic Law but an inferior teaching" (WND-1, 3). While the "Law" might seem to imply something separate from our everyday lives, it in fact exists nowhere apart from our own hearts.

SHAKYAMUNI'S MENTOR IS THE NAM-MYOHO-RENGE-KYO THUS COME ONE

> *Since I attained Buddhahood*
> *the number of kalpas that have passed*
> *is an immeasurable hundreds, thousands, ten thousands,*
> *millions, trillions, asamkhyas.*
> *Constantly I have preached the Law, teaching, converting*
> *countless millions of living beings,*
> *causing them to enter the Buddha way,*
> *all this for immeasurable kalpas.*
> *In order to save living beings,*
> *as an expedient means I appear to enter nirvana*
> *but in truth I do not pass into extinction.*
> *I am always here, preaching the Law.* (LSOC, 270–71)

Ikeda: Fundamentally, the Law and the Person (i.e., the Buddha) are inseparable.

Thus Come One, another name for Buddha, literally means "one who has come from the world of truth." In other words, Thus Come One is the manifestation in our day-to-day reality of the True Law. The universal life has the aspects of the Person and the Law, and these two aspects are inseparable.

This may get a little complicated, but since it is a key concept

I would like to pursue this point a little further. In one place in his preaching Shakyamuni says, "Those who see the Law see me, those who see me see the Law." This means that to perceive the Law with one's life is to encounter Shakyamuni, and that to encounter Shakyamuni is to perceive the Law. "Me," in the phrase "those who see me," fundamentally indicates the eternal Buddha who is one with the eternal Law.

In the "Life Span" chapter Shakyamuni reveals the eternal Buddha body when he says, "I am always here, preaching the Law" (LSOC, 271). In literal terms, this is referring to Shakyamuni who has been enlightened since the remote past described as an incredibly long period of time where numberless major worlds are reduced to dust and then each particle of dust is placed in different worlds and those worlds are reduced to dust once again. Ultimately it points to the Buddha of time without beginning, or the Buddha who has been enlightened since time without beginning.

The eternal Law at one with the eternal Buddha to which Shakyamuni became enlightened is the eternal life to which all Buddhas are enlightened. Just as did Shakyamuni, all Buddhas of the past, present and future have become enlightened to, and have taken as their mentor, the Buddha of time without beginning. This is the Buddha of Limitless Joy, the Buddha of absolute freedom of time without beginning, or the Nam-myoho-renge-kyo Thus Come One. President Toda said: "The life of Nichiren Daishonin and our own lives have neither beginning nor end. This is what is termed time without beginning. There is neither beginning nor end. The universe itself is a great entity of life." It has existed since time without beginning as the ultimate entity of compassion.

Embracing this great entity of life as his "mentor," Shakyamuni the human being became enlightened just as he was—as a human being. And the moment he became enlightened, he realized that all Buddhas throughout time and space became Buddhas with this "eternal Buddha," who embodies the principle of the oneness of the Person and the Law, as their mentor.

Suda: In the "Expedient Means" chapter of the Lotus Sutra, we also find the concept of "five kinds of Buddhas who preach the one Buddha vehicle." "Five kinds of Buddhas" specifically means: all Buddhas, the Buddhas of the past, the Buddhas of the future, the Buddhas of the present, and Shakyamuni Buddha.

Ikeda: By earnestly seeking and practicing the Law, we will certainly encounter the Buddha who is "always here, preaching the Law" (LSOC, 271).

Saito: "You should earnestly seek out the Law that I have left behind" is what Shakyamuni is in effect telling us. "When you do so, you will encounter the Buddha enlightened since the remote past." This is in fact the motif of the parable of the excellent physician and his sick children that is expounded in the "Life Span" chapter.

Suda: I see. I never made that connection before.

The gist of the parable of the excellent physician and his sick children is as follows. To save his children (the people) who have by mistake consumed poison and lost their minds, the excellent physician (the Buddha) goes away and has someone report that he died in a distant land. Grieving over their father's death, the children come to their senses and drink the good medicine (the Law) that their father had left for them and thereby recover their sanity. The father then returns and is reunited with his children who have been restored to health.

Endo: The Buddha is always in the world and never dies. To arouse in people a seeking mind for the Law, he uses as an expedient means his apparent entry into extinction. But once the people come to believe in and embrace the Law, the Buddha again appears before them. This is the meaning of the parable.

Ikeda: That's right. Through practicing the eternal Mystic Law, absolutely anyone can perceive in his or her heart the eternal Buddha who is "always here, preaching the Law." We can perhaps say that this is the true significance of the Buddha's decree—"return to Shakyamuni the human being!" The "Life Span" chapter's parable of the excellent physician and his sick children faithfully expresses this spirit.

Suda: As you have pointed out before, the "Life Span" chapter is a message for the people in the world after Shakyamuni's death, and in particular for the people of the Latter Day of the Law. Shakyamuni is saying, in other words, "After I have died, you must take my mentor as your own and advance along the same path as I have." This is in a sense Shakyamuni's will.

Endo: So Shakyamuni's not being in the world is really not an obstacle to attaining enlightenment.

Suda: Those in the world during Shakyamuni's lifetime could sense the eternal Law through direct personal contact with the Buddha and could advance along the path of enlightenment. But that is not possible for those of us living in the world after his death. I think that in this we find an important reason for why the "Life Span" chapter is said to be for those in the world after the Buddha's passing.

THOSE ALIVE IN SHAKYAMUNI'S DAY HAD PERSONAL CONTACT WITH THE BUDDHA

Endo: To give one example from Shakyamuni's time, after attaining enlightenment beneath the bodhi tree, he delivered his first sermon to five monks with whom he had formerly practiced austerities. Traditionally, this is called "the first turning of the wheel of the law."

The five ascetics had previously derided Shakyamuni on the grounds that he had "regressed from the path of difficult practices."

But it is said that when they laid eyes on Shakyamuni, they were struck by the undeniable brilliance of his character and immediately became his followers.

Ikeda: Shakyamuni's first words on that occasion were, "I have attained immortality."[11] With these words Shakyamuni was expressing how he felt having attained enlightenment. He must have perceived the great and eternal life of the universe pulsing in his heart. He must have sensed the eternal life force of the Thus Come One welling forth at each moment from the very depths of his being.

So moved were they by the great state of life they sensed flowing from Shakyamuni the human being that the five monks entered the path of Buddhism. Through the person Shakyamuni, they could connect to the eternal Law. It was only during Shakyamuni's lifetime that it was possible for people to have such a personal exchange between mentor and disciple.

Suda: To illustrate the kind of exchange that Shakyamuni had with his disciples, there was someone who was so impressed by Shakyamuni that it changed his entire life. I am referring to the notorious murderer called Angulimala. He was apparently given the name Angulimala on account of his supreme villainy. *Anguli* means finger and *mala* means necklace in Sanskrit. He was said to have killed a great many people and to have made a kind of ornament with his victims' fingers that he hung around his neck. It is said that a single phrase from Shakyamuni, "Come along,"[12] caused him to have a change of heart. As a result he became the Buddha's follower.

He thereafter began collecting alms as part of his practice. But people who bore a grudge against him because of his past actions pelted him with dirt and rocks and tore his robe to shreds. He returned to Shakyamuni covered with blood.

Shakyamuni encouraged Angulimala, saying: "You must persevere. You have to tenaciously endure this hardship. You are now receiving the effects of negative karma that ordinarily you would have to undergo in hell for years, for hundreds of years, for thousands of years."[13]

Endo: This is a clear example of the principle of 'lessening karmic retribution.'

Ikeda: Negative karma from past misdeeds doesn't just disappear immediately once a person begins practicing Buddhism. Still, it must have been very painful for Shakyamuni to see someone who had had a genuine change of heart and become a disciple receive such treatment, even if it were due to evil karma the person himself had created. Doubtless it was as painful for Shakyamuni as if he had received a wound to his own flesh.

Shakyamuni wanted above all to enable his followers to carry through with their practice without regression and advance along the path leading to the attainment of Buddhahood. For precisely that reason, he gave them encouragement of profound compassion. The suffering of the disciple is also the suffering of the mentor. This is the heart of a true mentor.

Angulimala keenly felt the Buddha's compassion. As a result he could endure this hardship.

Saito: There is another well-known episode that concerns Aniruddha,[14] a disciple who was losing his sight. Aniruddha was trying to thread a needle to mend his robe. But he was having difficulty because of his poor eyesight. He muttered in exasperation, "Isn't there anyone who wants to accumulate more benefit by threading this needle for me?" Someone replied, "Let me accumulate more benefit." He was taken aback when he realized that he was hearing the warm voice of Shakyamuni.

Aniruddha felt ashamed and tried to refuse the offer. "Surely there's no need for you to accumulate any more benefit," he told Shakyamuni. But Shakyamuni told him that this was not the case, and that the pursuit of truth and the pursuit of happiness were never-ending. With that, he threaded the needle.[15]

Ikeda: That's a marvelous vignette. It conveys a sense of the actual person Shakyamuni, who, if he saw a disciple having difficulties, would by no means simply ignore the person; on the contrary, he would do everything he could to warmly help him or her.

In any event, Shakyamuni's teachings differed considerably depending on whom he was addressing. All the same, through personal exchange with Shakyamuni, his disciples were able to advance along the correct path. Those alive during Shakyamuni's lifetime pursued the Law—the Buddha's mentor—inspired by the fresh and profound sense of the Buddha they gained through their direct contact with Shakyamuni.

AFTER SHAKYAMUNI'S DEATH, THE LAW BECOMES THE MENTOR

Saito: By contrast, after Shakyamuni's death the Law necessarily becomes fundamental. That is inevitable. The only way to attain Buddhahood is to have a direct connection with the Law and, in effect, make the Law one's mentor.

Ikeda: Yes. After Shakyamuni's passing, therefore, the practice of the Buddha's disciples came to center on the issue of how to perceive the eternal Law that is one with the eternal Buddha.

The so-called Hinayana Buddhist Order, which came into existence after Shakyamuni's death, comprised primarily Shakyamuni's direct disciples and those monks who carried on after them. It may be that at first they earnestly observed the practice of strictly regulating the self based on teachings, that Shakyamuni left behind. But that spirit was gradually lost over time. They departed from the original teachings, which is to look within the self to perceive the Law at one with the Buddha to which Shakyamuni had awakened; and it may be that as a result there arose a tendency to see Shakyamuni as somehow a different kind of being than they were.

In any event, at some point they forgot about struggling to embody the eternal Law at one with the eternal Buddha to which Shakyamuni the human being had awakened. This is a generalization, but it seems likely that this is the essence of what took place.

SHAKYAMUNI'S DEIFICATION RESULTED IN BUDDHISM'S DEHUMANIZATION

Saito: Because direct contact with the Buddha was impossible, in time the concept of the "great Buddha" took on a life of its own. People thought that Shakyamuni alone had attained the Buddha's enlightenment, and that it was far beyond them to ever become Buddhas themselves.

Endo: The enlightenment toward which they strove was the highest enlightenment of voice-hearers—the stage of arhat. The state of the Buddha was seen as unattainable.

Suda: In the meantime, the precepts gradually grew in complexity. Also, to maintain the order, the monks apparently created an air of mystery around their temples, going so far as to expound teachings arrogating authority to themselves. At the same time, they placed the Buddha on a pedestal rending him inaccessible to ordinary people.

Ikeda: Still, things weren't quite as bad as they could have been as long as Shakyamuni's direct disciples were around. The first compilation of sutras is said to have taken place about a century after Shakyamuni's death. By then Shakyamuni's deification may have already been fairly well advanced. Also, the project might have been prompted by fear that memory of Shakyamuni the human being, which had grown increasingly dim, was fading away entirely.

Saito: The Sanskrit term that, in the Chinese Buddhist canon, is translated as "World-Honored One" is *bhagavat,* an ancient Indian literary term. This was apparently an appellation that disciples used in addressing a teacher. But as Shakyamuni's deification became solidified, people came to refer to him instead as the "supreme deity" or as the "god of gods."

Suda: When we come to Mahayana Buddhism, we find an emphasis on a personal Buddha as a "savior" figure who leads people to enlightenment.

Endo: As was pointed out earlier, however, these Buddhas are not the same as Shakyamuni. They include Amida, Vairochana and Mahavairochana. They are personal Buddhas of deep compassion; moreover, they are described as supreme beings who continually save people over the span of eternity.

Ikeda: They may have arrived at these Buddhas in attempting to approximate the "eternal Law at one with the eternal Buddha" that Shakyamuni made his own mentor. In that sense, we can see them each as a partial expression of the life of the original Buddha enlightened since the remote past.

Suda: In terms of the doctrine of the Buddha's three bodies or enlightened properties,[16] according to one interpretation, Mahavairochana represents the Dharma body, or the property of the Law; and Amida represents the bliss body, or property of wisdom. By contrast, Shakyamuni of the "Life Span" chapter who has been enlightened since the remote past is the Buddha who inherently possesses all three enlightened properties. From the standpoint of the "Life Span" chapter, therefore, all other Buddhas represent partial views of enlightenment.

Saito: Regarding these pre–Lotus Sutra teachings, the Daishonin says, "All partially explain the phenomena inherent in one's life. They do not explain them as the Lotus Sutra does" (WND-1, 629). The same can perhaps be said of the Buddha's bodies or enlightened properties taken individually. Why don't we review this concept of the three bodies another time?

Endo: These teachings explain nothing but idealized Buddhas— Buddhas exhibiting special appearances and characteristics. This becomes a common concept in Buddhism.

Ikeda: From one standpoint, these Buddhas are expressions of people's ardent spirit of yearning for the Buddha; or perhaps they were formulated in response to that longing. Nichikan says that these Buddhas are "adorned with distinguishing features and characteristics in accord with the sentiments of the people of the time."

Suda: The problem is that as a result of this Mahayana Buddhist movement, people came to make light of Shakyamuni, the originator of Buddhism. Instead, they revered imaginary Buddhas as "gods." Ultimately, this closed off the path whereby people could discover the "Law at one with the Buddha" within their own lives.

Endo: Moreover, the teaching of such Buddhas, rather than encouraging people to place importance on their own inherent strength, only reinforced the tendency to depend on the Buddha's compassion for salvation. The Pure Land or Nembutsu school of Buddhism, in which people seek salvation through the benevolence of Amida Buddha, is a case in point.

Ikeda: In short, both the Hinayana and Mahayana teachings completely deviate from the spirit of Shakyamuni's teaching to make the Law and the self our foundation.

If I may generalize, while the Hinayana teachings emphasize seeking the Law, they needlessly alienate the Buddha from human beings. The Mahayana teachings, on the other hand, while they seek to revive the relationship between the Buddha and human beings, fail to extend people's understanding to the extent that they themselves can embody the Law. Neither approach is adequate. This underlines the significance of the "Life Span" chapter's teaching of casting off the transient and revealing the true.

Endo: Buddhism is not the only place we find such tendencies as you have just described. Any religion may succumb to the flawed notion of subordinating people through dogma or authority.

Ikeda: That's right. The Lotus Sutra's spirit is to resist the dehumanization of religion and religion's tendency to become divorced from reality but instead to steadfastly redirect religion to focus on the human being.

Suda: I recall the Daishonin's declaration in "On Practicing the Buddha's Teachings" that he has "launched the battle between the provisional and the true teachings" and "the battle goes on even today" (WND-1, 392). The true legacy of Buddhism can be found only within unceasing spiritual struggle.

Saito: The Daishonin constantly proclaimed: "Return to Shakyamuni!" He refutes adherents of the True Word school who revered Mahavairochana Buddha, saying, "Who were the parents of the Thus Come One Mahavairochana, and in what country did he appear when he expounded the Mahavairochana Sutra?" (WND-1, 349).

Endo: He condemns as utterly confused those who try to do away with the actual person Shakyamuni while making much of imaginary Buddhas of uncertain origins. "Return to Shakyamuni!" means "Return to the human being!"

Suda: The Daishonin waged a desperate struggle to revive the humanistic spirit of Buddhism.

Ikeda: That suggests just how strong the tendency of religion is to depart from the human being. And when that happens, religion becomes little more than a means for controlling people.

Suda: That's a truly frightful prospect.

Saito: While various arguments can be made about the principal cause for this phenomenon, the following can certainly be cited as contributing factors: corruption of the clergy, increasing rigidity in the organization of the religious body, and a stagnant spirit of faith. When these coincide, a religion becomes alienated from the people and grows authoritarian.

Suda: The Nikken sect is a classic example of a school in which these factors are all in evidence. They have a dissolute high priest making wild claims; for example, that he is equal to Nichiren Daishonin. This alone sends a clear message that they are not the least concerned with fundamental issues of human life and existence.

President Toda: "I Am Merely an Upstanding Common Mortal"

Ikeda: I recall how a newspaper reporter once sarcastically asked President Toda, "Since you're the president of the Soka Gakkai, that must make you a 'living Buddha,' doesn't it?"

"Hah!" he retorted with a hearty laugh. "If a living Buddha were to eat sushi or drink whiskey, that would be terrible. There is no such thing."

"I am merely an upstanding common mortal," he would often say. "Religious leaders who claim to be gods and the like are frauds."[17]

Saito: There isn't anyone who is superhuman—that was his firm conviction. I am impressed by how important the kind of humanism expressed by Buddhism will be for religion in the twenty-first century. This is indeed just as you are always telling us.

Ikeda: Moreover, it is not at all uncommon to find instances of powerful people using religion as a sign of authority to make themselves appear somehow superior to others. When clergy or leaders of society try to pass themselves off as better than others or as special, the people are invariably plunged into misery. This is a lesson of history, as the witch hunts and the oppressive regimes of dictators such as Hitler and Stalin make abundantly clear.

Blaise Pascal put his finger on the essence of this tragedy, saying, "Man is neither angel nor beast, and it is a misfortune that whoever tries to play the angel ends by playing the beast."[18]

Endo: Those who try to pass themselves off as superhuman or as "angels" are in fact, beasts; they come to behave in a way that is subhuman. From this standpoint, we find that the principle of casting off the transient and revealing the true signifies Shakyamuni displaying the great and eternal life that is at one with the universe while never for a moment departing from his status as a human being.

Ikeda: In philosophical terms, it urges us: "Direct your gaze on the eternal without departing from the present reality!" "Seek out the supreme that is at one with life's inherent truth!" "Discover the universal right where you are!" That is the spirit of casting off the transient and revealing the true.

THE "LIFE SPAN" CHAPTER UNIFIES THE HINAYANA AND THE MAHAYANA

Saito: Although both the Hinayana teachings and the provisional Mahayana teachings make repeated attempts to get at the truth and have produced significant philosophical results, ultimately they are distorted by biases. Through the "Life Span" chapter's teaching of casting off the transient and revealing the true, these two bodies of teaching are for the first time largely unified.

Ikeda: That's right. The "Life Span" chapter beckons us to return to Shakyamuni the human being. And yet, through the concept of the eternal Buddha, it develops a religious world more profound than that afforded through the Buddha's deification. Without departing in the least from the human being, it opens up a path whereby people can limitlessly expand or transcend the narrow limitations of their humanity.

Saito: Thinking in these terms, it occurs to me that while we tend to place importance on the aspect of Shakyamuni's revealing his true identity as the eternal Buddha, the aspect of his "casting off the transient" is equally important. In "casting off the transient," we can sense Shakyamuni's determination to discover the truth without departing from the actual person; that is, to always base himself on "Shakyamuni the human being."

Ikeda: To "cast off" has the meaning to open. Opening up the transient could be compared to removing the clouds blocking the sun. When the clouds are dispelled, the "true identity," like the brilliant light of the sun, appears. Just because there are clouds in the sky, it doesn't mean that you look for the sun somewhere else. You don't stop looking for the sun in the sky; for that is where its true identity resides.

Suda: I understand the meaning of 'return to the human being,' but I imagine that many people may be a little unclear as to what precisely is meant by the expression "eternal Buddha" or by the "Buddha who is always here, preaching the Law." Some may associate these terms with a kind of superhuman being.

Endo: Actually, general Buddhist scholarship treats Shakyamuni of the "Life Span" chapter as a kind of deity.

Ikeda: Nichiren Daishonin inscribed the Gohonzon for precisely this reason. Nothing could be more real, more concrete than the Gohonzon. The Daishonin made it possible for us ordinary people of the Latter Day, by chanting the Mystic Law to the Gohonzon, to become one with the "Buddha who is always here, preaching the Law."

The Gohonzon embodies the oneness of the Person and the Law. In terms of the Person, it is the manifestation of the Buddha of absolute freedom since time without beginning; in terms of the Law, it is the manifestation of actual 'three thousand worlds in a single moment of life.' Therefore, President Toda referred to the eternal Buddha of time without beginning as Mr. Three Thousand Worlds in a Single Moment of Life.

When we embrace the Gohonzon and exert ourselves for kosen-rufu, the "eternal Buddha who is always here, preaching the Law" comes forth from our lives.

President Toda commented on the passage of the "Life Span" chapter, "Ever since then [the remote past] I have been constantly in this saha world, preaching the Law, teaching and converting" (LSOC, 266), as follows: "This is the 'universe that is at one with the Gohonzon.' The life of Nam-myoho-renge-kyo has since the remote past been at one with the universe."[19]

He also said: "When we pray to the Gohonzon and receive the life of the Gohonzon in ourselves, then, because our lives themselves are Nam-myoho-renge-kyo, the power of the Gohonzon wells forth within us. Then we can observe the affairs of the world without any serious error in judgment."[20]

Revealing Our True Identity
Every Morning and Every Evening

Endo: The *Record of the Orally Transmitted Teachings* quotes Fu Ta-shih,[21] "Morning after morning we rise up with the Buddha, evening after evening we lie down with thr Buddha. Moment by moment we attain the way, moment by moment we reveal our true identity" (OTT, 83). We who are dedicating our lives to faith in the Gohonzon can sense the truth of these words more profoundly and immediately than any Buddhist scholar can.

Ikeda: It's a matter of "revealing the true" at each moment. Every morning and evening we actualize the principle of casting off the transient and revealing the true. We cause the life of the eternal Buddha of time without beginning to manifest in our hearts and we continuously advance toward kosen-rufu. From a broad perspective, this means that we are in fact reading the "Life Span" chapter with our lives each day.

Saito: Over the course of two millennia, the spiritual channel that Shakyamuni opened gradually drifted away from humanity and dried up. The humanism of Nichiren Buddhism has caused it to be revitalized as a great river that will endure for eternity.

Ikeda: Yes. The Daishonin's teaching refutes all philosophies and religions that force people to kneel down before religious authority and enables people instead to open up the sacred great life within themselves. It was for this reason that the Daishonin encountered great persecution. His was a great struggle for human rights, undertaken with indomitable courage.

In "The True Aspect of All Phenomena," he says: "A common mortal is an entity of the three bodies, and a true Buddha. A Buddha is the function of the three bodies, and a provisional Buddha" (WND-1, 384). I think we will have the chance to discuss this profound doctrine in detail later on; but in essence he is saying that the common mortal is the true Buddha. Let's interpret this as the ultimate declaration of the humanization of Buddhism.

Nichiren Buddhism is a humanistic religion that will illuminate the third millennium, beginning with the twenty-first century, and the entire ten thousand years and more of the Latter Day of the Law.

NOTES

1. Their dialogue was published under the title *Ningen kakumei to ningen no joken* (The Human Revolution and the Human Condition) by Ushio Publishing Company, Tokyo, in 1976.

2. At the Third SGI of Germany Executive Conference, held in Frankfurt am Main on May 24, 1994.

3. André Malraux, *Anti-memoirs*, trans. Terence Kilmartin (New York: Holt, Rinehart and Winston, 1968), p. 228.

4. Bodhisattva Hachiman: Originally, a Japanese deity of the harvest. He is often called Great Bodhisattva Hachiman. In Buddhism, Hachiman is regarded as a deity who protects the votaries of the Lotus Sutra.

5. André Malraux, p. 228.

6. *Arhat:* Defined variously as "one worthy of respect," "one who has nothing more to learn," "destroyer of the bandits of the illusions of thought and desire," "no rebirth" (because an *arhat* has freed himself from transmigration in the six paths), and "worthy to receive offerings."

7. Amida: Skt Amitayus, "Infinite Life," or *Amitabha,* "Infinite Light." The Buddha of the Pure Land of Perfect Bliss in the western region of the universe.

8. Mahavairochana: (Skt) A Buddha mentioned in the Dainichi and Kongocho sutras, worshipped by adherents of esoteric Buddhism.

9. Vairochana: A Buddha who appears in the Kegon, Bommo and Dainichi sutras. The Shingon sect equates this Buddha with its central deity, Mahavairochana.

10. *Nanden daizokyo*, ed. Junjiro Takakusu (Tokyo: Taisho Shinshu Daizokyo Kanko-kai, 1935), vol. 7, pp. 68–69.

11. *Nanden daizokyo* (Tokyo:Taisho Shinshu Daizokyo Kanko-kai, 1938), vol. 3, pp. 16–17.

12. Ibid., vol. 11, part 1, p. 134.

13. Ibid., pp. 139–40.

14. Aniruddha: Also Anaritsu. One of the ten great disciples of the Buddha. Having once fallen asleep in the presence of the Buddha, he vowed that he would never sleep again. He eventually lost his eyesight, but acquired the ability to see intuitively.

15. *Kokuyaku issaikyo indo senjutsubu agonbu,* vols. 9–10, ed. Shinyu Iwano (Tokyo: Daito Shuppansha, 1969), p. 152.

16. According to Great Teacher T'ien-t'ai of China, the benefit of the Buddha specifically consists of the Buddha's three bodies or enlightened properties: the Dharma body or property of the Law (the truth to which the Buddha is enlightened), the bliss body or property of wisdom (the wisdom the Buddha has attained), and the manifested body or property of action (the physical form in which the Buddha appears in this world and his compassionate actions).

17. *Kokuyaku issaikyo indo senjutsubu agonbu,* pp. 372–73.

18. *Pascal's pensées*, trans. Martin Turnell (London: Harvill Press, 1962), p. 173.

19. *Toda Josei zenshu* (Collected Writings of Josei Toda) (Tokyo: Seikyo Shimbunsha, 1985), vol. 5, p. 431.

20. Ibid., pp. 373–74.

21. Fu Ta-shih (497–569):A Chinese priest of the Northern and Southern Dynasties period. His true name is Fu His, but he was also called Fu Ta-shih, which can be construed to mean a bodhisattva who will succeed the Buddha.

3   Establish a State of Life
        of Eternal, Indestructible Happiness

Suda: In April 1997, much to the delight of amateur astronomers the world over, Comet Hale-Bopp made its closest pass to the earth since its last appearance some 4,200 years ago. Reportedly the comet is on a trek around the sun that won't happen again for another two or three thousand years.

Endo: A human being, by contrast, rarely lives even a hundred years. No one alive today will live to see this comet come again.

Saito: When we contemplate the grand workings of the universe, we find ourselves forced to ponder the ultimate nature of the self and the meaning of human existence. I wouldn't be surprised if a great many people, prompted by the sight of the comet, began thinking along these lines.

Ikeda: As we grapple with difficult Buddhist concepts, it is also important that we have the inner richness that allows us to look up at the stars or the moon and compose a poem once in a while. When we open our minds and fix our gaze on the universe, we fix our gaze on our own lives.

Suda: Yes, I agree. But amid the stress of daily life, it is often difficult to find the time in the day or the space in our lives to ponder life from such a lofty perspective. And when you add our anxiety over the most trifling matters as we try to keep up with the demands of day-to-day living, it is hard not to fall into a more mundane mind-set.

Ikeda: And that's why religion is so important.

The year before Josei Toda died, the Soviet Union successfully launched the first man-made satellite (Sputnik, October 4, 1957). This became the talk of the world. When he heard what a fuss people were making over it, President Toda chided them, saying: "It's nothing to get so excited about. We just have one more tiny star in the sky. From the standpoint of the vastness of the universe as taught in Buddhism, it's no more than a tiny speck." President Toda talked about the universe as though it were his own backyard; it gave one a sense of the vastness of Buddhism, as well as the grand scale of President Toda's life.

People in conflict tend to make big deals of the smallest things. So we become joyful or sorrowful because of trivial matters, bouncing forth and back. Such small-mindedness can only produce misery.

Nichiren Daishonin says that with the passage of time, "even the large-hearted become narrow, and even those who seek the way adopt erroneous views" (WND-1, 845). In a sense, the purpose of Buddhism and of the movement for widely declaring and spreading Buddhism lies in opening and expanding hearts that have grown narrow. The greatest expression of broad-mindedness is the principle of three thousand realms in a single moment of life, a principle that allows us to thoroughly grasp the truth that one's mind and the universe are eternally one. The purpose of Buddhism is to enable us to achieve this understanding.

In terms of our topic, Nichiren Daishonin says that without the principle of casting off the transient and revealing the true, as clarified in the "Life Span" chapter, there is no actual three thousand realms in a single moment of life. Why is that? In our discussion today I hope we can delve a little further into the meaning of this fundamental principle.

SHAKYAMUNI AND THE TEACHING OF THREE THOUSAND REALMS IN A SINGLE MOMENT OF LIFE

Thus, since I attained Buddhahood, an extremely long period of time has passed. My life span is an immeasurable number of asamkhya kalpas, and during that time I have constantly abided here without ever entering extinction. Good men, originally I practiced the bodhisattva way, and the life span that I acquired then has yet to come to an end but will last twice the number of years that have already passed. (LSOC, 267-68)

Endo: OK. We previously learned about the significance of the principle of casting off the transient and revealing the true. To recap, we discussed how Shakyamuni became a Buddha by taking as his mentor the "eternal Law at one with the eternal Buddha." With the teaching of casting off the transient and revealing the true, Shakyamuni urged his disciples to follow his example and make the same eternal Law their mentor as well.

The powerful message here is: "Return to Shakyamuni the human being! Acquire for yourself the same foundation that enabled Shakyamuni to become a Buddha!" When I heard this, I felt as though I had truly grasped this principle for the first time.

Saito: The eternal Law is Nam-myoho-renge-kyo. The eternal Buddha is the Buddha of absolute freedom who has been enlightened since time without beginning, or the Nam-myoho-renge-kyo Thus Come One.

Ikeda: That's right. Nam-myoho-renge-kyo is the Law; but at the same time it is also the life of the Buddha. The Person and the Law are one. The oneness of the Person and the Law is the important point.

While we may speak of the Law as though it were independent, if it really were separate from the Person (the Buddha) it would be no more than a theoretical construct. What the Buddha realizes is the Law. The Buddha's wisdom is the Law. The Buddha and the Law can never be separate.

The Buddha from time without beginning, the Buddha existing eternally without beginning or end, is the life of the universe itself. This Buddha works ceaselessly to lead all to enlightenment. In fact, since that Buddha and we ourselves are one, then, we ourselves have been working to lead people to happiness and for widely declaring and spreading Buddhism since the remote past; not only in this lifetime. This awareness is the heart of the "Life Span" chapter.

When our viewpoint expands from the present to the entirety of the eternal universe, we awaken to life's profound mission. Similarly, Shakyamuni realized that he was in fact one with the eternal Buddha, and he described this self as undying. He said: "It is better to live a single day aware of the undying self than to live a hundred years ignorant of the undying self"; and, "Rather than living a hundred years ignorant of supreme truth, it is better to live a single day perceiving supreme truth."[1]

Endo: Here, "undying self" and "supreme truth" refer to the same thing.

Ikeda: That's right. Simply put, they both refer to the doctrine of the three thousand realms in a single moment of life. Shakyamuni gave partial explanations of this doctrine in various sutras, but the explanations in the pre-Lotus Sutra teachings are not satisfactory. There is a well-known passage relating to this point in *The Writings of Nichiren Daishonin*, "The Opening of the Eyes."

Suda: Yes. The Daishonin says:

> All the other sutras such as the Flower Garland, Wisdom, and Mahavairochana not only conceal the fact that people of the two vehicles can attain Buddhahood, but they also

fail to make clear that the Buddha attained enlightenment countless kalpas in the past. These sutras have two flaws. First, because they teach that the Ten Worlds are separate from one another, they fail to move beyond the provisional doctrines and to reveal the doctrine of three thousand realms in a single moment of life as it is expounded in the theoretical teaching of the Lotus Sutra. Second, because they teach that Shakyamuni Buddha attained enlightenment for the first time in this world, referring only to his provisional aspect, they fail to reveal the fact stressed in the essential teaching that the Buddha attained enlightenment countless kalpas ago. (WND-1, 235)

The sutras before the Lotus Sutra discriminate against those of the two vehicles (voice-hearers and cause-awakened ones, or learning and realization), by concealing the fact that they can attain Buddhahood. The pre-Lotus Sutra teachings also do not reveal the fact that Shakyamuni attained enlightenment in the remote past. Therefore, there is no genuine equality in these teachings.

When the pre-Lotus Sutra teachings say that Shakyamuni attained enlightenment for the first time in India, they overlook and therefore do not explain his actual attainment in the remote past. In other words, they do not address the critical principle of casting off the transient and revealing the true.

Endo: Regarding the principle of enlightenment of the people of the two vehicles and the principle of Shakyamuni's actual attainment in the remote past, the Daishonin says, "These two great doctrines are the core of the Buddha's lifetime of teachings, and the very heart and marrow of all the sutras" (WND-1, 235).

We have learned that the enlightenment of the people of the two vehicles reveals the doctrine of three thousand realms in a single moment of life of the theoretical teaching, whereas Shakyamuni's actual attainment of enlightenment in the remote past reveals three thousand realms in a single moment of life of the essential teaching.

Saito: In this connection, the Daishonin says:

> The Expedient Means chapter, which belongs to the theoretical teaching, expounds the doctrine of three thousand realms in a single moment of life, making clear that persons of the two vehicles can achieve Buddhahood. It thus eliminates one of the two errors found in the earlier sutras. But it nevertheless retains the provisional aspect, and fails to reveal the eternal aspect, of the Buddha's enlightenment. Thus the true doctrine of three thousand realms in a single moment of life remains unclear, and the attainment of Buddhahood by persons of the two vehicles is not properly affirmed. Such teachings are like the moon seen in the water, or rootless plants that drift on the waves. (WND-1, 235)

The difficulty here is the question of why, in order to articulate the teaching of actual three thousand realms in a single moment of life, Shakyamuni had to employ the principle of casting off the transient and revealing the true. Why does the Daishonin refer to these teachings as rootless plants?

Ikeda: Let's consider this methodically. First, what is three thousand realms in a single moment of life of the theoretical teaching? We went through this earlier in our discussion of the second or "Expedient Means" chapter, but it might help to reconfirm the main points of that chapter here.

Saito: OK. The Great Teacher T'ien-t'ai of China established the principle of three thousand realms in a single moment of life based on the passage of the "Expedient Means" chapter that describes the true entity of all phenomena and the ten factors.[2]

The teaching of the true entity of all phenomena represents a radical departure from the pre-Lotus Sutra teachings because it bridges the hitherto insurmountable gap between the world of Buddhahood and the nine worlds.

The pre-Lotus Sutra teachings not only describe the beings of each of the Ten Worlds from hell to Buddhahood as existing separately; they go so far as to say that the Buddha and the beings of the nine worlds actually dwell in different lands. But the "Expedient Means" chapter of the Lotus Sutra brings things into focus, explaining that the Buddha and the beings of the nine worlds are in fact all entities of life who equally exhibit the same ten factors. This eliminates the discrimination found in the pre-Lotus Sutra teachings.

Ikeda: The ten factors are also termed the true aspect of the ten factors. The substance of the true aspect is none other than Myoho-renge-kyo itself. The factors of "inherent cause" and "latent effect," along with the other eight factors, exist in one's life at each moment. This is the simultaneity of cause and effect. This simultaneity is the marvelous Law of the lotus that we all are entities of that Law.

"All phenomena" in the phrase "the true aspect of all phenomena" indicates the Ten Worlds. While the phenomena of the universe are infinite, they are all included in the concept of life and environment endowed with the Ten Worlds. All phenomena of the Ten Worlds are the true aspect; that is, they are all aspects of the Mystic Law. That is the meaning of the true aspect of all phenomena.

Endo: Regarding the principle of the true aspect of all phenomena, in our discussion of the "Expedient Means" chapter, we touched on the true aspect of life as viewed from the enlightened state of Buddhahood. At that time, President Ikeda, you said:

> Here, all things are equal, transcending distinctions and differences between subject and object, self and others,

mind and body, the spiritual and the material. In its true aspect of life it is infinitely expansive and eternal, without beginning or end and transcending distinctions of the Ten Worlds.[3]

Ikeda: That's right. The true aspect accords with the dynamic life of the universe, without beginning or end. The true aspect of all phenomena reveals the Law through which all beings in the Ten Worlds can equally attain Buddhahood. This is three thousand realms in a single moment of life of the theoretical teaching.

WHY IS THE THEORETICAL TEACHING LIKE A ROOTLESS PLANT?

Suda: From that explanation, it seems that with the theoretical teaching, or first half, of the Lotus Sutra the doctrine of three thousand realms in a single moment of life has been all but completely elucidated. Why then does the Daishonin say that it would be like a rootless plant in the absence of the one remaining principle of casting off the provisional and revealing the true?

I believe it is because even though the theoretical teaching reveals that the nine worlds contain the world of Buddhahood through the explication of the doctrine of the enlightenment of the two vehicles, it does not teach the converse of this—that the world of Buddhahood contains the other nine worlds. As the Daishonin indicates where he says, "The doctrine of three thousand realms in a single moment of life begins with the concept of the mutual possession of the Ten Worlds" (WND-I, 224), the mutual possession of the Ten Worlds is the core of three thousand realms in a single moment of life. But we do not have the mutual possession of the Ten Worlds until it is clarified both that the nine worlds contain the world of Buddhahood and that the world of Buddhahood contains the nine worlds.

From the point of view that Shakyamuni attained enlightenment for the first time in India—that is to say, from the account of Shakyamuni as an ordinary person [representing the nine worlds], renouncing the world at age nineteen, carrying out Buddhist practice, and ultimately becoming a Buddha—we see only the aspect of the nine worlds containing the world of Buddhahood. Accordingly, to reveal the world of Buddhahood endowed with the nine worlds, Shakyamuni casts off his transient status and reveals his true identity.

Endo: That may be so. But isn't it also true that, on a theoretical level at least, the principle of the mutual possession of the Ten Worlds in some sense arises from the explanation of the true aspect of all phenomena that we find in the theoretical teaching? Since it is explained that all beings in the Ten Worlds are equally entities of, and fundamentally one with, the Mystic Law, it goes without saying that beings in the nine worlds possess the world of Buddhahood. Likewise, it also follows that beings in the world of Buddhahood possess the nine worlds.

Since the principal objective is to enable beings in the nine worlds to become Buddhas, the teaching of the enlightenment of the people of the two vehicles—that is, that the nine worlds contain the world of Buddhahood—naturally is given priority in the theoretical teaching. Therefore, part of the significance of casting off the transient and revealing the true lies in Shakyamuni's discussing, based on his own experience and in actual terms, the point that the world of Buddhahood contains the other nine worlds—which until that juncture had been merely "theory."

Ikeda: This is so complicated it seems you are all at odds with one another. Indeed, I sense an uncharacteristic lack of clarity about the true purpose of the teaching of casting off the transient and revealing the true.

Certainly, the doctrine of the true aspect of all phenomena is the key that reveals a correct view of life, according to which the nine worlds are endowed with the world of Buddhahood; and the world of Buddhahood, with the nine worlds. But a major contradiction arises between this teaching of Shakyamuni's and his apparent enlightenment within his lifetime in India.

Put another way, the teaching of the true aspect of all phenomena points directly to the vast life of the Buddha who exists eternally without beginning or end—the world of the original Buddha, whom Shakyamuni made his mentor. In short, the "Expedient Means" chapter teaches that the eternal Mystic Law and the external Buddha are one and the same.

Saito: In expounding this teaching, as long as Shakyamuni maintains the position that he attained enlightenment for the first time during his present lifetime, the "teaching expounded" and the "person expounding it" are not in agreement. And the only way for Shakyamuni to bring them into agreement is to reveal the realm of the Buddha from time without beginning, which the teaching of the true aspect of all phenomena implies.

In conclusion, the teaching of casting off the transient and revealing the true is a necessary link to, and provides actual proof of, the teaching of the true aspect of all phenomena.

Ikeda: That's why when Shariputra, who was regarded as the foremost disciple in wisdom, hears Shakyamuni preach the true aspect of all phenomena, he immediately realizes Shakyamuni's "true identity," which is implicit in this teaching. And by realizing Shakyamuni's true identity, he at the same time recollects his own true identity.

The Daishonin calls this Buddha the "Buddha of the true aspect of all phenomena" (OTT, 22). To make this even clearer, I'd like us to now return to "The Opening of the Eyes" and look at what Nichiren Daishonin says about the principle of casting off the transient and revealing the true.

The World of Buddhahood From Time Without Beginning and the Nine Worlds From Time Without Beginning

Endo: Yes, the Daishonin says:

> When we come to the essential teaching of the Lotus Sutra, then the belief that Shakyamuni first obtained Buddhahood during his present lifetime is demolished, and the effects of the four teachings are likewise demolished. When the effects of the four teachings[4] are demolished, the causes of the four teachings are likewise demolished. Thus the cause and effect of the Ten Worlds as expounded in the earlier sutras and the theoretical teaching of the Lotus Sutra are wiped out, and the cause and effect of the Ten Worlds in the essential teaching are revealed. This is the doctrine of original cause and original effect. (WND-I, 235)

"Cause and effect of the Ten Worlds," here, means the cause and effect of attaining Buddhahood. This can be thought of as the path of attaining Buddhahood whereby the world of Buddhahood (the effect) is attained through carrying out the practice of the nine worlds (the cause). But this "cause and effect of the Ten Worlds" is completely different before Shakyamuni casts off his transient status and reveals his true identity than after he does so.

Suda: In the first place, by casting off the transient and revealing the true, Shakyamuni rejects the view that he attained enlightenment for the first time in his present existence and in effect refutes the effects of the four teachings. The effects of the four teachings are the various states of Buddhahood as taught in the four teachings — Tripitaka, connecting, specific and perfect teachings—that is, in the pre-Lotus Sutra teachings and the theoretical teaching of the Lotus Sutra. These explanations of Buddhahood are all premised on the view that Shakyamuni attained Buddhahood for the first time in India. That premise is fundamentally overturned when we come to the Lotus Sutra's essential teaching.

Endo: Shakyamuni himself negates the view of Buddhahood that had prevailed until then, announcing in effect: "That is not the true nature of the Buddha's life!"

Saito: The Daishonin says that this also amounts to a refutation of the causes of the four teachings. The denial of Buddhahood described as effects in these teachings amounts to a denial of the authenticity of the causes or practices said to have led to these effects.

In this way, the essential teaching entirely refutes the causality of the Ten Worlds expounded in the pre-Lotus Sutra teachings and the theoretical teaching.

Endo: It is a momentous change of scene.

Saito: At the same time that he refutes the causes and effects he had preached up to that point, Shakyamuni reveals the original cause and effect—the True Cause and True Effect—of his enlightenment. In "The Opening of the Eyes," the Daishonin describes the content of this revelation as follows:

> It reveals that the nine worlds are all present in begin-
> ningless Buddhahood and that Buddhahood is inherent
> in the beginningless nine worlds. This is the true mutual
> possession of the Ten Worlds, the true hundred worlds
> and thousand factors, the true three thousand realms in
> a single moment of life. (WND-1, 235)

The principle of casting off the transient and revealing the true in the "Life Span" chapter clarifies the true aspect that possesses both the "beginningless Buddhahood" and the "beginningless nine worlds." On this basis, the Daishonin affirms that the true mutual possession of the Ten Worlds, the hundred realms and thousand factors, and three thousand realms in a single moment of life are established.

Suda: "Beginningless" literally means without beginning, or eternal, in contrast to "with beginning," or having a point of origin sometime in the finite past. The view of Shakyamuni as attaining Buddhahood for the first time during his lifetime in India suggests, erroneously of course, that his enlightenment has a definite beginning.

"Beginningless" Implies Simultaneity of Cause and Effect

Ikeda: Which passage of the "Life Span" chapter substantiates the key concepts of "beginningless Buddhahood" and "beginningless nine worlds?"

Endo: "Beginningless Buddhahood" is indicated by "it has been immeasurable, boundless hundreds, thousands, ten thousands, millions of nayutas of kalpas since I in fact attained Buddhahood" (LSOC, 265–66). Here, Shakyamuni is saying that an immeasurable period of time has passed since he attained Buddhahood; this is the revelation of his actual attainment in the remote past.

Suda: The passage "since I attained Buddhahood, an extremely long period of time has passed. My life span is an immeasurable number of asamkhya kalpas, and during that time I have constantly abided here without ever entering extinction" (LSOC, 267–68) has much the same meaning.

Saito: From these passages, the Daishonin states that the life of the Buddha is "beginningless."

Endo: The term *beginningless nine worlds* comes from the passage, "originally I practiced the bodhisattva way, and the life span that I acquired then has yet to come to an end but will last twice the number of years that have already passed" (LSOC, 268). This is saying that the life of the nine worlds (represented here by the world of Bodhisattva) also continues eternally.

Ikeda: The Buddha briefly speaks of the beginningless state of his life. Referring to this, the Daishonin says: "The nine worlds are all present in the beginningless Buddhahood." In other words, the world of Buddhahood didn't just suddenly appear; it exists inherently in life from time without beginning.

Buddhahood is inherent in the beginningless nine worlds. The nine worlds neither suddenly appeared nor will they at some point simply disappear. Rather, like the world of Buddhahood, they are eternal. This is the truth of all Ten Worlds, precisely described in the "Life Span" chapter.

If the Ten Worlds were not beginningless, they would not be inherently and eternally existing. On the contrary, they would be nothing originally and existing only in the present—truly the image of rootless plants.

It is only with this clarification of "beginningless Buddhahood" and of the "beginningless nine worlds" that the two distinct concepts of the nine worlds and Buddhahood become one, indivisible and equal. At this point of congruence, cause (the nine worlds) and effect (world of Buddhahood) are simultaneous. This is the "true mutual possession of the Ten Worlds."

Suda: Can we rephrase this as follows? If one subscribes to the view that Shakyamuni first attained enlightenment during his lifetime, his Buddhahood was attained as a result of having practiced for countless aeons. It is therefore without origin, existing only in the present. In terms of cause and effect, the cause of Buddhahood (the nine worlds) comes first, and the effect of Buddhahood (the world of Buddhahood) comes later; which obviously is not the simultaneity of cause and effect.

According to that view, before achieving the effect of Buddhahood one would possess only the nine worlds; which separates the nine worlds from the world of Buddhahood. And after the effect of Buddhahood is attained, one would possess only the world of Buddhahood; separating one from the nine worlds.

Ikeda: That's right. Within that view, there is no mutual possession of the Ten Worlds. And without the mutual possession of the Ten Worlds, there is no doctrine of three thousand realms in a single moment of life. That's why the Daishonin compares the doctrines of the mutual possession of the Ten Worlds and three thousand realms in a single moment of life found in the theoretical teaching of the Lotus Sutra to "rootless plants," or "the moon seen in the water."

The Daishonin calls the mutual possession of the Ten Worlds expounded in the theoretical teaching "mutual possession of the Ten Worlds of initial attainment"; and he calls the mutual possession of the Ten Worlds found in the essential teaching "mutual possession of the Ten Worlds of original attainment and original endowment." He thus indicates that these two doctrines are completely different. The key difference is whether there is recognition of the original Buddha whose life is without beginning or end.

Endo: The writing "On the Ten Dharma Worlds" says the following regarding the difference between "initial attainment" and "original attainment":

> The theoretical teaching expounds only the mutual possession of the Ten Worlds of initial attainment and nowhere reveals the mutual possession of the Ten Worlds of original attainment and original endowment. Therefore, the beings who receive this teaching

and the perfect Buddha who expounds it are all of initial attainment. Since this is the case, how can it be free from the flaw of "the erroneous view that enlightenment is something that they did not possess originally but have now acquired"? (WND-2, 166)

Both the multitude of beings who are taught and the Buddha who teaches are like rootless plants "that enlightenment is something that they did not possess originally but have now acquired." Neither are connected to the truth of the "mutual possession of the Ten Worlds without beginning or end."

Saito: The passage continues:

One should understand that when the Buddhas of the four teachings of doctrine become Buddhas of prefect endowment, they do so in terms of the news expounded in the theoretical teaching. Therefore in the theoretical teaching, pracitioners are ignorant of the Buddha who has been enlightened since time without beginning. (WND-2, 166)

Ikeda: Yes. This is important.

Saito: The Buddhas appearing in the four teachings (Tripitaka, connecting, specific and perfect) and the accounts of their enlightenment have validity only up to the theoretical teaching. The fact is that these are Buddhas of initial attainment. As the Daishonin says, "enlightenment is something that they did not possess originally but have now acquired," like rootless plants. These teachings explain neither the doctrine of eternity nor the true Buddha whose life is without beginning. The Daishonin, therefore, refutes these teachings for not recognizing the fact that the true Buddha exists originally and eternally in both body and mind.

THOSE CONFUSED ABOUT THE ORIGINAL BUDDHA ARE LIKE ANIMALS

Ikeda: The purpose of the essential teaching of the Lotus Sutra is to awaken people to the true Buddha whose life is without beginning. In fact, this is the ultimate purpose of all Buddhism. Without recognizing the original Buddha, we can never recognize the mentor of all Buddhas of past, present and future, nor truly awaken to the fact that we ourselves can attain Buddhahood. We would be like children who do not know their parents and who, as a result, do not know themselves either. It is just as the Daishonin indicates when he says, "The people of these schools who are ignorant of the teachings of the 'Life Span' chapter are similarly like beasts . . . Therefore, Mia-lo states: 'Among all the teachings of the Buddha's lifetime, there is no place . . . where the true longevity of the Buddha is revealed . . . If a son does not even know how old his father is, he will also be in doubt as to what lands his father presides over" (WND-1, 258).

Such people do not know the origin, the source, of their own lives, which are supremely worthy of respect and one with the great eternal universe. Unable to respect either themselves or others, they live out their lives in interminable conflict, harming others.

People like this, no matter how superior they act, are no better than talented animals. The Daishonin compares them to animals because they do not understand the relation of parent and child. At the beginning of "The Opening of the Eyes," the Daishonin says, "In the age before the Three Sovereigns,[5] people were no better than birds and beasts in that they did not even know who their own fathers were" (WND-1, 220).

Suda: It seems to me that this gets at the heart of what ails modern civilization. We have seen explosive growth in scientific technology and other spheres of human knowledge. Yet the basic conditions of people's lives have not substantially changed. Human society is still essentially animalistic.

Endo: We can now calculate the orbit of comets with remarkable accuracy. But by comparison little progress if any has been realized in the investigation of our inner universe.

Ikeda: Elevating humanity to become truly humane is the object of the Lotus Sutra and the object of our efforts to widely declare and spread Buddhism.

Saito: To confirm what has been said so far, only when we base ourselves on the perspective of life without beginning, or the eternal, can we genuinely understand the oneness or mutual inclusiveness of the nine worlds and the world of Buddhahood.

It occurs to me that, while ordinarily it is natural to proceed from cause to effect, that is not the case in the realm of the true Buddha from time without beginning, or the true aspect of life. This is a mystic realm in which the world of Buddhahood (the effect of Buddhahood) and the nine worlds (the cause of Buddhahood) actually exist simultaneously. This simultaneity of cause and effect flies in the face of conventional causality.

Endo: The world of the simultaneity of cause and effect could not be revealed without casting off the transient and revealing the true. The view that Shakyamuni attained enlightenment for the first time in India could only point to a consecutive sequence of causality, in which cause comes first and effect later. But the truth to which Shakyamuni became enlightened is the Mystic Law of the simultaneity of cause and effect. And it was to reveal this truth that he cast off his transient status and revealed his true identity.

Ikeda: This Law of the simultaneity of cause and effect is the life of the Nam-myoho-renge-kyo Thus Come One, the true Buddha from time without beginning.

Practicing this Law from time without beginning is the "original cause." And the effect of Buddhahood we attain through this practice is the "original effect." The doctrine of True Cause and True Effect points to this ultimate Law. Its purpose is to cast off the transient and reveal the true.

True Cause means the fundamental cause for becoming a Buddha, including all practices. So once we embrace this True Cause, it is not necessary that we practice for countless aeons before we can attain Buddhahood.

THE MYSTIC LAW SIMULTANEOUSLY CONTAINS BOTH THE CAUSE AND THE EFFECT OF BUDDHAHOOD

Suda: The meaning of the well-known passage in the "The Entity of the Mystic Law" (in *The Writings of Nichiren Daishonin*, vol.1) is now clear to me:

> This passage of commentary means that the supreme principle [that is the Mystic Law] was originally without a name. When the sage was observing the principle and assigning names to all things, he perceived that there is this wonderful single Law [*myoho*] that simultaneously possesses both cause and effect [*renge*], and he named it Myoho-renge. This single Law that is Myoho-renge encompasses within it all the phenomena comprising the Ten Worlds and the three thousand realms, and is lacking in none of them. Anyone who practices this Law will obtain both the cause and the effect of Buddhahood simultaneously.
>
> The sage practiced with this Law as his teacher and attained enlightenment, and therefore he simultaneously obtained both the mystic cause and the mystic effect of Buddhahood, becoming the Thus Come One of perfect enlightenment and fully realized virtues. (WND-1, 421)

Ikeda: Yes. Only when we arrive at the teaching in the depths of the essential teaching do magnificent lotus flowers "bloom" in the lives of all people. It is then that the Law of the "lotus flower" embodying the simultaneity of cause and effect becomes manifest.

Since this is a key point, I'd like to try to summarize things from another angle. The essential teaching explains that the life of the Buddha is eternally endowed with both the world of Buddhahood and the nine worlds. It is neither only the world of Buddhahood, nor only the nine worlds; rather they exist together eternally. The Daishonin calls this doctrine of the essential teaching "the teaching of cause and effect existing eternally together" (GZ, 871). By contrast, he calls the provisional teachings that precede the Lotus Sutra "teachings of the distinct natures of cause and effect" (GZ, 871).

Suda: The Buddhas appearing in the pre-Lotus Sutra teachings are said to possess states of life that can only be actualized by first eradicating the nine worlds. In other words, "if one wishes to attain Buddhahood, one must necessarily develop a loathing for the other nine realms of existence" (WND-2, 62). These Buddhas are said to have become Buddhas as a result of having practiced lifetime after lifetime over countless aeons and having completely eliminated the delusions innate to the nine worlds. The Daishonin calls these "teachings of the distinct natures of cause and effect" because they treat the cause of Buddhahood as if it were completely separate from the effect.

Endo: The Lotus Sutra, then, through the teaching of the true aspect of all phenomena in the "Expedient Means" chapter, clarifies that the world of Buddhahood and the nine worlds are both realities of the true aspect endowed with the ten factors of life. The Daishonin therefore designates the theoretical teaching of the Lotus Sutra as the "teaching of the identical nature of cause and effect" (GZ, 871).

But in the theoretical teaching, Shakyamuni's stance is the same as in the pre-Lotus Sutra teachings; namely, that he had practiced for countless aeons in the past and attained enlightenment for the first time in his present existence.

Saito: In other words, in the theoretical teaching, even though he says that the world of Buddhahood and the nine worlds have an identical nature, there is no clear indication of what the relationship between the two might be in terms of Shakyamuni's own life.

Suda: And only when we get to the essential teaching is it revealed that Shakyamuni's true identity is that of the Buddha possessing the nine worlds.

THE BUDDHA ORIGINALLY POSSESSING ALL TEN WORLDS

Saito: The Buddha revealed in the "Life Span" chapter is not a Buddha who has distanced himself from and extinguished the nine worlds but the Buddha originally possessing the life of the Ten Worlds. The Daishonin says, "The heart of the 'Life Span' chapter is the originally existing Ten Worlds" (GZ, 834).

Ikeda: That's right. The Buddha of the "Life Span" chapter teaches that all beings of the Ten Worlds are essentially a Buddha (WND-I, 458).

This Buddha is originally endowed with the world of Buddhahood, the states of bodhisattva, voice-hearers and cause-awakened ones, as well as hell, hunger and animality, and so on. Shakyamuni did not at some point suddenly become a Buddha; nor did the nine worlds cease to exist in his life at some moment of enlightenment.

The Ten Worlds are also called the ten Dharma worlds. "Dharma world" indicates the universe, the entirety of phenomena. The entire universe expressed as the Ten Worlds is a great entity of life, a great Buddha whose life is without beginning or end and who continually acts with compassion. For precisely this reason, all beings, whichever of the Ten Worlds is their dominant tendency, are one with this Buddha.

When we realize that our lives are one with the great and eternal life of the universe, we are the Buddha. The purpose of Buddhism is to enable all people to come to this realization. But people suffer because of their attachment to the small self and their narrow-mindedness. The Lotus Sutra exists to help us break through this shell of delusion and cause the sun of the great life of time without beginning—eternity—to rise in our hearts.

Since the Buddha we are talking about is the Buddha originally possessing the Ten Worlds, the "true identity" revealed in the "Life Span" chapter is not the identity of Shakyamuni alone but the actual identity of all beings of the Ten Worlds.

In the line, "it has been immeasurable, boundless hundreds, thousands, ten thousands, millions of nayutas of kalpas since I in fact attained Buddhahood" [LSOC, 265–66], "I" literally means Shakyamuni but implicitly it stands for all beings of the Ten Worlds. Thus, we ourselves are unquestionably the eternal Buddha.

Suda: That's why in *The Record of the Orally Transmitted Teachings,* the Daishonin says, "'I' here refers to each and every being in the Ten Worlds" (OTT, 126).

THE TEACHING FOR THIS LIFETIME VERSUS THE ETERNAL TEACHING

Ikeda: What is the meaning of "I"? What is the meaning of "self"? These questions are not just abstract philosophy but go to the root of our human existence.

One view would be to think only in terms of one's present existence, identifying the self in terms of one's parents, or the particular day, month and year of one's birth. In terms of the future, likewise, one would think of the self as encompassing the span of time until one's death.

I once accompanied President Toda on a trip to encourage members in the Sendai area. As always, even aboard the train, Mr. Toda made me study. I recall that on that trip I was reading "The One Hundred and Six Comparisons." I asked President Toda about Shakyamuni having attained enlightenment for the first time in India compared to Shakyamuni having attained enlightenment in the remote past. President Toda remarked: "We might say that the view of his attaining enlightenment for the first time is an argument about the present. It considers everything only in terms of the present existence."

For example, President Toda said, we may think of marriage as a bond existing only in the present existence. Similarly, we might think about our having taken faith, our being born and dying, our relations with our parents and siblings and so on, all only in terms of the present existence. This underlies the view that Shakyamuni attained enlightenment for the first time in India.

Thinking this way produces only unhappiness—for the individual, for society and for the world. If everything were limited to just our present existence, people might conclude that they should merely live frivolously and only for enjoyment; and if things came to a deadlock, they would be justified in resorting to any underhanded tactic at their disposal to get ahead; and that if every attempt to get ahead failed, then there would be no point to go on living. Many people's actions, attached only to things as they are, evince such an attitude.

On the other hand, President Toda continued, "The view of Shakyamuni as having actually attained enlightenment in the remote past is premised on an eternal perspective of life." According to this view, for example, we marry the person we marry because of a past relationship. Also, there is nothing coincidental about our having taken faith in the Daishonin's teaching. In the past we formed a relationship with the Lotus Sutra; in fact, we have been Bodhisattvas of the Earth since the remote past. That is why we have embraced the Mystic Law in this existence. The same will be true in the future as well. We are eternal friends and comrades.

There are countless stars in the universe, billions and billions. After our present existence comes to an end, we can freely be born anywhere we wish in the universe. And we can work there to help people become happy and attain enlightenment.

The lives of all people continue eternally. When we understand this, we understand what a great crime it is to create nuclear and other weapons of mass destruction.

The understanding that life continues eternally prompts us to think not about fighting with one another but about learning how to get along with, encourage and assist one another; and about how to pool our energies and construct peaceful and happy lives. When we understand that all people are Buddhas, heinous crimes such as murder become unthinkable. Likewise, it simply could not happen that people would pointlessly destroy the environment if they understood that all life possesses the Buddha nature. This is the spirit that the Lotus Sutra teaches.

Saito: The Lotus Sutra is itself a fundamental message of peace. And the "Life Span" chapter, in particular, holds the key to elevating the lives of all people.

Don't Lose Sight of the Big Picture

Endo: I think we can also talk about "initial attainment" and "actual attainment in the remote past" in terms of faith. Most people initially embrace faith in the Daishonin's teaching on account of illness or worries in their families or personal lives.

Suda: I can't imagine that many people take faith out of a sense of mission from the remote past.

Endo: As we overcome our worries, we gain confidence and

advance in our practice and study. As a result, we gradually come to realize that we have been born in this life in accord with a vow that we made in the past to work to widely declare and spread Buddhism. It seems that this is similar to the point of view of actual attainment in the remote past.

Ikeda: That's exactly right. Certainly there is a great difference between understanding something theoretically and understanding it through actual practice and experience. When hungry, knowing the right proportions of water and grain, knowing the precise cooking temperature does not satisfy us. A pot of delicious steaming rice does.

Similarly, even if we understand the Lotus Sutra theoretically, unless we take action to widely declare and spread Buddhism, it won't do us any good. Indeed, failure to take action is the very proof of not understanding!

On the other hand, eternal Buddhahood manifests in the depths of the lives of those who take action daily to widely declare and spread Buddhism, for the Mystic Law and for the happiness of others—regardless of how much theory they "know." Such action is the source of inexpressible joy and vitality, courage and wisdom. It is the origin from whence a sense of exuberance wells forth, infusing and permeating their lives. Their lives are filled with a visible brilliance, good fortune and benefit.

Those who truly embrace the Mystic Law are most noble just as they are. And it is in their lives that the world of the great and eternal life of the "Life Span" chapter appears. This is the true condition of immortality.

We should never allow ourselves to become totally consumed by our immediate circumstances. When we become completely caught up by immediate circumstances, our vision is clouded by the view of "initial attainment." Rather, we should live with our gaze fixed on eternity and the universe, without being knocked off balance by our immediate concerns.

It is important to view this present existence based on that fundamental awareness. Seen from the vantage point of eternity, the present existence is the most important. This life is short; from the standpoint of eternity, it is but a moment. But by maintaining a steadfast practice throughout this existence, we can firmly establish Buddhahood as the basic tendency of our lives. Then we can continue to enjoy the state of life of the Buddha eternally. That's why it's so important that we practice wholeheartedly in the present.

REVEALING THE STATE OF ABSOLUTE HAPPINESS

Suda: The "Life Span" chapter explains this transformation.

Ikeda: It could be termed a revolution in the state of life. President Toda said:

> It's only natural that we should want to make a lot of money, live in a fine house and be healthy. And it is a true religion that enables us to realize these wishes...
>
> The difference is that in our case, even though we may desire these same things, in the future we will be able to attain a state of life of absolute happiness. We cannot truly say that we desire a state of absolute happiness. But even so, we still attain this state, no matter how badly we might want not to!
>
> Absolute happiness is a state such that, whatever your situation, you feel an immense sense of worth and satisfaction; and wherever you are, to be alive is itself a joy ...Even when we encounter situations that make us angry, we become angry joyfully. When we establish such a state of life, our life is one of boundless joy.[6]

When we aspire only for relative happiness, we are basing ourselves on the view of "initial attainment." This view, taken alone, is like a rootless plant. It is empty and fleeting.

Absolute happiness means realizing the state of actual attainment in the remote past. To achieve that state, we need to spiritedly struggle to widely declare and spread Buddhism, not lead a self-centered existence. This is what it means to practice faith in the essential teaching. By practicing with a spirit of not begrudging our lives, we can break through the darkness of the small self. And to the extent that we do so, the life of the great self wells forth in us.

Endo: "We become angry joyfully"—that's quite a state of life.

Ikeda: In reality, this is what it means for the nine worlds to be endowed with the world of Buddhahood. When we are angry, we are in the world of anger. Joy is the world of Buddhahood.

Also, since the world of Buddhahood is endowed with the nine worlds, attaining Buddhahood does not mean the end of worries or suffering. Many difficult and unexpected things happen in the course of life. But because we embrace the Mystic Law, we can enjoy these waves of difficulty as we can joyfully "surf" them. It is in fact that variety and unpredictability that make life truly interesting.

The important point here is awareness. Because the Ten Worlds are inherent in our lives, through believing in the Mystic Law of time without beginning we can immediately call forth the world of Buddhahood, no matter what world we happen to be in at the time. As long as we do not forget the awareness that we gain through faith, even the world of anger becomes an enlightened land.

While enduring the extreme cold of prison, Mr. Makiguchi, our founding president, wrote in a letter to his family dated January 17, 1944: "Single-mindedly practicing faith is my occupation these days. As long as I do this, I do not have any worries. Basing my heart on faith, even in hell I feel peace and ease."[7]

It is definitely not a matter of length of practice. Even senior leaders or people of longtime practice will no longer be successful if they lose faith and their hearts become corrupt.

As long as our mind of faith shines, then, whether we are investigating the truth in the worlds of voice-hearers and cause-awakened ones or battling corrupt authorities in the world of anger, all our actions ultimately accord with the wisdom of the Buddha.

On the other hand, should we lose our faith, only ugly egoism will remain. There have been any number of people who have lost their faith, succumbing to desires surrounding their immediate circumstances. What is the value for such people in their having read the "Life Span" chapter daily? It would seem that they missed the point entirely. In the future they are sure to suffer. They are truly pitiful.

Saito: Our faith, our lives, should never be like a rootless plant. I think this means never forgetting the mentor-disciple relationship. Herein lies the essence of the "Life Span" chapter. That's because, fundamentally, the "Life Span" chapter seeks to reveal Shakyamuni's own mentor, "this wonderful single Law [*myoho*] that simultaneously possesses both cause and effect [*renge*]" (WND-1, 421) that is one with the Buddha of time without beginning.

This "single Law," however, is not explicitly stated in the sutra itself. The sutra only goes so far as to indicate Shakyamuni's true identity as the Buddha who attained enlightenment in the extremely remote past where numberless major worlds are reduced to single particles of dust, each particle of dust is placed one by one in different worlds, and then those worlds are reduced to dust once again.

Ikeda: That's why Shakyamuni is called the teacher of the True Effect. On a literal level, the "Life Span" chapter explains the original effect that Shakyamuni gained in the remote past through practicing the Mystic Law. But it does not clarify the original cause that enabled him to achieve this effect.

Put another way, there is no object of devotion in the twenty-eight–chapter Lotus Sutra. While it certainly does present a succession of brilliant teachings, in conclusion the sutra is not at all clear about what should be made the object of devotion. This has long been a point of much discussion and controversy.

In a sense, it is natural that the sutra doesn't explain an object of devotion. The people in Shakyamuni's day could all attain Buddhahood through the Lotus Sutra. They intuitively understood what the object of devotion was. But those in the world after Shakyamuni's passing, and particularly those of the Latter Day of the Law, had no such understanding.

Endo: That's why the Daishonin had to expound the Buddhism of the True Cause.

THE UNIVERSAL SCALE OF THE TEACHING OF THE TRUE CAUSE

Ikeda: To put it figuratively, Shakyamuni as described in the "Life Span" chapter, who attained enlightenment in the remote past, is like fully ripened fruit. This fruit has a wonderful appearance, but the seeds that produced it are nowhere to be found in the passages of the sutra. They are hidden. It will take the teaching in the depths of the sutra to reveal the seeds within the fruit.

I think we will have the chance later on to discuss this point from various angles. But from the standpoint of the theory of causality that we discussed earlier, the Daishonin refers to the Buddhism of the True Cause that he revealed as the "doctrine of a single moment of life that encompasses within itself both cause and effect" (GZ, 871).

Suda: This is in contrast to the "doctrine of the distinct nature of cause and effect" (of the provisional teachings), the "doctrine of the identical nature of cause and effect" (of the theoretical teaching of the Lotus Sutra), and the "doctrine of cause and effect existing eternally together" (of the essential teaching of the Lotus Sutra).

Ikeda: The "doctrine of cause and effect existing eternally together" is the essential teaching of Shakyamuni's Lotus Sutra. The "doctrine of a single moment of life that encompasses within itself both cause and effect" is Nichiren Daishonin's ultimate teaching. The difference between these is crucial.

From a literal standpoint, the essential teaching is saying only that Shakyamuni's life eternally possesses both Buddhahood (the effect) and the nine worlds (the cause). It does not explain the original cause that enabled him to attain Buddhahood.

That original cause is "this wonderful single Law [*myoho*] that simultaneously possesses both cause and effect [*renge*]." The person who reveals this original cause directly and without distortion is the "teacher of the True Cause." Nichiren Daishonin declares, "I, Nichiren, am the teacher of this doctrine" (GZ, 863).

Endo: This is from the passage of the "The One Hundred and Six Comparisons" that goes, "The 'Life Span' chapter in the depths of our lives means the original cause in the depths of the 'Life Span' chapter of the Buddhism of harvest. I, Nichiren, am the teacher of this doctrine" (GZ, 863).

Ikeda: The "Mystic Law of the True Cause" is itself the "object of devotion of all Buddhas throughout time" concealed in the depths of the "Life Span" chapter. It is true three thousand realms in a single moment of life. This one Law is, at the same time, both the True Cause and the True Effect. The cause and effect of Buddhahood occur simultaneously. The only way to attain the effect of Buddhahood, that is, to become a Buddha, is by becoming a person of the strongest possible faith. Faith, the cause of Buddhahood, is itself the effect of Buddhahood. Faith itself is the embodiment of the world of Buddhahood. Our mind of faith is fully endowed with both the cause and the effect of Buddhahood.

Saito: That, in other words, is the "doctrine of a single moment of life that encompasses within itself both cause and effect."

Ikeda: We could say that this is the meaning of the "doctrine of a single moment of life that encompasses within itself both cause and effect" as viewed from the standpoint of living beings.

Fundamentally, we have the moment of life, or *ichinen*, of the Buddha from time without beginning whose body and mind are one with the entire universe, and who is endowed with the original cause and original effect of enlightenment, as well as with all phenomena in the Ten Worlds. In that sense, the teaching of three thousand realms in a single moment of life in the depths of the sutra encompasses the entire universe.

We can say that three thousand realms in a single moment of life of the theoretical teaching tries to indicate the three thousand realms existing in a single moment of life of unenlightened beings of the nine worlds. And that three thousand realms in a single moment of life of the essential teaching tries to indicate the three thousand realms contained in the mind of the individual Buddha Shakyamuni. Both of these doctrines of three thousand realms in a single moment of life thus reflect the reality of individual beings.

By contrast, the implicit and ultimate doctrine of three thousand realms in a single moment of life views all beings in any of the Ten Worlds as expressions of a single moment of universal, eternal life. This implicit doctrine of three thousand realms in a single moment of life is the true "actual doctrine of three thousand realms in a single moment of life" that enables all Buddhas of past, present and future to attain enlightenment.

Suda: That is on a scale that boggles the mind.

The True Cause Is the Buddhism of the Sun

Ikeda: To illustrate, if the implicit Buddhist teaching revealed by Nichiren Daishonin is compared to the sun, then the theoretical and essential teachings of the Lotus Sutra could be likened, respectively, to the planets and the moon, which reflect the light of the sun in varying degrees.

Saito: Profound doctrinal meaning attaches to the fact that Nichiren Daishonin compares his Buddhism of the True Cause to the sun and Shakyamuni's Buddhism to the moon.

Ikeda: All Buddhas over the three existences without a single exception attain Buddhahood by causing this sun to rise in their hearts. Our practice is not to gaze upon the moon or the stars and think about the sun, but to directly cause the sun to rise in our hearts by continually basing our lives on the Mystic Law.

Suda: We don't have to practice for countless aeons to attain Buddhahood. We can attain Buddhahood in this very lifetime.

Ikeda: Yes. Therefore, Nichiren Daishonin says repeatedly that those who chant Nam-myoho-renge-kyo "will be able to attain Buddhahood readily" (WND-I, 884). He also states, "There can be no doubt that those who correctly practice the Mystic Law will easily become Buddhas equal to Shakyamuni" (GZ, 817); and "you can readily become as noble a Buddha as Shakyamuni" (WND-I, 1030).

What a wonderful Buddhist teaching this is! How truly fortunate we are! What a wonderful jewel the Daishonin has bestowed upon humankind!

This teaching represents the true humanization of Buddhism.

NOTES

1. Hajime Nakamura, *Budda no shinri no kotoba, kankyo no kotoba* (The Buddha's Words of Truth, Words of Inspiration) (Tokyo: Iwanami Shoten, 1988), p. 26.

2. Ten factors: (1) appearance (*nyo ze so*): the external manifestation of life; (2) nature (*nyo ze sho*): the spiritual or mental aspects of life; (3) entity (*nyo ze tai*): the totality of life consisting of appearance and nature; (4) power (*nyo ze riki*): inherent energy; (5) influence (*nyo ze*

sa): externally directed action; (6) inherent cause (*nyo ze in*): the direct cause for things to occur; (7) relation (*nyo ze en*): the causes or conditions that activate the inherent cause; (8) latent effect (*nyo ze ka*): the result produced [in the depths of life] by inherent cause and relation; (9) manifest effect (*nyo ze ho*): the concrete, perceptible manifestation of the latent effect; (10) consistency from beginning to end (*nyo ze honmatsu kukyo to*): the perfect integration of these nine factors in every moment of life.

3. Daisaku Ikeda, et al. *The Wisdom of the Lotus Sutra* (Santa Monica, Calif.: World Tribune Press, 2000), vol. 1, p. 173.

4. The four teachings of doctrine: A classification of the Buddhist teaching by T'ien-t'ai according to content and consists of the Tripitaka teaching, the connecting teaching, the specific teaching and the perfect teaching. These correspond to the Hinayana, the introductory Mahayana, the Mahayana teaching specifically for bodhisattvas, and the perfect teaching which encompasses and unifies the other three.

5. Three Sovereigns: Fu Hsi, Shen Nung and Huang Ti, legendary rulers of ancient China said to have realized model governments.

6. *Toda Josei zenshu* (Collected Writings of Josei Toda) (Tokyo: Seikyo Shimbunsha, 1984), vol. 4, pp. 443–44.

7. *Makiguchi Tsunesaburo zenshu* (Collected Works of Tsunesaburo Makiguchi) (Tokyo: Daisan Bummeisha, 1987), vol. 10, p. 284.

PART II:

"The Life Span of the Thus Come One" Chapter:

THE TEN WORLDS

4   The Pursuit of Happiness

Ikeda: We are following the supreme path in life. Whether we can truly elevate our lives depends totally on whether we realize this solemn fact.

What is the purpose of Buddhism? It is to enable all people to become happy and cultivate lives of supreme joy. Tolstoy writes: "Rejoice! Rejoice! One's life's work, one's mission is a joy. Toward the sky, toward the sun, toward the stars, toward the grasses, toward the trees, toward animals, toward human beings—you may as well rejoice."[1] Our mission in life is to experience joy! This was one conclusion that Tolstoy reached.

We who embrace the Mystic Law understand the true meaning of these words, for the Lotus Sutra enables us to cultivate in our lives "the greatest of all joys" (OTT, 212).

Endo: The state of life Shakyamuni manifested as he meditated beneath the Bodhi tree was one of boundless joy that nothing could disturb.

Ikeda: That's right. The expression "Shakyamuni's attaining enlightenment for the first time" in India under the bodhi tree has a lofty ring to it. But to put it in plain terms, it means that the sun of supreme joy solemnly rose in Shakyamuni's heart.

A Fierce Struggle With Negativity

Suda: I once visited the place where Shakyamuni is said to have attained enlightenment, a location one sutra describes as "not far from the city of Gaya" (LSOC, 261). In fact, it is ten kilometers south of the present-day city of Gaya (located in the state of Bihar in northeast India). Because Shakyamuni attained enlightenment there, the spot was later named "Gaya of the Buddha," or Bodh Gaya.

Endo: In like fashion, the tree at the spot came to be called the *bodhi* tree in commemoration of Shakyamuni's having attained enlightenment there. This kind of tree was originally called the Asvattha tree, which reportedly means "place to perceive immortality," and was revered as a tree of wisdom.

It seems that the Buddha's followers later planted root clippings from this tree across the country. Currently, the tree standing at Bodh Gaya grew from a root clipping taken from a tree in Sri Lanka, far to the south, which itself was grown from a clipping of the original tree. Further complicating things, some indications suggest that the tree in Sri Lanka may not have been the original tree but a transplant grown from the original Sri Lanka clipping. That would make the present tree at Bodh Gaya the great-grandchild, as it were, of the tree under which Shakyamuni sat.

Ikeda: I, too, have visited Bodh Gaya. Shortly after becoming president of the Soka Gakkai, I made a trip to the birthplace of Buddhism (in 1961). Vowing to accomplish the westward transmission[2] of Nichiren Daishonin's teaching, I buried a capsule containing a copy of the writing "On the Three Great Secret Laws" and a stone marker at the site.

Saito: True to the vow you made then, the Buddhism of the Sun has today spread not only across India, but throughout Asia and other countries of the world. Considering that it took many hundreds or even a thousand years for the Buddhism of Shakyamuni to spread through Asia, this accomplishment in the course of just thirty or forty years will no doubt impress future historians as truly remarkable.

Ikeda: You, the younger generation, need to follow in my footsteps. It is essential that people carry on this work.

At any rate, it was from Bodh Gaya that Shakyamuni began his struggle to lead all people to enlightenment. What do you suppose Shakyamuni's spiritual struggle at Bodh Gaya was like?

Endo: Well, let's see. Before that, Shakyamuni is said to have completely eradicated desires as a result of carrying out grueling ascetic practices. Realizing that such practices could not lead to true happiness, however, he abandoned them.

Suda: He had discarded both desire and ascetic practices. What, then, was Shakyamuni seeking? And to what did he awaken?

Ikeda: This is very significant.

Shakyamuni was seeking happiness for all. "Where does the path of true happiness for all people lie?" he asked himself. He understood that people could become happy neither by simply allowing their lives to be consumed in the flames of desire nor by causing pain to their bodies through asceticism.

He was seeking the path of the Middle Way that would allow people's lives to shine brilliantly. And it was with the aim of finding such a path that he diligently applied himself to his practice.

Suda: Shakyamuni is said to have spent a period of seven days sitting cross-legged in meditation beneath the bodhi tree.

Ikeda: "Meditation" sounds calm and peaceful, but it is by no means an easy path. It is a fierce struggle against the pull of negativity and darkness. Shakyamuni squarely confronted, fought and defeated the "destroyer of life," a function pervading the universe.

In so doing, he conquered the darkness that is called unhappiness.

Saito: Buddhist texts describe how the devilish forces cunningly tried to capture Shakyamuni's mind. A devil by the name of Namuci approached Shakyamuni and whispered to him: "You are thin and emaciated, and your color is bad. Clearly you are on the brink of death. If you go on meditating in this fashion, you don't have even one chance in a thousand of surviving."[3]

Shakyamuni certainly had no guarantee that at the end of his practice he would find enlightenment. Because his was the path of a pioneer, no one knew what lay ahead. And if he were to die, that would definitely spell an end to his efforts to pursue the goal of human happiness.

Ikeda: But at the last minute, Shakyamuni recognized the devil for what it was and loudly proclaimed: "Devil, a coward might be defeated by you, but a courageous person will win. I will fight. I would rather fight you and lose my life than be defeated and live on!"[4] At these words, the devil immediately retreated.

Dawn was approaching. Just as Venus began shining in the eastern sky, he at last attained enlightenment.

Buddhism is a struggle with all kinds of devilish, negative forces inherent in life. Without struggling against and overcoming such enemies, there is no enlightenment, there is no true joy, there is no human revolution, there is no Buddhism. Unless we struggle with all our might against the forces of darkness and negativity, we cannot become Buddhas.

The Sun of Great Joy Has Arisen!

Saito: During the course of this struggle, Shakyamuni uttered three poems, one at sunset, one in the middle of the night, and one at dawn. As to the content of these poems, the Buddhologist Dr. Koshiro Tamaki of the University of Tokyo describes them as "expressions of the Dharma."[5]

Dharma means Law. The fundamental law of the universe became manifest in Shakyamuni himself, permeating his entire being and infusing his life.

Suda: The poem he uttered at sunset goes, "When the Dharma truly manifests in a practitioner who continues to meditate earnestly, at that time all of his doubts and illusions disappear. For he has understood the law of dependent origination."[6]

The poem in the middle of the night goes: "When the Dharma truly manifests in a practitioner who continues to meditate earnestly, at that time all of his doubts and illusions disappear. For he has realized the eradication of all kinds of karmic relations."

The final poem, which he spoke at dawn, goes: "When the Dharma truly manifests in a practitioner who continues to meditate earnestly, at that time he has demolished the forces of the devil and abides in peace. He is just like the sun that shines in the sky."

Endo: "The sun has risen in my heart!" he declares. This is a historic moment.

Ikeda: This is the dawn of the sun of joy that illuminates all humankind. Buddhahood is a state of supreme joy.

After passing a time in this state of exultation, Shakyamuni resolutely began preaching the Law. But he found that no matter how he tried to explain the truth to which he had awakened, it was extremely difficult for others to accept the Law that he perceived in his own heart. Therefore, he sought to develop the capacity of the people by expounding expedient teachings that were easy to grasp.

In the "Life Span" chapter, he directly and fully expresses this sunlike state of life. The "Life Span" chapter could therefore be termed the "chapter of great joy." It is both the climax and summation of Shakyamuni's entire life.

Symbol of the "Universe of Life"

Saito: In the "Life Span" chapter, Shakyamuni employs an image of the incredibly vast expanse of the universe—described as innumerable major world systems—to explain the eternity of his life. This would seem to symbolize the infinite and boundless life space that Shakyamuni has attained.

Ikeda: That may be so. Through the concept of universal space, Shakyamuni comes up with a vivid image of the "eternal Law at one with the eternal Buddha," that is, of the vast state of life of Buddhahood that he perceives within himself.

Suda: In the sutra, we find this in the concept Shakyamuni uses to explain the inconceivably long period of time since he first attained enlightenment. The description begins:

> Suppose a person were to take five hundred, a thousand, ten thousand, a million nayuta asamkhya major world systems and grind them to dust. Then, moving eastward, each time he passes five hundred, a thousand, ten thousand, a million nayuta asamkhya worlds he drops a particle of dust... (LSOC, 266)

Endo: If he had just said that his life was eternal, it wouldn't have had nearly the impact. But the description of countless major world systems ground to dust causes an image to immediately spring to mind. One feels, "What an awesome state of life!" From this account, we may imagine racing across the universe in a rocket ship.

Saito: The life space described in the "Life Span" chapter is a state of life of boundless joy. Each moment is joyful. Therefore, Shakyamuni's "life-time," although it is described as virtually eternal, would seem extremely short.

Ikeda: Simply put, "life-time" may be identified with subjective time.

Endo: Yes. For instance, hell is a state of life in which there is very little joy—virtually zero. The life space of a person in this state is infinitesimally small, as though confined within a tiny prison cell. The "life-time" of such a person creeps ahead with agonizing slowness.

Suda: Certainly, when you have a toothache, for example, a minute can seem like an hour.

Endo: On the other hand, Buddhahood is characterized by joy so abundant as to be well nigh inexhaustible. The "life-time" of one in this state is therefore extraordinarily fast.

Saito: The rate at which time passes differs depending on our state of life. "Life-time," in other words, is relative.

Ikeda: The greater the energy in a person's life, the more vigorously his or her "life-time" moves ahead.

On another level, it has been proven theoretically that time is relative, as we see, for example, in Einstein's theory of relativity. According to the theory, if you were to travel through the universe on a rocket ship, as your speed increased, the rate of time's passage would change. This is the so-called Urashima effect in Japan.

Endo: That's right. What we call the Urashima effect, also known as the "clock paradox" or "twins paradox," is a hypothesis we arrive at from the theory of relativity. It refers to the phenomenon whereby the time aboard a spaceship traveling at a rate approaching the speed of light passes more slowly than time passes on Earth. You could have a situation where a number of years had passed on Earth, while aboard the ship it seemed as though only a day had passed. Thus a person traveling through space at such a fantastic speed would, upon returning to Earth, find himself dislocated in time, just as in the Japanese folktale of Urashima Taro.

STATE OF LIFE IS ALL IMPORTANT

Ikeda: That certainly is relativity.

In any event, the world that we perceive will be different depending on which of the Ten Worlds we are in. The way we receive impressions of the world around us, both spatially and temporally, changes radically. We could call this the mystery of "state of life."

"State of life" is the prime focus of Buddhism. Buddhism does not look at people in terms of ethnicity or race. Neither does it view people in terms of level of schooling or social standing. Its gaze is trained directly on the condition of people's hearts, on the state of their life itself.

Does having a lot of power and influence make someone great? Among powerful people, there are more than a few whose lives are ravaged by the worlds of hunger and animality. On the other hand, ordinary citizens dwell in the joyous worlds of bodhisattva and Buddhahood.

Does graduating from a prestigious university make someone superior to others? Are people of certain ethnicity or race automatically superior? Are people of certain social classes automatically inferior? Definitely not. And yet, throughout all of human history, people have been viewed with just such prejudices. How great, indeed, are the tragedies that such thinking has produced!

Suda: The history of the twentieth century—whether we look at Nazism or Japanese militarism or the countless bloody class struggles that have occurred—is a history of tragedies resulting from such discriminatory biases.

Saito: Discrimination is the cruel product of prejudice and bigotry. We find similar discriminatory tendencies in the extreme emphasis that many people in Japan today place on educational background.

Ikeda: Buddhism, through the doctrine of the Ten Worlds, views all people in terms of the state of their life. It is therefore wholly impartial. The sufferings of hell, for example, are the same, regardless of whether the person is wealthy or poor.

Also, Buddhism recognizes the existence of Buddhahood in all people as a potential. The compassion to strive to help people cultivate and manifest this state is key to the doctrine of the Ten Worlds. And the essence of this doctrine is found in the "Life Span" chapter. Why don't we discuss the Ten Worlds in terms of state of life?

Urashima Taro and the Ten Worlds

Suda: The Urashima effect was mentioned earlier. The story of Urashima Taro from which "Urashima effect" derives its name might provide a good segue to a discussion of the doctrine of the Ten Worlds.

Ikeda: Indeed. It's a classic tale for the Japanese. What do we find when we view the story in terms of the Ten Worlds?

Endo: The story begins with how the fisherman Urashima Taro comes upon a couple of children pestering a turtle on the beach. In terms of the Ten Worlds, the children harassing the turtle would probably be in a state of animality. For, as the Daishonin says, "It is the nature of beasts to threaten the weak and fear the strong" (WND-1, 302).

Suda: Yes. And the turtle being toyed with would be in the world of hell. To get the children to leave the turtle alone, Urashima Taro gives them some money. His actions in doing so would seem to represent one aspect of the world of bodhisattva. The children who listen only after being given money could now be said to be in world of hunger.

Endo: Several days later, the turtle, mindful of its debt, visits Urashima. Grateful, it offers to take Taro on a tour of the dragon king's palace.

Saito: To remember and repay one's debts of gratitude—that must be the world of humanity. To requite one's obligations is proof of one's humanity.

Ikeda: Though a turtle, it still has the world of humanity.

Saito: Yes. By contrast, some people forget their indebtedness to others and thereby descend to the level of animals. In "The Opening of the Eyes," the Daishonin teaches the importance of requiting one's debts, saying, "Even these creatures understood how to repay a debt of gratitude" (WND-1, 244).

Suda: At the palace of the dragon king, Taro is welcomed by a princess, with whom he spends an enjoyable time drinking and dancing. Here, he is definitely in the world of rapture, or heaven.

Incidentally, inclusion of the dragon king's palace is thought to indicate the influence of Buddhist texts. "Devadatta," the twelfth chapter of the Lotus Sutra, for example, mentions the "palace of the dragon king Sagara" (LSOC, 224) at the bottom of the ocean.

Endo: Taro has such a wonderful time that he forgets about returning home. Before he knows it three years have gone by. Since he is dwelling in a rapturous world, the time passes in what seems an instant. Eventually, Taro informs the princess of his departure and leaves bearing under his arm a small chest she has given him as a memento.

When he returns to his land, Taro is astonished at what he finds: the world is completely different. During the three years he spent in the palace of the dragon king, three hundred years had passed on Earth. Earth time had left him behind and gone far ahead. This is what is meant by the Urashima effect in physics.

When he realizes what has happened, Urashima Taro becomes despondent. All of his relatives are gone. He has not a single friend. And everywhere he turns, he sees strange and unfamiliar things.

Ikeda: It might be said that Taro's state of life at this moment is that of hell. Everything he sees and hears amounts to an outright denial of his very existence. There is no place for him in the world. In the bat of an eye, Taro's life space has completely vanished.

Suda: At that point, Taro opens the little chest, which represents his last hope. Smoke billows out, Taro's hair instantly turns white, and he is transformed into a tottering old man. He suddenly fades into senility, and in a daze he sits down on the beach. This is a really dramatic last scene.

Ikeda: What world would you say he is in at that point?

Endo: That's a tough one. I see Taro, who was already in the state of hell, as having fallen into a state of even deeper despair. But that would make it an extremely sad ending.

Suda: And it would mean that the princess had given him a really cruel gift.

Ikeda: This ending might indicate entrance into the realm of the two vehicles, or the worlds of voice-hearers and cause-awakened ones. Nichiren Daishonin says: "The fact that all things in this world are transient is perfectly clear to us. Is this not because the worlds of the two vehicles are present in the human world?" (WND-1, 358). While the story itself does not say so, it might be that the aged Taro has glimpsed something of the impermanence of existence that he had not comprehended before.

Saito: The story concludes, "Those joyous days were gone forever." That is certainly not a happy ending. All the same, the ending seems to suggest that, having wandered through the realm of the six worlds, he has finally arrived to where he can perceive the existence of the worlds of voice-hearers and cause-awakened ones.

Suda: From another perspective, the story invites us to reflect deeply on the meaning of life and human existence.

Ikeda: When we internalize Buddhism's perspective on life, we can understand the essence of anything we see or hear from a much deeper perspective. This is an important reason for Buddhist study. The question "What is true human happiness?" forms the basis of the doctrine of the Ten Worlds.

HELL—A WORLD OF HOPELESSNESS AND RAGE

Ikeda: Next, let's consider each of the Ten Worlds in light of the sutras and Nichiren Daishonin's writings. As the major premise, we should bear in mind that only with the Lotus Sutra's revelation of the principle of the mutual possession of the Ten Worlds can we talk about the Ten Worlds as conditions of human life. Let's delve into the significance of the mutual possession of the Ten Worlds on another occasion; however, without understanding that each world is endowed with all Ten Worlds, the beings in each of the Ten Worlds can only be understood as dwelling in distinct and separate realms, and as having absolutely no contact with or relation to one another.

Saito: In other words, because those in the world of humanity— meaning us—have all of the Ten Worlds in our lives, the Ten

Worlds can be understood as states or conditions of life. Moreover, because of this we can talk about changes in state of life.

Suda: The names of each of the Ten Worlds appear in "Benefits of the Teacher of the Law," the nineteenth chapter. It states:

> [T]hey will gain twelve hundred ear benefits with which to purify their ears so they can hear all the different varieties of words and sounds in the major world systems, down as far as the Avichi hell, up to the Summit of Being, and in its inner and outer parts... [M]en's voices, women's voices,... voices of heavenly beings,... asura voices,... voices of hell dwellers, voices of beasts, voices of hungry spirits,... voices of voice-hearers, voices of pratyekabuddhas, voices of bodhisattvas and voices of Buddhas. (LSOC, 293)

Ikeda: That's right. We need to help people overcome their sufferings and become happy by using the "voices of bodhisattvas and voices of Buddhas." We cannot simply remain silent.

Endo: Based on this passage, the Great Teacher T'ien-t'ai of China formulated the doctrine of the Ten Worlds—namely, hell, hunger, animality, anger, humanity, rapture, learning, realization, bodhisattva and Buddhahood—existing in people's lives.

Of the Ten Worlds, the six worlds from hell to rapture, known as the "six paths," are based on the worldview of Brahmanism, which was widespread in India in Shakyamuni's time. According to Brahman teaching, all beings dwell in places or realms that belong to one of the six paths and into which they are born according to their past actions, or karma. The key idea is that of retribution according to the law of cause and effect; people are held to transmigrate through these six paths according to the causes they make.

The worlds from voice-hearer to Buddhahood, known as the

"four noble worlds," represent the states of those beings who have freed themselves from this transmigration in the six paths.

Suda: Why don't we consider these states one at a time. First there is the world of hell. This comes from a Sanskrit term *naraka*, which literally means an underground prison.

Ikeda: A variant of this term *naraku* survives in the modern Japanese expression to *fall into the abyss.* The Japanese equivalent of *hell* is composed of two characters meaning "earth" and "prison." "Earth" means the lowest place; and "prison" indicates the state of being bound and shackled, totally immobilized. Hell is the most miserable state, one in which a person is bound hand and foot with suffering.

Endo: In "The Object of Devotion for Observing the Mind," Nichiren Daishonin says "Rage is the world of hell" (WND-1, 358). Rage corresponds to anger, one of the three poisons — greed, anger and foolishness. I think this refers to the state of those who, when things do not go as they imagine, harbor resentment and animosity toward whomever or whatever they suppose upset their plan.

Saito: Yes, only this rage has no positive energy to be turned toward others directly. On the contrary, it causes people to be consumed by deadlock and futility, trapped in emotions that can find no outlet.

Ikeda: While there are many gradations even in the world of hell, in general, hell indicates a state in which merely living is painful; where whatever you see makes you miserable. Those in this state have an extremely weak life force and, in fact, approach the condition of death. We could describe this "rage" as the wail of a life that has exhausted every possible avenue.

Endo: One can hear this despairing groan in the tortured voices of youth who try to commit suicide or among delinquents. "Life is just too painful," they may say. "There is no place for me in this world."

When their "life space" approaches absolute zero, people may conclude they have no alternative but to die. This truly is the state of hell. It breaks my heart when I think of people in such a state.

Ikeda: Such people need someones—anyones—to be at their side. They need someone who will be with them and listen to them; someone who will offer even just a few words of encouragement. That's all it may take for the flame of life to spring up anew in the heart of someone suffering deeply. Just knowing someone cares about them causes their "life space" to expand.

When people have a genuine sense that, no matter how difficult their present circumstances, they are not alone but are vitally connected with others and with the world, they can stand up without fail. This is the power inherent in life. It is important, therefore, that we form good relations, that we develop bonds with people who can have a positive influence on our lives and our Buddhist practice—what we call "good friends."

"He Carried Within Himself His Own Little Hell"

Suda: Devadatta represents the world of hell. Though a disciple of Shakyamuni, Devadatta was a person of great evil who out of envy even tried to kill his mentor.

Saito: In light of the law of cause and effect, since Devadatta persecuted the Buddha, we can say that he was in the world of hell. But looking at him as an individual, we must also conclude that he must have been suffering in a hellish state.

Ikeda: Devadatta probably felt that as long as Shakyamuni was around, nothing would go as he wished. Though Devadatta might try in his small-minded way to gain status and recognition, Shak-yamuni was always there towering impossibly far above him like the Himalayas. Devadatta, far from respecting someone of higher attainment than himself, could not even tolerate such a person's existence. This is the ugliness of male jealousy.

Such hatred and resentment caused Devadatta's heart to close and freeze over like ice. This is what the mind of someone in the world of hell is like. The feeling would be akin to that of being bound hand and foot, totally helpless to change your frame of mind through your own efforts. This is truly the state of hell.

Saito: According to a biography of Joseph Stalin, whenever the Soviet dictator met someone more outstanding than him, or who possessed some remarkable ability, he was filled with violent envy and hatred.

The author describes Stalin in these terms, "while maintaining an air of calm, he would be panic-stricken"; and, "on the outside he wore the impression of a hard smile, while inside he was full of foreboding, carrying within himself his own little hell."[7]

Ikeda: "He carried within himself his own little hell." That's a magnificent way of putting it.

Unable to trust anyone, Stalin was constantly filled with fear and trepidation. He believed he might be betrayed at any moment. Such doubt and suspicion can in themselves reduce one to a state of desperate agony. One's sense of self becomes incredibly small when writhing in the "hell of mistrust," as if bottled up in a tiny space.

Of course, we can also view the jealousy displayed by Devadatta and Stalin as characteristic of the world of anger as well as of the world of heaven, inasmuch as the desire to willfully manipulate others exemplifies the devil of the sixth heaven, representing the corrupting and exploitative nature of power that is heaven's negative side.

The world of hell indicates a weakness and a profound inner

suffering that a person feels totally powerless to resolve. Hell is sometimes said to exist under the ground; but in fact it is a state in which one's life sinks further and further down under its own weight.

Those who suffer—whether due to family discord, sickness or the flames of jealousy—and whose hearts swirl with rage at whatever has brought on that suffering, certainly cannot recognize that the actual cause for the suffering exists in their own lives. They lack the life force to perceive it in those terms and, consequently, feel resentment and anger toward others.

Some people direct the flames of rage at themselves and their inability to do anything about their suffering. They have no strength to take responsibility for their misery and resolve the situation. Instead, they feel only unassignable resentment at their own impotence, a groan of despair.

Endo: To be without freedom—the condition of someone who is in prison.

Ikeda: By contrast, for those who believe in the sanctity of life and believe in people, their minds will be as broad and expansive as the sky—even if they are in jail. This was of course true of Nichiren Daishonin as it was of Tsunesaburo Makiguchi and Josei Toda.

Nelson Mandela, the former president of South Africa, spent ten thousand days (twenty-seven years) living in prison under conditions that can only be described as hellish. Only his dauntless conviction that he would ultimately realize a victory for human dignity supported him during that time.

"An hour felt like a year," he says. Unless you have experienced life behind bars, you cannot truly understand these words. And yet, President Mandela did not lose the warmth of his gaze. This is proof of his triumph as a human being.

Saito: People faced with trying circumstances or beset by difficulties tend to think they alone are miserable. As a result, they often resent others and society in general and retreat into their own shell.

The world of hell that Buddhism describes does not indicate a set of external circumstances or an environment one is presented with. Rather, I think it indicates the weak life force in which people are buffeted about and controlled by their surroundings, unable to take a single step to extricate themselves.

Ikeda: That's right. It doesn't refer to anything external.

Nichiren Daishonin says:

> First of all, as to the question of where exactly hell and the Buddha exist, one sutra states that hell exists underground, and another sutra says that the Buddha is in the west. Closer examination, however, reveals that both exist in our five-foot body. This must be true because hell is in the heart of a person who inwardly despises his father and disregards his mother... (WND-I, 1137)

The Ten Worlds exist within our lives. That's why apart from changing ourselves from within, there is no other way to realize true happiness.

HUNGER—ENSLAVEMENT TO GREED

Endo: Next is the world of hunger.

Hunger derives from the Sanskrit word *preta*, which originally meant "corpse." In Buddhism, the term came to signify a realm of misery, like that of hell or animality, into which dead people might fall. *Preta* also means "ancestral spirit." In India, it was thought that many ancestral spirits were hungry and desirous of food. It seems that that's why the dead came to be referred to as "hungry spirits."

Suda: The Japanese Bon (or Urabon, Skt *ullambana*) Festival, a ceremony to appease the souls of deceased ancestors who have fallen into the realm of hunger, is sometimes referred to as "giving alms to hungry spirits" (Jpn *segaki*).

Saito: The Daishonin says that the world of hunger is characterized by greed (WND-1, 358), another of the three poisons. T'ien-t'ai says, "This state of life is filled with hunger and thirst; that's why they are called hungry spirits."[8] It is the state of beings tormented by a hunger nothing can assuage.

Ikeda: Those in the world of hunger are pulled this way and that by desires. Thus they suffer and lack a feeling of inner freedom. They become slaves to their desires.

Endo: Yes. But it seems that compared to the world of hell, the person's "life space" is somewhat larger, even if only slightly. The person has escaped from a state of complete captivity and hopelessness and is at least living in pursuit of something.

Suda: Desire is, after all, a manifestation of vital energy, too. But, being unable to quench their desires, people in hunger invariably experience severe frustration. Lacking enough to eat, adequate clothing or shelter—these are dire issues of the modern age.

Saito: Yet there is hunger even in so-called affluent societies. In 1996, *Newsweek* said of modern American society, "The paradox of our time is that we are feeling bad about doing well."[9]

Ikeda: People's desires are limitless. There is the fundamental desire to live. There is also the instinctive desire for food, the materialistic desire for possessions, and the psychological desire for attention, as examples.

Suda: There is also the desire for power, the desire for fame, and the desire to control. People also desire to be respected and loved.

Ikeda: We could not live without desires. In many cases, these desires become the energy that enables us to advance and realize self-improvement. That's why it is said of the world of hunger, "This path is connected with other paths and leads to both good and evil."[10]

The real issue, therefore, is how we use desire. Those in the world of hunger do not use desire to create value; rather, they become its slave. On account of desire, they suffer themselves and cause injury to others. That's why the world of hunger is called an "evil path."

Saito: Modern civilization could be described as one of unbridled desire. The result is the perverse situation in which desire, having swollen to gargantuan proportions, reigns like a master to which people are enslaved.

Endo: Incidentally, regarding what causes lead to hunger, Nichiren Daishonin says, "Persons who, becasue they are greedy for fame and profit, preach from such impure motives, will suffer retribution in this realm" (WND-2, 196). In other words, he is saying that those who preach with impure motives because they are consumed by desire for fame or profit will fall into the world of hunger. This well describes the priests of the Nikken sect.

Suda: In the same writing, the Daishonin also says, "Those who in the past cut down trees that had been planted to give shade and coolness, or who had cut down trees in the gardens and groves used by the company of monks, will suffer retribution here" (WND-2, 197). This passage also seems apropos to Nikken, who had some 280 cherry trees cut down on the head temple grounds.

Saito: The Daishonin condemns priests consumed by the desire for wealth, calling them "Law-devouring hungry spirits" (WND-1, 191). The Nikken sect, which preys on lay people while wallowing in decadence, is truly an order of hungry spirits.

ANIMALITY—THE STUPIDITY TO BE CAUGHT UP IN ONE'S IMMEDIATE CIRCUMSTANCES

Suda: What kind of state, then, is animality?

Saito: Originally, of course, the term refers to the state of animals such as birds or beasts. In "The Object of Devotion for Observing the Mind," the Daishonin says, "Foolishness is that of animals" (WND-1, 358). Of the three poisons, it corresponds to stupidity. In human terms, those in this state are in essence so caught up in their immediate circumstances they lose sight of the underlying principles that govern all things.

Endo: As the Daishonin indicates when he says, "It is the nature of beasts to threaten the weak and fear the strong" (WND-1, 302), animality is the state of those who live instinctively, unable to judge true and false, good and evil. While it would seem that the "life space" of those in this state is somewhat more expansive than that of those in the world of hell or hunger, they are still caught in an evil path.

Ikeda: They lack a sound standard for judging good and evil, a firm moral or ethical foundation. As a result, they act instinctively and without any sense of shame.

To "threaten the weak and fear the strong" is certainly an inherent part of the logic of power. It's a psychology of survival of the fittest. It could be said that those in this state, while human, have lost their humanity.

Suda: The barbarity of war is the ultimate manifestation of the "logic of power." Facing combat, soldiers may initially experience pangs of conscience as the consequences of injuring or even killing another person looms before them. But such feelings are often subordinated to a fear of their superior officers. This allows them to justify the barbarous acts they may commit on the basis of orders from a superior. Their conscience becomes anesthetized. Through the institutionalization of such bestiality, forces such as the Nazis and Japan's wartime military have gone so far as to commit large-scale atrocities—far beyond what any animal would ever be capable of.

Ikeda: The most dangerous bestiality dwells within human beings. Dostoevsky writes, "People talk sometimes of bestial cruelty, but that's a great injustice and insult to the beasts; a beast can never be so cruel as a man, so artistically cruel."[11]

Endo: I think that's certainly the case. Animals will fight and kill to protect themselves and survive. But they also have a social side, in that they will care for another; although I suppose that this is probably instinctive.

There was an interesting case involving a flock of ordinary starlings. It seems in one flock one bird had an injured leg. Observers noted that when the birds discovered a large store of food, they all waited until the bird with the bad leg arrived, and only then did they began eating.[12]

Ikeda: From time to time we hear about cases of people who have grown up entirely in the wild.

Suda: Yes. I recall the case of a French boy who had been abandoned by his parents and grew up in the jungle. Apart from searching for food and nests, he did not show the slightest interest in the world around him. His hearing was normal, but he reportedly did not display any interest in sounds that had no relation to food. Also, he showed no affection or attachment toward anyone.

Ikeda: People only become human if they are educated as human beings. It is not birth that makes us such. Only when we are raised as human beings do we become human. That's why education is so important.

The Japanese writer Yuyu Kiryu described the world as "the path of animality." Because there are all too few truly "human" beings, people start wars simply to prove who is strongest. We find ourselves tossed about in a society locked in the grip of animality.

To ensure that such are never again repeated, we have to produce a steady stream of humane people, of people overflowing with humanity. That is my conviction and my heartfelt prayer. Kosen-rufu is in a sense a great movement of human education on the success of which the fate of humankind depends.

Suda: Those in the world of animality are called "foolish" because, by living according to instinct, happiness forever eludes them.

Ikeda: Even though they imagine that they are moving toward happiness, in the final analysis they are heading in precisely the opposite direction. They only see what is right before their eyes, and they get lost easily and ultimately come to grief.

In "Letter from Sado," the Daishonin says: "Fish want to survive; they deplore their pond's shallowness and dig holes in the bottom to hide in, yet tricked by bait, they take the hook. Birds in a tree fear that they are too low and perch in the top branches, yet bewitched by bait, they too are caught in snares" (WND-1, 301). Because they fly toward the bait in front of their eyes, in the end they are destroyed and undone. This is what is meant by "foolishness."

Suda: Certainly many people live in just this manner.

Endo: Regarding the causes and effects of the world of animality, the Daishonin proclaims: "Those who are stupid and shameless, who simply accept alms from believers and do nothing by way of return will suffer retribution by being born in this realm" (WND-

2, 197). This exactly describes the corrupt priests of the Nikken sect.

People Who Willingly Enter
the Sea of Suffering

Ikeda: The Daishonin says, "warfare [occurs] as a result of anger" (WND-1, 989). The spirit of hell gives rise to war. Even with the end of World War II, Japan remained a cruel society of the three paths—hell, hunger and animality.

It was President Toda who stood up alone on the scorched earth of the three evil paths and declared, "I want to eradicate poverty and sickness from the face of the Earth!" "I want to eliminate the word *misery*!" He went out among the people proclaiming: " Human revolution is the only way!" "The only way is for people to revolutionize their state of life!" And he succeeded in fundamentally pointing society in the direction of peace and prosperity.

I have followed in President Toda's footsteps. All along, I have fought with the spirit that my life and the life of President Toda are one and inseparable. And in so doing, I have put aside every selfish concern.

Endo: I once heard the following experience.

In the winter of 1957, a woman by the name of Tamiko Hayashi was so worn out by the difficulty of her life that she had decided to commit suicide. Wanting to see her mother one last time before she died, she boarded a train with her last 100-yen bill in hand. This was, of course, before she took faith in Nichiren Buddhism.

The train was bound for Ogori Station from Nagoya. Mrs. Hayashi, wearing trousers and an apron, felt ashamed of her shabby appearance and shrank from the eyes of others. With her she had her two-year-old daughter.

Every time the train stopped at a station, vendors selling box lunches would come around. Although the mother and daughter were famished, they had no money to buy food.

A young man boarded the train at Maibara or at Kyoto. He was not by any means well dressed. The youth sat down directly opposite Mrs. Hayashi and her daughter. The young man opened up a thick book with a black leather binding (she later learned that it was the collected writings of Nichiren) and began intently writing something.

Whenever Mrs. Hayashi's young daughter saw someone selling box lunches, she would say, "Mommy, I'm hungry." Each time they arrived at a station, she asked for the impossible. Feeling wretched and helpless, the mother scolded her, telling her firmly, "No!"

After a while, the youth signaled a vendor and bought two box lunches. "Lucky him," thought the mother. "He can buy not just one but two. Isn't he fortunate!" The young man then handed her one and said, "Please feed this to your child." For a moment Mrs. Hayashi was speechless. What was happening seemed totally incomprehensible.

Around them there were many people wearing fine clothes. But they had all regarded her and her daughter with complete indifference. She thought: "But this young man, even though he is not well off himself, gave a box lunch to us, a couple of miserable strangers. It's a wonder that there could be such a person in the world." Mrs. Hayashi still vividly recalls the sense of surprise and appreciation she felt then.

It was all she could manage to say, "Thank you very much." Ashamed of her appearance, she found it impossible to say anything further. To this day she remembers what was in the box lunch. It was two-thirds rice, with the remainder side dishes and fried fish.

She also retained an indelible memory of the look in the eyes of the young man. "They were beautiful eyes that beamed with gentleness." The young man got off the train at Osaka. As he alighted, he told her, "Good luck!" A feeling of inexpressible warmth filled her heart. The sound of his voice, too, was unforgettable. Mrs.

Hayashi looked again at the youth's eyes. "How warm they are," she thought. At that instant, her intention to take her own life dissipated.

At Ube she spent a month with her mother. Then she returned to Nagoya. Shortly thereafter, Mrs. Hayashi heard about Buddhism from a Soka Gakkai member and began practicing. At the time, an offering of 500 yen was required to receive the Gohonzon. But Mrs. Hayashi didn't even have that much money. She worked and prayed and worked and finally received the Gohonzon in January 1958.

The following year, on March 22, 1959, a lecture on the writings of Nichiren was held at the Matsuba Elementary School in Toyohashi. The lecturer was Daisaku Ikeda (who was then the general administrator of the Soka Gakkai).

Mrs. Hayashi was pregnant with her second child and already quite large when she went to Toyohashi. The podium was far away and she could not make out the leaders' faces. But the moment she heard you begin speaking, President Ikeda, she felt a rush of joy: "Ah, that's the young man I met on the train! There's no doubt about it!"

The voice of the youth she heard on the train that had prompted her to give up thoughts of suicide was unforgettable to her. At that moment she made her resolve, her lifelong vow: "Even if I should be the last member of the Soka Gakkai in the world, I will always continue following Mr. Ikeda."

The daughter who received the box lunch (Misako Okada) is also practicing today and is a block leader. And the son whom Mrs. Hayashi was carrying at the time of the lecture in Toyohashi (Masami Hayakawa) is a district leader.

TRANSFORMING ONE'S STATE OF LIFE REQUIRES ALL-OUT EFFORT

Saito: That's a wonderful story. I am deeply moved. It is truly awesome the way you have given profound encouragement to so many people, President Ikeda. I, too, am determined to earnestly take on the challenge of transforming my state of life.

Suda: This anecdote well illustrates how a momentary encounter can change people's hearts, even their state of life.

Ikeda: I'm really glad that Mrs. Hayashi and her daughter have found happiness. I find that I simply cannot help trying to encourage people whom I meet. That is the Soka Gakkai spirit.

At any rate, if you truly want to transform your state of life, then you have to put every ounce of strength you've got into it. There's no way you can do so if your practice is half-hearted. Painful though it may be, it is only by struggling to thoroughly polish and temper your life that you can attain a state of great joy. I hope that young people, in particular, will diligently strive to cultivate themselves, with the attitude: "If I don't develop myself now while I am young, then when will I do so?"

We need to exert ourselves strenuously for kosen-rufu with the spirit, "I will elevate my state of life without fail." By carrying out that sort of practice, we can come to truly understand the doctrine of the Ten Worlds.

NOTES

1. Translated from Japanese: Leo Tolstoy, *Torusutoi no kotoba* (Words of Tolstoy), trans. Fumihiko Konuma (Tokyo: Yayoi Shobo, 1993), p. 94.

2. Buddhism spread after Shakyamuni's death from India to eastern regions gradually through China, Korea and Japan. Nichiren Buddhism in the Latter Day of the Law in turn spreads from Japan to western regions as if Buddhism is returning to its home in India (WND-1, 401; WND-2, 936).

3. Translated from Japanese: *Nanden Daizokyo*, ed. Junjiro Takakusu (Tokyo: Taisho Shinshu Daizokyo Kanko-kai, 1971), vol. 24, p. 154.

The *Group of Discourses* (Sutta-Nipata), vol. 2, trans. K. R. Norman (Oxford: The Pali Text Society, 1992), pp. 45–46.

4. Ibid., pp. 157–58.

5. Here and below, the source is: Koshiro Tamaki, *Bukkyo no kontei ni aru mono* (That Which Lies at the Foundation of Buddhism) (Tokyo: Kodansha, 1986), p. 22.

6. Law of dependent origination (*engi*): The interdependence of things. It teaches that all beings and phenomena exist or occur only because of their relationship with other beings or phenomena.

7. Translated from French: *Victor Serge, Portrait de Staline* (Paris: Editions Bernard Grasset, 1940), pp. 180–83.

8. *Hokke mongu* (Words and Phrases of the Lotus Sutra), vol. 4.

9. *Newsweek* (U. S. version), January 8, 1996, p. 24.

10. *Kokuyaku issaikyo Indo senjutsubu ronshubu,* vol. 1, ed. Shinyu Iwano (Tokyo: Daito Shuppansha, 1977), p. 114.

11. Fyodor Dostoevsky, *The Brothers Karamazov* (New York: Random House, 1943, 1945), p. 283.

12. Maurice Burton, *Just Like an Animal* (London: Dent, 1978), p. 26.

5 Turning a Society of Anger Into a Society of Humanism

Saito: In the last chapter we talked about the three evil paths of hell, hunger and animality. Let's move on to the world of anger.

Ikeda: I hope we can really study this in earnest. The purpose of Buddhist study after all is to expand one's state of life. And the doctrine of the Ten Worlds is like a mirror. As we gaze into it, we can see the true aspect of our own lives. It also enables us to perceive correctly the lives of others and society, and understand what we can do to contribute to others' well-being.

Suda: Yes. In contrast to the three evil paths, the worlds of anger, humanity and heaven (or rapture) are termed the three good paths. Together these make up the six paths.

Endo: What seems odd to me is that while the world of anger is considered one of the four evil paths when grouped together with hell, hunger and animality, it is also considered as one of the three good paths. How can it be both good and evil?

Ikeda: We will need to give that some thought. Perhaps we can begin by considering the fundamental meaning of these terms.

ANGER—THE ARROGANCE TO LOOK DOWN ON OTHERS

Endo: "Anger" in the "world of anger" derives from the Sanskrit term *asura*. In ancient India, *asura* originally represented a class of benevolent deities. But in later mythology, they came to be regarded as belligerent demons who ceaselessly fight with gods.

Suda: Nichiren Daishonin explains that the world of anger is characterized by "perversity," written with Chinese characters that mean fawning and crooked (WND-I, 358). An example of perversity can be seen in the case of a disloyal person who hides his or her true feelings while making a show of loyalty. Such behavior is certainly fawning and crooked.

Endo: The mystic demon *asura* is the picture of haughtiness— certainly the opposite of fawning. But, at first glance, someone in the world of anger might appear to be humble.

Ikeda: Indeed, and therein lies a problem. The world of anger is fundamentally an arrogant state of life.

But arrogance can be understood in any number of ways; Buddhist tradition, for example, identifies seven or nine types of arrogance. Nonetheless, anger, in essence, indicates one's attachment to the illusory assumption that he or she is better than others.

Those in the world of anger think of themselves as the most wonderful people. The energy of the world of anger is directed toward sustaining and enhancing this image. To ensure that others think of them in similarly glowing terms, they can never reveal their true feelings but act in a fawning, obsequious manner.

Endo: In other words, inner feelings and outward appearance are out of accord. As a result, such people say things that are not in their hearts. This is a tendency we do not find in people in the three evil paths. It is a fairly sophisticated, even intellectual, operation.

Saito: In *Great Concentration and Insight,* the Great Teacher T'ien-t'ai of China says:

> Since the mind of a person who is in the world of asuras desires in every moment to be superior to everyone else and cannot bear to be inferior to anyone else, he belittles and despises others and exalts himself just as a kite flies on high and looks down. Moreover, he outwardly displays benevolence, righteousness, propriety, wisdom, and good faith, and develops an interior kind of goodness of mind, and yet puts into practice the way of asuras." (WND-2, 197)

In their hearts, they cannot tolerate the existence of someone more capable or more respectable than themselves. They cannot truly respect others, because they believe that they alone are worthy of respect. A burning desire to surpass all others is their exclusive focus.

Outwardly, however, they do not give the least hint of such an obsession. They conduct themselves as virtuous people of benevolence, justice, propriety, wisdom and fidelity. By so doing, they try to convince others that these are their true qualities, and they may even come to believe this themselves.

Endo: They may even delude themselves into believing they are better than others because they are so humble.

Suda: As there is clearly a great disparity between what is in their hearts and what we see, fundamentally, people in the world of anger are dishonest.

Ikeda: Those who abandoned their faith and betrayed the Soka Gakkai, turning against their fellow members, were all people whose lives were entirely consumed by such a state of anger. We must never allow ourselves to be deceived by appearances.

Saito: As "fawning and crooked" suggests, their hearts are genuinely twisted.

Ikeda: That's right. And, since their hearts are crooked, they can see neither themselves nor others correctly. Looking at things through the distorted lens of arrogance, they think they are larger than life. As a result, they neither desire to learn from others nor are they capable of honest self-reflection, both of which are the means to grow as human beings.

In *The Record of the Orally Transmitted Teachings,* Nichiren Daishonin cites a passage from the *Annotations on the Words and Phrases of the Lotus Sutra* regarding the difference between "arrogance" and "self-importance": "'Because these people conceal their failings, flaunt their virtues,' refers to overbearing arrogance. 'Incapable of self- reflection' refers to self-esteem [self-importance]" (OTT, 35).

Saito: Hiding one's own faults while advertising one's virtues is arrogance. Arrogant people haughtily assert that they have attained the effects of Buddhist practice when they have not. Such attachment to one's own arbitrary views and the inability to self-reflect is certainly self-importance.

Ikeda: "Expedient Means," the second chapter of the Lotus Sutra, says that the people of an impure age are "arrogant and puffed up with self-importance, fawning and devious, insincere in mind" (LSOC, 70–71). In other words, while having a strong sense of self-importance and inflated pride, their minds are crooked. They are dishonest and insincere. This well describes the state of affairs in society.

Suda: In modern Japanese, *gaman,* the term originally meaning "self-importance," has an entirely different connotation. For example, mothers often use this term to admonish their children to be patient. This is a remarkable change of meaning. The intention is certainly not to encourage children to develop an overweening sense of self-importance.

Fear of Exposure

Ikeda: At some point, *gaman* came to mean "to endure" and not self-importance. I wonder why that happened. Perhaps it has to do with the way arrogant people can summon forth a tremendous amount of energy or willpower to protect their inflated self-image.

Saito: It would be wonderful if such people could channel that energy into self-improvement. But unfortunately they use it merely to protect the illusion to which they are so attached.

Ikeda: That is the misery of the world of anger. The hearts of those in this state are always filled with fear—fear that their true nature will be exposed. In "Letter from Sado," Nichiren Daishonin says: "An arrogant person will always be overcome with fear when meeting a strong enemy, as was the haughty asura who shrank in size and hid himself in a lotus blossom in Heat-Free Lake when reproached by Shakra" (WND-1, 302).

On the other hand, those with the heart of a lion king are totally fearless. That's because they are concerned not with protecting themselves but with protecting the Law and the people.

Endo: Someone in the state of anger has a gargantuan sense of self: "An *asura* stands 84,000 *yojana*[1] in height, and water of the four oceans comes no higher than his knees."[2] Yet this is only its subjective sense of self, not its true form.

Suda: Arrogant people labor under illusions of personal grandeur. But when their arrogant illusions are shattered by the presence of someone possessing genuine strength—such as the god Shakra in the above example—they become so small that they can hide themselves in a lotus flower.

Endo: A person in that state is like a deflated balloon.

Saito: Looking at things in this way, the *asura* would seem to embody characteristics found in a great many people today. I am struck in particular by the strong similarities between Buddhism's depiction of the world of anger and Dr. M. Scott Peck's analysis of "evil" in his book *People of the Lie: The Hope for Healing Human Evil.*

Endo: I've read that, too. His main point is that the corrupt individual who casually tells lies is definitely not an exception but appears in all walks of life.

Saito: That's right. The characteristic of such people, according to Peck, is that "deep down, [they] feel themselves to be faultless."[3] He also says:

> Utterly dedicated to preserving their self-image of perfection, they are unceasingly engaged in the effort to maintain the appearance of moral purity. They worry about this a great deal . . . While they seem to lack any motivation to be good, they intensely desire to appear good. Their "goodness" is all on a level of pretense.[4]

Suda: In other words, outwardly they display a mind of minor goodness.

Endo: A little earlier we discussed the energy of self-importance. In this connection, Peck writes that one is "struck by the extraordinary willfulness of evil people."[5] He also says: "They are likely to exert themselves more than most in their continuing effort to obtain and maintain an image of high respectability. They may willingly, even eagerly, undergo great hardships in their search for status."[6]

Ikeda: The problem is that such efforts all emerge from their egoistic hearts. Buddhism teaches that the heart is most important.

Even if two people are making comparable efforts, the resulting effects will differ greatly if one person is motivated by some value transcending the self, such as good or beauty, or the well-being of others, while the other is solely motivated by ego.

From our standpoint, faith means determining that our fundamental objective in life is to advance kosen-rufu and then thoroughly dedicating ourselves to that cause.

By contrast, those whom I mentioned earlier who abandoned their faith and actually betrayed the Soka Gakkai had succumbed to the mistaken notion that the organization for kosen-rufu somehow exists to help them further their own private interests. Full of arrogance and unable to respect their fellow members, such people have used the organization, used their positions, and used me personally to try to flaunt their supposed greatness.

Saito: And when you have seen through their pretenses, President Ikeda, these people tended to react with strong personal animosity toward you.

Suda: They ought to have sincerely self-reflected, but instead they began attacking you out of bitter resentment.

Endo: Doesn't that psychology also spring from the desire to protect a self-image based on illusion? In the book I mentioned, Dr. Peck says, "The evil attack others instead of facing their own failures . . . Instead of destroying others they should be destroying the sickness within themselves."[7] Such people, he says, "are characterized by their absolute refusal to tolerate the sense of their own sinfulness."[8]

Suda: That certainly is the image of someone who cannot self-reflect. As a result of this inability, the person deeply resents others.

Saito: Up to now, we have tended to identify anger with a strong desire to prove oneself better than others. This may actually offer a profound insight into human nature. Could it be that anger is some fateful side of human nature directly linked with self-awareness?

The three evil paths are states of life in which people are completely overwhelmed by their environment. But those in the world of anger have one foot free; they have a self that is in some degree sheltered from the influence of their environment or immediate circumstances.

Suda: That's probably why anger is not counted as one of the three evil paths.

Saito: But the moment they gain such subjective self-awareness, there is a strong tendency for people to become dominated by the desire to be better than others.

Ikeda: How can this tendency be overcome? That is the jumping-off point for entering the world of humanity. Ultimately, it is when we learn to channel the energy that had formerly been directed toward winning over others into winning over ourselves that we enter the world of humanity.

But before we begin discussing the world of humanity, why don't we give some thought to the envy that is the hallmark of anger?

A "Society of Envy" Will Decline

> *Since hatred and jealousy toward this sutra abound even when the Thus Come One is in the world, how much more will this be so after his passing?*
>
> *Medicine King, you should know that after the Thus Come One has entered extinction, if there are those who can copy, uphold, read, and recite this sutra, offer alms to it and expound it for others, then the Thus Come One will cover them with his robe, and they will also be protected and kept in mind by the*

Buddhas who are now present in other directions. These people will possess the power of great faith, the power of aspiration, the power of good roots. You should know that these people will lodge in the same place as the Thus Come One, and the Thus Come One will pat them on the head with his hand. (LSOC, 203–04)

Ikeda: Nichiren Daishonin, describing his contemporaries says, "their thoughts [are] filled with jealousy" (WND-1, 873). Indeed, the same could be said of people today.

A country dominated by envy—and this does not apply only to Japan—is sure to decline. That's because people in such a society, rather than respecting those who have achieved some measure of success or attainment, desire only to drag them down. The ancient Greek city-state of Athens offers a good example.

Endo: The practice of ostracism well illustrates the deep-seated envy and jealousy that permeated Athenian society and the destruction that it wrought. In the name of constraining tyranny, people could vote to determine that someone was a potential tyrant—the person with the greatest number of votes was consequently banished from the city, nominally for a ten-year period.

Suda: In fact, President Ikeda, you once shared a passage from Plutarch's *Lives of the Noble Greeks* that explained what a nefarious system this was.

During one ostracism, an illiterate man approached Aristides, a person of exemplary virtue. The man, not realizing to whom he was talking, asked Aristides to write the name *Aristides* on the sherd used as a ballot, naming him as the person he wished to banish. Aristides asked the man if Aristides had ever done him any injury. "None at all," the man replied, "Neither know I the man; but I am tired of hearing him everywhere called the Just."[9] Aristides, saying nothing, returned the sherd with his own name on it. Aristides in fact received the greatest number of votes and was thus banished from Athens.

Plutarch writes:

> The spirit of the people, now grown high, and confident with their late victory, naturally entertained feelings of dislike to all of more than common fame and reputation. Coming together, therefore, from all parts into the city, they banished Aristides by the ostracism, giving their jealousy of his reputation the name of fear of tyranny.[10]

Ikeda: This is an important historical lesson.

As the country prospered, the people became conceited and swollen with self-importance and lost the spirit to respect others. When someone even slightly better than the norm appeared, the citizenry would try to pull the person down out of envy. As a result, people of the highest caliber disappeared from Athens, with only people of inferior ability remaining.

Eventually, Athens found itself without people who could manage the affairs of state. It declined and finally was defeated in war. And so the curtain fell on Athens' glorious history.

Saito: Jealousy is truly fearful. As we've seen, it can destroy a country.

What is the true nature of envy? There is much discussion on the subject. The Japanese philosopher Kiyoshi Miki writes: "A person feels envy toward someone who has a higher standing or a more fortunate situation than he... Moreover, envy prompts a person not to try to improve his own position but rather to try to drag others down to his own level."[11]

It Is Better To Be Envied Than To Be Envious

Ikeda: Rather than seeking to elevate themselves and become better people in their own right, they try to drag others down. Such arrogance benefits no one under any circumstances. Even if we pursue this course with all our might, no good will come of it. Injuring others won't improve one's own lot in the least.

The doctrine of the Ten Worlds concerns itself primarily with the pursuit of happiness. No true happiness can be found in the desire to be better than others, which characterizes anger. People in this state constantly chafe at those who are better than them, while fearful that their true nature will be exposed. To cover up their cowardice, they try to drag others down. The truth is, however, the more they do so, the more miserable they themselves become.

Suda: Why?

Ikeda: People are envious because they are inwardly aware that in some regard the other person is superior. There is a saying that envy is a [perverse] form of praise; to envy someone is to inwardly recognize the person's superiority. Those in anger deny this reality.

Suda: They make no attempt to assess just how petty their own lives are. It seems they have a good deal of pride.

Ikeda: This pride makes those in anger miserable. The more they realize the superior qualities of others, the more they envy and resent them; and, consequently, the more they become aware of the dreariness and pointlessness of their own existence. The angst that they feel at this awareness compels them to turn on others with added fury. It's a vicious cycle.

In truth, to the extent that we can genuinely respect what is lofty and admirable in others, we can develop good qualities in ourselves. Goethe laments of his contemporaries who were engaged in scholarly and literary activities: "True greatness is hateful to them; they would fain drive it from the world, so that only such as they might be of importance in it."[12]

Saito: Certainly, no good comes of envy. As Kiyoshi Miki writes: "I know of no emotion that is at once as busy yet as unproductive as envy."[13] He is describing the power of envy that drives people to spend their time doing all kinds of pointless things.

Ikeda: What causes a person to reach such a point? That is the crux of the matter.

Endo: Earlier we said that someone in anger is cowardly. Is it perhaps the case that the roots of envy are also to be found in a lack of self-confidence?

As evidence, envious people have a hard time recognizing that they are attacking others out of envy. Instead, they invariably find some pretext to justify their actions. That's because the moment they recognize that they are jealous, they must recognize that they are inferior to others. And for those who seek to always be better than others, this can be unbearable.

Saito: Therefore, envious people don masks of righteousness.

Suda: Certainly. Here in Japan, unscrupulous journalists are a good example. They think nothing of lying to bring someone down. Moreover, outwardly they always strike an upstanding pose, pontificating about social justice, freedom of speech and so on. When they find someone to pick on, they employ every base means available to them to injure the person. The conclusion is decided from the outset.

In the view of one critic, such journalists are not reporting facts but merely making up stories and mass-distributing them.

Endo: How many people have had their human rights violated by such unethical individuals! It would seem that persecution by the tabloid media is the modern equivalent of Athenian ostracism. If nothing is done about the situation, it seems to me, contemporary society is sure to decline, as did ancient Greek society. The more outstanding someone's actions, the more these people will envy and try to drag the person down.

FALSE EQUALITY

Saito: It seems to me that malicious and base tabloid journals are symptomatic of a society steeped in envy. Conversely, envy swirling through society makes it possible for such malice to exist in the first place. Isn't a false egalitarianism a key ingredient in the soil from which it emerges? By false egalitarianism, I mean the negative sense of equality that demands that everyone be lined up shoulder to shoulder in perfect conformity.

Suda: You're suggesting that this kind of equality produces the envy that prompts people to try to pull down anyone who stands out.

Ikeda: Certainly, such conformism may be at the root of bullying in Japanese schools. If a student is in some way different from others, he or she is immediately singled out for harassment. In such an environment of conformism, unless people get in with the majority, they will become social outcasts.

In a sense, bullying and envy directed toward those who stand out stem from conformism. In that light, it is very interesting that Athens was the birthplace of democracy.

Suda: I guess the pursuit of equality under democracy intensifies envy because it tries to force everyone into a mold.

Ikeda: Of course, that's not true equality. True equality starts from the recognition that each person is unique—like cherry, plum, peach and damson blossoms.[14] Equality allows each person to fully manifest his or her individuality; and democracy impartially gives all people this opportunity.

If people are evaluated based on a rigid set of criteria in the name of democracy, then those who do not meet that criteria have no place to go.

Saito: Japan's current education system functions in large measure to rank individuals based on test results. Today, success in life, or happiness, means entering the top schools and working at the leading companies, where academic credentials are the key determinant. Under the circumstances, while it might appear people are being treated equally, that is not in fact the case, and there will always be winners and losers.

There is no medicine for curing the sense of defeat felt by those who lose. The "winners," on the other hand, will automatically feel superior to others in all areas, even though their only real success may be in having done well on examinations.

Suda: It would seem that this is the soil from which envy and bullying grow.

Endo: In the past, being a good student didn't count for anything in the society of children. Rather, it was things like throwing stones well or knowledge about insects that could win one a certain measure of respect and status among one's peers. No wonder there was little reason for children to gang up on those who were good at studying.

Ikeda: Conformism is narrow-mindedness. Envy and bullying, and the cruel struggles of anger are born of such narrow-mindedness.

What is needed is the broad-mindedness to respect others. The ultimate articulation of such broad-mindedness is the Lotus Sutra, which explains that all people possess the world of Buddhahood. And its ultimate expression is the world of Buddhahood.

Conformism is a major issue not only in Japan but around the world. The tendency is for people to make economics their sole standard of value and to classify countries as "advanced" or "developing" on that basis. But if we change the standard, the map of the world changes entirely. For example, if we viewed the countries of the world instead in terms of degree of family harmony or degree of respect for nature or some other criterion, then the ones that qualified as "advanced" and "developing" would be completely different.

In the twenty-first century, it will be imperative that the peoples of the world learn to respect one another based on a pluralistic outlook.

A Bulwark for Protecting Human Rights

Endo: This is a necessary word of caution for Japan, in particular, since the Japanese have a strong tendency toward conformism. The combination of conformism and a tradition of collectivism is a sure recipe for fascism. It produces an unwillingness to tolerate people's individual refusal to go along with the majority, which amounts to trampling on their human rights.

Suda: To put it another way, in Japanese society the more everyone is the same, the more comfortable everyone feels. The psychology is analogous to that of a group of people all jaywalking together; because of their number, they don't feel afraid.

Ikeda: Because of the very real danger that Japan may again slip into nationalism, we have to fight hard now to foster individuals who possess sound conviction.

Saito: Nationalistic elements in Japan attack the Soka Gakkai precisely because it has become a bulwark for the protection of human rights.

Ikeda: We have to struggle bravely with the indomitable spirit of lion kings. The Lotus Sutra enables us to manifest the power of bounding lions. Only Bodhisattvas of the Earth and Buddhas can manifest "the lion's ferocity" (LSOC, 258).

Toward evil, we have to fight with the intensity of *asura* or a charging demon. Buddhism concerns itself with winning. We have no choice but to win. When we thoroughly exert ourselves for kosen-rufu, the life of *asura* manifests the function of Buddhahood. This is the principle of the mutual possession of the Ten Worlds. The Buddhas and bodhisattvas existing throughout time and space heartily applaud when they see such valiant, dedicated efforts.

On the other hand, to fight solely for oneself is lowly and base. To look down on and harm others based on one's ego is the nature of Devadatta. Those dominated by the spirit to appear to be better than others are themselves miserable.

Saito: In that position one is certainly miserable.

I suppose that Devadatta, who became Shakyamuni's archenemy, had the deep-seated desire to be "better than" Shakyamuni. Toward that end, he soiled his hands through evil machinations. Still, Shakyamuni was perfectly calm and self-possessed. Every time he saw Shakyamuni's composure, Devadatta must have been filled with chagrin and driven further down the path of anger, reminded of his own pettiness. In the end, he tumbled into a state of hell.

Suda: Devadatta advocated practices[15] more severe than those advocated by Shakyamuni, and he maintained an upright and humble appearance. This is the working of a "mind of minor goodness."

Ikeda: Those in the world of anger deceive themselves and deceive others; they live a life of lies built upon lies. They can neither experience true fulfillment nor expand their state of life. Clinging to their own puny illusory sense of self while making a false show of strength, they lead a pitiful existence.

Endo: Another passage in the book we talked about a moment ago, *People of the Lie*, reads:

> Forever fleeing the light of self-exposure and the voice of their own conscience, they are the most frightened of human beings. They live their lives in sheer terror. They need not be consigned to any hell; they are already in it.[16]

Ikeda: An arrogant mind is always bobbing this way and that. It never knows a moment's calm. The envious try to upset the lives of others while they themselves live wildly fluctuating lives.

The Daishonin describes the befuddled vision of the Lotus Sutra's enemies, saying: "People like this Acharya Owari fail to recognize their own faults, and in their jealousy of others they believe that the huge mountain is turning around when it is only their own eyes that are spinning" (WND-2, 727).

Saito: The mirror for discerning this is the doctrine of the Ten Worlds. Many people, influenced by those filled with envy whose eyes are spinning, cannot correctly judge the grandeur of a mountain.

Ikeda: Such is the state the sutra describes where it says, "Since hatred and jealousy toward this sutra abound even when the Thus Come One is in the world, how much more will this be so after his passing?" (LSOC, 203).

Our examination of anger has become quite lengthy, but this is perhaps inevitable because, as the sutra says, hatred and jealousy abound. It is a subject with a great deal of relevance to the state of affairs in the world today.

HUMANITY—THE PATH OF SELF-MASTERY

Saito: This brings us to the world of humanity. In contrast to anger, which is characterized by the desire to appear to be better than others, humanity indicates a state of life victorious over the self. When I first heard this, it struck me as quite a revelation.

Ikeda: Strictly speaking, humanity is the first step toward attaining a state of self-mastery, the culmination of which is to be found in the worlds of bodhisattva and Buddhahood.

Citing a familiar Buddhist concept, the Daishonin says, "Those who give their allegiance to the three treasures and abide by the five precepts will be born in the world of human beings" (WND-2, 197). The teachings of both the three devotions[17] and the five precepts[18] signify the effort to advance along the correct path in life. When we follow this path, our lives become stable; we are not tossed about this way and that, the way someone with an arrogant mind is.

Broadly speaking, the teaching of the three devotions indicates a spirit of faith. Haughty people in anger cannot recognize anyone as better. They cannot bow their heads to anyone. Ultimately, they become the slaves of their own arrogance and captives of evil. Those in humanity, by contrast, humbly and sincerely respect those of higher attainment and ability and, consequently, accrue inner wealth.

The teaching of the five precepts is not a way of binding our lives from without. The precepts could be described, rather, as a standard or vow that is internalized, a path in life. When we understand that breaking the five precepts produces the effect of suffering and therefore control ourselves with our own intellect, we are in the world of humanity.

Suda: In Sanskrit, *human being* is signified by the term *manusya*, which means "thinking being" or "one who thinks." From that standpoint, I guess that intellect is the key condition of humanity.

Nichiren Daishonin says, "The wise may be called human, but the thoughtless are no more than animals" (WND-1, 852). Beings in this state possess a greater ability to discern correctly the good and evil of things than do those dwelling in the three or the four evil paths.

Saito: T'ien-t'ai cites "the ability to widely recognize causes in anticipation of future effects" as the distinguishing characteristic of humanity. In other words, to dwell in humanity means to understand the principle of cause and effect to a certain degree.

Endo: The May 1997 issue of the *Daibyakurenge* carried an interview with Professor Sallie King (of James Madison University in Harrisonburg, Virginia) on Buddhism's philosophy of human rights. The article contained a discussion of the five precepts.

Professor King noted, for example, that if one were to undertake the first precept of Buddhism, not to harm others, it would obviously be for the other person's good. But such restraint would, at the same time, also be in one's own interest. Because, as she rightly points out, the karmic consequences of harming others would accrue to the perpetrator. In this sense, the Buddhist perspective of human rights, which has, at its foundation, the good of all people, is different from that in the West.

Ikeda: The modern significance of Buddhism becomes all the more clear. Buddhism clarifies the path of fulfillment for both oneself and others; it reveals the correct path in life for human beings. Because we are advancing along the correct path, we lead stable lives, realizing progressive improvement and growth.

Regarding humanity, in "The Object of Devotion for Observing the Mind," the Daishonin says, "calmness is that of human beings" (WND-1, 358).

Suda: It is a state of calm and tranquillity, as when one takes a moment's rest after a hard day's work.

Endo: For me, I associate the "calmness" that the Daishonin speaks of with the last scene in the novel *Shin Heike monogatari* (New Tale of the Heike), by the popular Japanese writer Eiji Yoshikawa.

It is the scene where Abe-no-Asatori and his wife, Yomogi, peasants who have observed the continuous struggles between the

Minamoto and Taira clans for hegemony over a half century, have an intense discussion. While viewing the cherry flowers of Mount Yoshino, and looking back on the tumultuous past, the couple feel an acute sense of happiness.

> When it comes to human happiness, where we are at right now is the happiest point that can be reached... Why, even so, do people all shed blood and fight over rank and power?
>
> There is no use comparing individual differences in talent, or the different professions and missions that people pursue in life. Those who thoroughly dedicate themselves to their work in life are all respectworthy; that's what is important. There is no difference among them as human beings.[19]

To me, this ordinary elderly couple who had miraculously managed to survive in an age rife with war represents the world of humanity.

Ikeda: That's a famous scene. While perhaps ordinary and unremarkable, they display a splendid radiance as human beings.

Those in anger vie with one another in their quest for status and power, spilling blood and doing injury to one another. But the two of them lived true to their hearts. Without comparing themselves to others, they strove to follow through on their own path. Even in a society characterized by anger, those who persist in following such a path attain peace of mind, the world of humanity.

Peace of mind or calmness definitely cannot be gained without diligent effort. Unless we make steadfast effort, our state of life will inevitably be colored by our environment or those around us.

Suda: Certainly, the tendency is for someone in humanity to quickly be pulled down into one of the three evil paths or the world of anger by external influences. This is evident in our everyday lives. It is extremely difficult to maintain a calm and tranquil self. At the slightest obstacle, one may become downcast or filled with rage.

LIVING HUMANELY MAKES US HUMAN

Ikeda: That is precisely the challenge of leading a humane existence. This is all the more difficult because this is the Latter Day of the Law, and we are surrounded by negative influences. For precisely this reason, to live as human beings we need to follow a path of continuous advancement. This path is none other than our Buddhist practice.

When a top stops spinning, it falls over. It is only stable when it is rotating at a high speed.

Being born human does not make one a human being. Don't we really only become human when we make tenacious effort to live as human beings? In the early twentieth century, two girls who had been raised by a pack of wolves were rescued by residents of a small village near Calcutta. The girls were about two and eight years old at the time. When they were found, while their features were human, in their actions and activities they were no different from wolves. During the day, they would sleep in the corner of a dark room or would lie perfectly still. At night, they would prowl around the vicinity and would howl repeatedly. They could neither eat with their hands nor stand up on two feet.

Saito: I heard about that. Later, efforts were made to help them behave as humans, but their habits as wolves reportedly stayed with them largely unchanged all their lives.

Ikeda: That's right. Pitifully, the younger of the two children died shortly thereafter. While the elder girl lived another nine years, even at age seventeen she reportedly managed to use only four or five words.

Saito: It may be that being born as a human being means nothing more than that one has the potential to become human.

Ikeda: That's why education is so important. We need humanistic education to become human beings.

Endo: Come to think of it, I once heard the following story. A child returned home after getting a perfect score on a test. Right off the bat his mother asked him how many children in the class had gotten perfect scores. When he answered that many had, she replied, "Then it's only natural that you should have gotten a perfect score."

Suda: A child, it seems, can never do well enough.

Endo: Often parents don't try to see what their children have learned or how they have developed. Instead, they are concerned only with how their children compare to their peers. This approach would seem to lend itself to producing people who dwell in anger.

Ikeda: It is becoming increasingly difficult to lead a simple, humane existence. In terms of the structure of the doctrine of the Ten Worlds, the world of humanity is right in the middle. From that vantage, one can either ascend to higher states of life or descend into the lower worlds. It could be said, therefore, that humanity occupies the central position.

For precisely that reason, Nichiren Daishonin repeatedly tells us that since we have had the rare good fortune to be born in the world of humanity, we should strive to attain a still higher state of life.

For What Purpose Were We Born As Human Beings?

Suda: Yes. For example, the Daishonin says, "Those who are born in the three evil paths are more numerous than the dust particles of the great earth, while those who are born as human beings are fewer than the particles of dirt one can put on a fingernail" (WND-2, 142).

Endo: He also says, "Now I have already obtained birth in the human realm, something difficult to achieve, and have had the privilege of hearing the Buddhist teachings, which are seldom encountered. If I should pass my present life in idleness, then in what future life could I possibly free myself from the sufferings of birth and death and attain enlightenment?" (WND-1, 125).

Ikeda: Therefore, it's important that we exert ourselves earnestly while we are hale and hearty. To the extent that we courageously take action for kosen-rufu, we solidify within our lives the path leading to eternal happiness.

In Buddhism, the human body is called the "correct vessel of the noble paths" — that is, it is the vessel of the Law for carrying out Buddhist practice. When we fill that vessel with the great life of Buddhahood, we realize the true significance of having been born as human beings.

Saito: In that sense, can we perhaps say that the meaning of humanity lies in striving to attain a still higher state of life?

Elevating the State of Life of All People

Ikeda: Yes, I think so. A higher state of life would mean the worlds of heaven, voice-hearers, cause-awakened ones, bodhisattva and Buddhahood.

At any rate, there is something wondrous about the function

of one's state of life. Whether we are aware of it, our state of life to a great extent determines our actions, thoughts, relationships and path in life, as well as our emotions.

State of life, moreover, is not only a property of individuals. A society, too, has a state of life, the Ten Worlds. Kosen-rufu is not only a struggle to change the state of life of individuals but a movement to change the state of life of an entire country, to elevate the state of life of humankind. It is a grand and unprecedented experiment.

I am reminded of certain words of Shozo Tanaka. [The legislator Tanaka made a name for himself as a friend of the people in the Ashio Copper Mine Incident, which resulted in widespread environmental damage. He devoted his life to opposing abuses of people's rights by the authorities.]

In his later years, he said: "Nations are like people. People are not necessarily respected because they are stout. They are respected for their knowledge and virtue. Nations are like people. People are respected not because of their physical strength but because of their intellect, no matter how skinny they are."[20]

Victimizing the people both at home and abroad, Japan, in racing ahead along the path of anger toward developing a rich nation and a strong military, became arrogant and lost its spirit. It lost sight of the path of humanism.

Tanaka declared: "Japan still sustains its body but has lost its spirit. Japan no longer exists."[21] He wrote these words four months before his death. Thirty-two years later, Japan had indeed collapsed.

Because we do not want this tragedy to be repeated, we are crying out to our compatriots: "Abandon arrogance! Humbly pursue the path of humanism!"

NOTES

1. *Yojana*: (Skt) A unit of measurement used in ancient India, equal to the distance that the royal army was thought to be able to march in a day. Approximations vary as widely as 9.6, 16 and 24 kilometers.

2. Nichikan, "Sanju Hiden Sho" (The Threefold Secret Teaching).

3. M. Scott Peck, M.D., *People of the Lie: The Hope for Healing Human Evil* (New York: Simon and Schuster, 1983), p. 73.

4. Ibid., p. 75.

5. Ibid., p. 78.

6. Ibid., p. 77.

7. Ibid., p. 74.

8. Ibid., p. 71.

9. Plutarch, *Lives of the Noble Greeks*, ed. Edmund Fuller (New York: Nelson Doubleday, Inc., 1959), p. 99.

10. Ibid., p. 98.

11. *Miki Kiyoshi zenshu* (Collected Works of Kiyoshi Miki), "Jinseiron Noto" [Thoughts on Life] (Tokyo: Iwanami Shoten, 1966), vol. 1, pp. 267–68.

12. Johann Peter Eckermann, *Words of Goethe* (New York: Tudor Publishing Company, 1949), p. 129.

13. *Miki Kiyoshi zenshu*, ibid., p. 270.

14. Buddhism teaches that each of us has our own unique personality and mission. In Nichiren's writings, it states: "Cherry, plum, peach or damson blossoms—in its own entity, without undergoing any change possesses the eternally endowed three bodies" (OTT, 200).

15. Devadatta sought to present himself as surpassing the Buddha and to gain recognition in society by advocating five practices. As detailed in the *Shibunritsu*, they were: to wear robes of rags; to seek food only by begging; to eat only one meal a day; to always sit out in the open; and to partake of neither salt nor the five flavors.

16. Peck, *People of the Lie*, p. 67.

17. Three devotions: Devotion to the three treasures of the Buddha, the Law and the *sangha,* or community of Buddhist followers.

18. Five precepts: Prohibitions against killing, stealing, illicit sex, lying and consumption of alcohol.

19. *Yoshikawa Eiji zenshu* (Collected Writings of Eiji Yoshikawa) (Tokyo: Kodansha, 1982), vol. 39, pp. 213–14.

20. *Tanaka Shozo zenshu* (Collected Works of Shozo Tanaka) (Tokyo: Iwanami Shoten, 1979), vol. 11, p. 131.

21. *Tanaka Shozo zenshu* (Tokyo: Iwanami Shoten, 1977), vol. 13, p. 446.

6   From the Six Paths to the Four Noble Worlds

Endo: Now let's discuss the world of heaven and the worlds we've come to know as the two vehicles of voice-hearers and cause-awakened ones. The word *heaven* evokes a realm bathed in cheerful rosy hues. But I'm not sure what color I would associate with the worlds of voice-hearers and cause-awakened ones.

Ikeda: How about gray?

Saito: Yes, gray would be it. Such a realm, as I imagine it, would be rather dark and gloomy.

Suda: That's probably because in the Daishonin's writings there are many descriptions of people of the two vehicles being severely reprimanded by Shakyamuni Buddha.

Endo: Still, the two vehicles, or two paths, are included among the four noble worlds.[1] That's because those in these states have gone beyond endless transmigration through the six paths.[2] As a matter of fact, their state of life is quite high. And, to that extent, they should be happier than those dwelling in the six paths.

Ikeda: Why, then, do you suppose the progression is from rosy to gray? Wouldn't it be better to simply remain in the world of heaven? I expect our discussion will hinge on this point.

Ultimately, there is nothing wrong with the world of heaven. Problems arise, however, when, filled with self-satisfaction and complacency, we become attached to or are held back by this state of life.

It probably goes without saying that everyone desires the bliss of a heavenly existence—good health, abundance, a happy home, a joyful life—circumstances I hope and pray everyone will enjoy. Unfortunately, no rose can bloom forever. With the passing of time, its color is certain to fade and its petals to scatter as it experiences the four seasons or sufferings — birth, aging, sickness and death — that are an integral part of all life.

Saito: It has been said that as the joy of heaven fades, its inhabitants experience the five types of decay.[3] Buddhist texts use the image of flowers wilting to convey this.

Ikeda: The joy of heaven is ephemeral like a mirage or a dream. A life spent in pursuit of a mirage is itself a mirage.

The purpose of Buddhist practice is to establish an eternally indestructible state of happiness; not a fleeting happiness that perishes like a flower but an internal palace of happiness that will last throughout all time. This diamond palace, this treasure tower soaring to magnificent heights, is built through faith.

Heavenly flowers of joy blossom within that palace according to the season. Because in this state we actualize the principle that earthly desires are enlightenment, the more worries we have, the greater the sense of fulfillment we feel. The true purpose of the four noble worlds lies in constructing such a "diamond-like heart."

In other words, it is our human revolution—changing from someone buffeted about by the environment to someone who can positively influence his or her surroundings—that enables us to construct an unshakable palace within. The seeking mind represented by the two vehicles could be said to constitute the foundation on which this eternal palace within is built.

Suda: Perhaps rather than the color gray, a more appropriate simile would be a subdued silver.

Endo: The state of the world today could be likened to a bubble that has burst. The ephemeral prosperity we have enjoyed has taken a heavy toll. When you think about it, any society that would encourage its people to play out their desires to the hilt only engenders suffering. That is certainly the state of affairs in Japanese society today. I think it is also why Japan today so clearly illustrates the teaching about transmigration in the six paths.

Ikeda: That's what is commonly called the devilish power of desire. What happiness has the pursuit of such desires brought?

If you can imagine a "heaven of desire" produced from having all of your desires fulfilled, you will find at its summit the devil king of the sixth heaven. A life or a society devoted solely to the pursuit of desire is ruled by this devil king. No condition is more horrid and miserable.

Saito: In modern civilization, the unbridled pursuit of desires is generally regarded as something good. And the goal of society is simply to reach the world of heaven. But modern civilization has reached a deadlock. That should be clear to anyone.

Ikeda: The fundamental cause for this deadlock is that people are focused entirely on the external, material world and fail to direct their gaze within. Above all, they avert their eyes from the universal sufferings of birth, aging, sickness and death that constitute the fundamental problems of human existence.

The Lotus Sutra, and particularly the "Life Span" chapter, can open people's closed eyes. Only when we fix our gaze on grappling with questions of life and death do we awaken to the true meaning of existence. When we squarely face the profound reality of life and death, we realize how shallow are our concerns for momentary satisfaction. This is very common.

The Brilliance of Life as Perceived
From the Abyss of Death

He sees living beings seared and consumed by birth, aging, sickness, and death, care and suffering, sees them undergo many kinds of pain because of the five desires and the desire for wealth and profit. Again, because of their greed and attachment and striving they undergo numerous pains in their present existence, and later they undergo the pain of being reborn in hell or as beasts or hungry spirits. Even if they are reborn in the heavenly realm or the realm of human beings, they undergo the pain of poverty and want, the pain of parting from loved ones, the pain of encountering those they detest—all these many different kinds of pain.

Yet living beings, drowned in the midst of all this, delight and amuse themselves, unaware, unknowing, without alarm or fear. They feel no sense of loathing and make no attempt to escape. In this burning house which is the threefold world, they race about to east and west, and though they encounter great pain, they are not distressed by it. (LSOC, 94–95)

Suda: To look death in the eye can change the way we live, as many SGI members can attest, such as Makoto Sato, who was head of the Soka Gakkai organization in Toyama Prefecture. In June 1979, Mr. Sato was diagnosed with terminal cancer of the upper jaw. He transferred from a hospital in Toyama Prefecture to one in Tokyo. On that day, he learned the truth of his condition.

Saito: Did he hear it from the doctor?

Suda: No, Mr. Sato heard the news from his wife, who had been informed by the doctor a little earlier. She broke it to him as the two of them were strolling through the bustling Shinjuku district.

Endo: It must have come as quite a shock.

Suda: Mr. Sato had had some inkling as to the gravity of his condition, but still he was stunned. Yet, for some reason, he was not overcome with fear. On the contrary, he described how at the moment he heard the news, everything around seemed to take on a kind of glow. The asphalt streets seemed to shine in the rays of sunlight that broke through the overcast skies of the rainy season. He felt he had never seen the trees so green or the streets so lovely. He described feeling the urge to speak out to passersby and embrace everyone.

Endo: That sounds remarkable.

Suda: At the same time, he said, he felt a shudder as though he were about to mount the gallows. But Mr. Sato did not run away from the reality of his life. With his entire being, he began waging an all-out struggle against the "devil of death."

His surgery, which was supposed to last eight hours, took only two-and-a-half hours and was highly successful. His teeth, gums and upper jaw were surgically removed, and the replacement of the gauze in his mouth every day caused him such excruciating pain that he almost fainted.

Still, he read the writings of the Daishonin with his fading eyesight, engraving one passage after another in the depths of his life. After the operation, he was afraid his speech would be impeded but it turned out that talking became part of his rehabilitation. Mr. Sato remarked, "Speaking at Gakkai activities was the greatest aid to my recovery."

Even in his circumstances, he was anxious about his fellow members of Toyama Prefecture. Since coming to the hospital in Tokyo, he had not had a single chance to return. Aware that he had not been back for some time, President Ikeda, you invited him to go on a guidance trip with you through Toyama and the Hokuriku region. When you arrived, the first thing you did was introduce him to everyone, saying, "I've brought Mr. Sato with me today." I hear he was overcome with tears.

After that, Mr. Sato officially transferred to Tokyo and began devoting himself in earnest to speaking at seminars, giving individual guidance and doing other activities in his new community west of Tokyo.

Ikeda: I met him many times at the Tachikawa Culture Center. I will always remember his spirited, animated gait. One could sense that he felt immense joy to be alive.

Suda: Mr. Sato himself once remarked: "Before experiencing the very border between life and death, I could not understand the true profundity of the Buddhism or President Ikeda's guidance. To live, Buddhism teaches, is a formidable struggle. But all too many people fail to realize this. I still have a lot of work I need to do for kosen-rufu. Therefore, I cannot waste my time."

Saito: For many people, certainly, it is only when death is staring them in the face that they ask themselves: "What has the purpose of my life been?" "Why didn't I live and practice faith more earnestly while I was healthy?"

Ikeda: That's it exactly. Unless we practice faith with the attitude "now is the last moment of my life," we will have cause for regret. Unless we thoroughly exert ourselves for kosen-rufu while we are healthy and can take action, we will regret it for countless aeons to come.

Suda: Mr. Sato died in 1992. But until his death, he put all his energy into giving individual guidance. Describing his attitude, he said, "When I meet someone, the thought that I may never have the chance to meet the person again in this life fills me with the ardent desire to teach the person as many passages of Nichiren Daishonin's writings as possible."

In particular, if he learned that someone was in the final stage of terminal cancer, Mr. Sato would encourage the person passionately as if it were his own problem. Those who received his encouragement and were revitalized have now fanned out throughout the entire country.

He would give people passages from Nichiren Daishonin's writings that he had copied onto memo stationary: "The reason that you have survived until now when so many have died was so that you would meet with this affair" (WND-1, 829); "And could not this illness of your husband's be the Buddha's design, because the Vimalakirti and Nirvana sutras both teach that sick people will surely attain Buddhahood?" (WND-1, 937); "Life is limited; we must not begrudge it" (WND-1, 214). Those receiving these pages often reported that while they had been familiar with the passages, when they received them in this form, individually handwritten, it struck a fresh chord in their hearts.

Saito: That's a wonderful account.

Ikeda: It illustrates what it means to live a truly noble life. When one gazes into the chasm between life and death, status, fame and wealth count for absolutely nothing. All that remains is one's bare self stripped of all external adornment. Only through Buddhism can we change our lives on this essential level.

RELIGION IS BORN OUT OF FEAR OF "HEAVEN"

Ikeda: Why don't we consider the basic meaning of "heaven"?

Endo: The term *heaven* is the translation of the Sanskrit term *deva*, a realm in which heavenly beings dwell. The same term is also translated as "deity." It originally means "shine," in the sense of radiating light.

Saito: Whether we call it "heaven" or "deity," when we think of it as the place where the Buddhist gods might dwell, that makes a lot of sense. The *deva* or the Buddhist gods, which include the god of the sun and god of the moon, must have been conceived as beings with a power transcending that of people on the earth.

Suda: In India, from ancient times it was believed that those who performed good acts in the present life would be reborn in heaven.

Endo: Brahman and Indra were representative Indian gods believed to dwell in the world of heaven. They were incorporated into and given new roles by Buddhism as Bonten and Taishaku, respectively.

Ikeda: "Heaven" or "deity" could be thought of not as a place but as a universal force. People, gazing up at the skies, have always been captivated by the awesome grandeur of the heavens. They have prayed to make the power of the universe their ally. Also, fearful of the destructive power that nature sometimes shows, they have prayed to avoid disaster.

People feared and worshipped the great power of nature. Sensing the existence of a destiny they were powerless to change through their own efforts, they prayed to their gods for their lot to improve. From such prayer religion was born. Prayer was not born of religion; rather, religion was born of prayer. In other words, the concept of "heaven" suggests the perception of a great existence transcending human beings.

Many animals live on four limbs with their eyes turned to the ground. Human beings stood up on two legs and directed their gaze out into the universe. They aspired toward "heaven." Metaphorically speaking, I think we can characterize the evolutionary advancement of human beings in these terms. In that sense, the shining "heavens" must have become a kind of ideal.

Suda: Certainly, many new thinkers who lived around the same time as Shakyamuni—for example, the six non-Buddhist teachers[4]—

put forward the view that the purpose of practice was to gain rebirth in heaven.

Ikeda: In Buddhism, "heaven" is not seen as a place one goes after death but rather as a state of life we may experience from moment to moment. Also, Buddhism designates the life-conditions attained through the practices of the six non-Buddhist teachers as belonging to the world of heaven.

Endo: You are referring to the six heavens of the world of desire (a realm swirling with desire), the eighteen heavens of the world of form (a realm in which one has overcome domination by desire but is still bound by physical restrictions), and the four heavens of the world of formlessness (a realm in which one is still subject to spiritual restrictions). Together these make up the twenty-eight heavens.

Suda: The Lotus Sutra says of the threefold world of desire, form and formlessness, "There is no safety in the threefold world; / it is like a burning house" (LSOC, 105). Since the six paths are included within the threefold world, the two terms are identical in meaning.

Saito: Of these, the world of desire swirls with the desire to live, instinctive desire, material desire and desire for social advancement.

The world of heaven is primarily a state of rapturous joy experienced through the fulfillment of such desires. For example, when we are satisfied after a good meal, we are in the world of heaven.

Suda: Nichiren Daishonin says, "Joy is that of heaven" (WND-1, 358).

Ikeda: Different kinds of joy accompany the fulfillment of different desires. There is, for example, pure intellectual desire that transcends the desires of the "world of desire"; there is desire for beauty; and there is spiritual desire to attain a sublime state of life.

Endo: The pursuit and fulfillment of such lofty desires must be found in the worlds of form and formlessness.

Saito: This could be described as a state in which one seeks the truth and this desire is fulfilled. This is still within the world of heaven.

Suda: How is that different from the life-condition of the two vehicles of voice-hearers and cause-awakened ones? In particular, it seems that the world of formlessness and the two vehicles are similar in that they both indicate conditions of spiritual attainment.

Two Different Views of Attainment

Ikeda: People of the two vehicles with their higher life-condition do not view the state of life they have attained as an absolute goal. They do not become attached to it.

While those in the world of formlessness view their state as a condition of final attainment, those in the worlds of voice-hearers and cause-awakened ones view their state as an "intermediate path" that they have taken in seeking to advance further toward the state of Buddhahood. They are not captive or shackled to what they have attained thus far. They perceive the principles of nonsubstantiality and dependent origination operating in all phenomena.

Suda: Viewing all things from the standpoint of dependent origination means viewing them as coming into being through a synergy of internal causes and external relations, and as mutually interdependent.

Saito: When a new cause or relation is involved, the situation immediately changes. Therefore, they perceive everything as existing through the temporary interaction of internal causes and relations. This is termed the "temporary fusion of internal cause and relation."

Ikeda: That's certainly true of human beings. The features that we think of as constituting our "self" are really no more than a temporal aspect that we assume. No one can escape change. A healthy person will someday become sick and die. A young person, in what seems but an instant, becomes old.

We may ask ourselves, "Just who am I?" But the person we were ten years ago is not the person we are today. There is no such thing as an unchanging self. Buddhism therefore teaches that we should discard attachment to the self.

Suda: That's the doctrine of selflessness.

Ikeda: Selflessness means being without self. This concept reflects the point of view that there is no eternally unchanging fixed self. Rather, there is continual change. This position views the self as essentially nonsubstantial, or empty.

Saito: But unenlightened beings, supposing the self to be unchanging, become attached to the self and to their possessions. In other words, they perceive all things as substantial. This is the state of life of beings in the six paths.

Ikeda: The same is also true of people's attachment to wealth, status, fame and the like: nothing is more empty; they are as ephemeral as bubbles on the water. Yet beings in the six paths become attached to them and live under the illusion that such things will belong to them in perpetuity.

To sum things up, those in the six worlds perceive all phenomena as substantial. Those in the worlds of voice-hearers and cause-awakened ones perceive all phenomena as essentially empty; that is to say, in light of the truth of nonsubstantiality. Those in the world of bodhisattva perceive phenomena as provisional; that is, in light of the truth of temporary existence. And those in the world of Buddhahood perceive phenomena in light of the truth of the Middle Way, which integrates the truths of nonsubstantiality and temporary existence. I expect that we will have the chance to discuss this later in greater detail.

Endo: To illustrate what is meant by the statement that those in the six paths perceive phenomena as substantial, take the case of a baseball pitcher. While young, he may make a name for himself for having a very powerful fastball, but he will gradually lose his strength as he ages. Nevertheless, he will maintain an image of himself as always having the same strong fastball. Then years later, when he's much older, he pitches at a crucial moment what he imagines to be his usual fastball. But it isn't. It is a decidedly weak pitch that leads his team to defeat.

Ikeda: Some people, even after they retire, cannot shake their sense of themselves or their pride as, say, managers or employees of a leading company. They become rather difficult to get along with. It is not unusual in Japan to find people whose entire identity is so bound up with the company they work for that, after they retire, all that remains is an impoverished sense of identity. In many cases, such people cannot begin a new phase in life because they cannot examine this self with clear eyes, leaving them frustrated and miserable.

People tend to view not only themselves but others as well in such static terms. No matter how someone might have grown and changed, others tend to see the person as he or she was in the past. It is the insight of the two vehicles, that is, the wisdom of the truth of nonsubstantiality, that refutes such a static view. The true enlightenment of the two vehicles lies in the perception that there is nothing at all in the world that does not undergo change. As a result, it is incumbent upon us to forever strive to advance and improve.

Saito: So when people of the two vehicles believe that the state they have attained is an end in itself and thereby grow complacent, ironically they no longer can be said to belong to the two vehicles.

Ikeda: That's right. At that point, they revert to the six paths. This is similar to how beings of the world of formlessness, once they believe that they have arrived at the highest summit of the world of heaven, begin to descend.

Suda: Nichiren Daishonin says in "The Opening of the Eyes":

> The devout followers of the non-Buddhist teachings… ascending to the worlds of form and formlessness, believe they have attained nirvana when they reach the highest of the heavens. But although they make their way upward bit by bit like an inchworm, they fall back from the heaven where there is neither thought nor no thought, and descend instead into the three evil paths. Not a single one succeeds in remaining on the level of the heavens… (WND-1, 222)

Ikeda: Although they have carried out difficult practices, earnestly ascending step by step, in the end they fall head over heels. Why do you suppose that is?

There are many different perspectives. But simply put, there is probably something unnatural or forced in the state of life they have attained as a result of carrying out such arduous practices. And because it is forced, they cannot remain long in that state. To illustrate, if people with little money manage to stay at a first-rate hotel by resorting to unreasonable measures, then even though they may enjoy fine living there for a time, eventually the truth will come out and they will have to return to their shabby homes. Using the same analogy, it could be said that the purpose of Buddhist practice, rather than being to check into a nice hotel, is to securely rebuild one's home. Through our practice we develop a self that is like a splendid palace. To do so, we must first understand the fundamental causes of our suffering—the places where the roof leaks or where there are drafts—and fundamentally repair these areas, and so create a comfortable and homey state of life.

In other words, Buddhist practice lies in perceiving that the cause of suffering is none other than one's own illusions and then struggling to transform the self so as to conquer these illusions. Those in the world of formlessness are people who strive in their own way to change their state of life but who lack the wisdom of the true law of life. For that reason, there is something unnatural or forced about their efforts. They stand up as straight as they can; but because they lack firm footing, they tumble down again to their former state.

Saito: The law of life enabling one to change the self into a "palace" is the Mystic Law.

Ikeda: That is indeed the conclusion we reach.

Suda: This is the meaning of the Daishonin's statement to the effect that, without the Lotus Sutra, one could never escape from transmigration in the six paths (WND-2, 161). It is through the Mystic Law that people of the two vehicles, too, can for the first time move beyond the six paths.

THE "FIRST STEP" IN THE BIRTH OF BUDDHISM

Ikeda: In any event, desires and pleasures are of many different kinds. Consequently, the states of life that accompany their fulfillment also differ widely. It can be said that the state of joy we experience upon achieving a lifelong goal is that of heaven. For instance, a child may have the goal of achieving the best grades in the class, or of mastering a difficult physical challenge, such as the horizontal bar in gymnastics. Musicians in an orchestra may attain the state of heaven through thoroughly polishing their musical sensitivity and skill, performing in wonderful harmony and attaining a high level of musical expertise.

Saito: While these are certainly on different levels, in a sense they are alike in that each is a kind of self-actualization.

Suda: To dedicate one's life to achieving some target—we can say that this itself is a part of what it means to lead a humane existence.

Endo: Earlier, we said that those in the world of anger strive to "win over others," while those in humanity, heaven and the four noble paths aim to "win over themselves." It could be said that the world of heaven is the effect produced through a tenacious struggle to win over the self.

Since it is a state of inner fulfillment reached in the course of achieving one's own goals, the "life space" is broader than that of the world of humanity. Even so, those in this state have not transcended the six paths.

Ikeda: Let's try to recapitulate what has been said thus far. In Shakyamuni's time, attaining the state of heaven was a widely held ideal. This state was above all understood as signifying fulfillment of the world of desire.

Saito: Toward that end, adherents of traditional Brahmanism carried out various prayers and practices.

Ikeda: In terms of secular desire, the palace where Shakyamuni grew up must have seemed to the people of the time as akin to a heavenly realm. But when he ventured from the gates of the palace, Shakyamuni saw people suffering from old age and sickness. He also saw a corpse. Confronted by the reality of the four sufferings—birth, aging, sickness and death—Shakyamuni understood the emptiness of desire. In other words, he perceived that everything is subject to change. Thereupon, he renounced the heavenly lifestyle in which he had grown up and embarked upon his religious quest.

At the time, there were new thinkers who aspired to attain a lofty state of life transcending secular desire. These were the six non-Buddhist teachers. It is said that after renouncing the world, Shakyamuni received instruction from two of these individuals. But at length he discerned that the teachings they espoused did not ultimately offer a solution to the sufferings of life and death.

Endo: The world of desire had proved to offer no solution. Nor did the worlds of form and formlessness.

Ikeda: "Where, then, does true human happiness lie?" From this inquiry, the great teaching that is Buddhism was born.

Suda: The birth of Buddhism, then, lay in Shakyamuni's progression from the world of heaven to the realm of the two vehicles.

Ikeda: Yes, in the transition from the six paths to the four noble paths.

Endo: Could the first step in that direction have been Shakyamuni's perception of life's impermanence, as indicated by the account of his early life? Nichiren Daishonin says: "The fact that all things in this world are transient is perfectly clear to us. Is this not because the worlds of the two vehicles are present in the human world?" (WND-1, 358).

Ikeda: As was true in Shakyamuni's case, fixing one's gaze on death is probably the first step to be taken in seeking the eternal.

We live in a civilization dedicated to the pursuit of desire, of attachment to the world of desire. People take it for granted these days that life ought to become increasingly comfortable and easy. If they cannot lead a peaceful and easy existence, it is certainly not for wanting to do so.

Difficult as it may be for people today to imagine, there have in fact been times in which people sought not an easy life but another kind of existence. Making this point, the author and social critic Aldous Huxley writes:

> The first thing that strikes one about the discomfort in which our ancestors lived is that it was mainly voluntary... Men could have made sofas and smoking-room chairs, could have installed bathrooms and central heating and sanitary plumbing any time during the last three or four thousand years. And as a matter of fact, at certain periods they did indulge themselves in these comforts. Two thousand years before Christ, the inhabitants of Cnossos were familiar with sanitary plumbing. The Romans had invented an elaborate system of hot-air heating, and the bathing facilities in a smart Roman villa were luxurious and complete beyond the dreams of the modern man... If the men of the Middle Ages and early modern epoch lived in filth and discomfort, it was not for any lack or ability to change their mode of life; it was because they chose to live in this way, because filth and discomfort fitted in with their principles and prejudices, political, moral, and religious...
>
> One can never have something for nothing, and the achievement of comfort has been accompanied by a compensating loss of other equally, or perhaps more, valuable things...
>
> The modern world seems to regard it [comfort] as an end in itself, an absolute good. One day, perhaps, the earth will have been turned into one vast feather-bed, with man's body dozing on top of it and his mind underneath, like Desdemona,[5] smothered.[6]

Suda: His point is that to simply seek an easy life kills the spirit.

Modern Society Tries To Conceal Death

Ikeda: In that connection, what is problematic about the world of heaven is that it functions to conceal the reality of the four sufferings. Because the state of heaven is accompanied by momentary joy, it has the propensity to cause us to divert our eyes from the great problems lying at the heart of existence. In fact, often the world of Hell is more effective in opening our eyes to the reality of life and enabling us to comprehend quickly the path leading to the four noble worlds.

Suda: Certainly, those whose lives on the surface appear very happy may have considerable difficulty embracing faith.

Saito: Material abundance and spiritual joy are important. But the question is whether simply possessing such happiness is enough to enable one to overcome the sufferings of life and death. Sadly, the answer is "No."

Endo: A religious scholar once asserted that in creating a work of art, a master painter can attain a transcendent state in which he or she can sense the eternity of life. He said: "Attachment to life cannot disrupt the artist's frame of mind in such a sublime state of life. Nor does fear of death occupy any quarter... The problem of life and death melts away of its own."[7]

This scholar himself was later diagnosed with cancer and told he had only six months to live. At that point, he later recounted, he was swept by feelings and emotions he had never imagined.

Ikeda: That's the case of Hideo Kishimoto.[8] It's quite famous.

Endo: He writes:

> I then understood the strength of my attachment to life. When one's life is exposed to direct danger, how the

heart seethes and rages! The entire body wages a desperate resistance, which extends to the cells at the very tips of one's hands and feet.[9]

And so he began a ten-year struggle against illness.

At first, the only way I could find to help myself cope with the shock that I had cancer and sustain myself spiritually was by frantically throwing myself into my work. I pushed myself relentlessly like a wounded boar. By living vigorously and keeping busy with my work, with the sense of fulfillment it brought me, I tried to resist the fear of death that assailed me. The desire to live well—that was my sole source of sustenance. I thought that, insofar as possible, I would thereby try to distract myself from my fear of death ... But the more I tried to avoid thinking about the darkness of death, the larger the prospect of death, like a gaping portal, loomed before me.[10]

Dr. Kishimoto's son relates that, a year before his father died, the latter was so busy that to talk with him, the son had to make an appointment two days in advance to get ten minutes of his time.

Several months before he died, Dr. Kishimoto wrote: "As a result of this cancer, a disease that I never thought I would contract, I was overwhelmed by the sense of hunger for life and I found myself standing before the implacable darkness of death."[11] He also said: "For the ten-year period during which I continued to battle the recurrence of cancer, I came to understand with my entire being the horror of this state of hunger."[12]

Ikeda: A "hunger for life" that no amount of working or thinking can assuage—these are the sentiments of someone who has squarely faced the reality of his own death.

Suda: People can rarely muster this extraordinary courage to face death directly.

Ikeda: Dr. Kishimoto also offers insightful comments about various trappings of the modern age that, as he puts it, "try to conceal death."

Endo: One of these, according to Dr. Kishimoto, is an improved standard of living. Through hard work, we can attain lives of comfort and convenience and enjoy an agreeable environment. With the advance of medical technology, the average life span has increased. As a result, he says, death has become further and further removed from the reality of people's daily lives.

Ikeda: In a broad sense, I think it could be said that such boons of civilization represent the aspect of heaven in society. Dr. Kishimoto argues that such things that prompt us to avert our eyes from death are deceptions that, while entirely free of malice, are at the same time the most dangerously misleading.

Endo: Yes. He suggests that modern civilization deceives people into believing there is no need to come to terms with death.

Ikeda: But the roots of this "society of deception" are clearly in decay, and suffering people are on the increase. For instance, while each year in Japan approximately ten thousand people die in traffic accidents, twice that number annually commit suicide.

Also, there is a frightening degree of apathy or indifference about matters of life and death in our society. It is only becoming more pronounced and widespread, not only in youth but in the older generation as well. We hear about many appalling incidents evidencing a cold-blooded apathy toward other human beings.

Saito: It seems to me that a death of the spirit and a death of sensitivity afflict growing numbers of people.

Ikeda: I feel that it is becoming increasingly apparent that modern civilization is paying the price for having paved over life's fundamental issues.

Conquering the Fear of Cancer's Recurrence

Endo: At the start of our discussion, the experience of Mr. Sato of Toyama was introduced. I keenly feel that facing death is much easier said than done. Probably it was because Mr. Sato of Toyama (see p. 148) had lived out his life in the Soka Gakkai that he could conclude his life so vigorously.

Saito: Likely no one else can understand the pain and shock people feel when they are told they have cancer. Many SGI members have fought and overcome cancer through faith. In such a struggle, the encouragement of family members and friends becomes a great source of support.

Ikeda: Encouragement is very important; it is a source of untold strength. Probably no one could remain perfectly calm when faced with the prospect of imminent death. Death makes anyone uneasy and anxious. It is frightening. That's normal and natural.

Someone who says "I am not afraid of death" is usually putting on a false front. On the other hand, if one cowers in fear at the prospect of death, then one cannot defeat the demons of illness and death. Only through faith can we truly overcome our fear of death.

But even if sick people intend to chant daimoku, anxiety will often stand in their way. At such times, having someone who will pray together with them or offer heartfelt encouragement will go a long way toward alleviating their worries and filling them with courage.

Endo: That's really true. For someone who has had cancer, the greatest concern is that the cancer will recur. It seems that the shock people feel when they learn that their cancer has returned is even greater than the shock they felt when learning for the first time of their condition.

Yoshinobu Matsuura of Toyohira Ward, Sapporo, whose experience has appeared in the *Seikyo Shimbun*, was operated on for cancer of the liver. In just four months' time the cancer recurred. At that time, he was reportedly frozen in shock. Even though he made struggling against the disease the focus of his life, he found that he simply could not muster the energy to chant daimoku. The pessimistic sense that he had no chance of recovery grew only stronger.

The words of a senior in faith finally aroused Mr. Matsuura's spirits: "If you take it easy like this, the cancer will also feel comfortable and will be content to remain inside your body indefinitely. You should fight for kosen-rufu and thereby drive the cancer away!"

He understood then that he had been defeated by himself—by the weak part of his nature that had decided his condition was incurable. In the end, he realized that by winning over himself, he could defeat the devil of illness. From that point on, he reportedly began exerting himself in kosen-rufu activities like a new person.

Ikeda: He achieved a splendid victory. When we stand up to battle the devil of illness, we are winning over the self.

Endo: He had the attitude that with every daimoku he chanted, he was driving out the cancer cells. He exerted himself with the same spirit in introducing other people to Nichiren Buddhism and promoting subscriptions to Soka Gakkai publications. Each day he waged an earnest struggle, and in the end he realized a splendid recovery.

One Day of Life Is More Precious Than All the Treasures in the Universe

Ikeda: For someone who has once come to the brink of death, each day takes on immeasurable value and importance. This is something that those who avoid facing death wholly fail to grasp. Nichiren Daishonin says, "One day of life is more valuable than all the treasures of the major world system" (WND-1, 955). Therefore, it is important that we make the most of each and every day.

A Buddhist text says, "Each day we should earnestly set about accomplishing everything that we need to do that day, since for all we know our death may come tomorrow."[13]

Saito: This is what is meant by "now is the last moment of one's life" (see WND-1, 216) with the awareness that the present moment is the last moment of our lives and, therefore, is infinitely valuable.

Ikeda: Life changes constantly and flashes by in an instant. We should carefully reflect on these words of the Daishonin:

> How long does a lifetime last? If one stops to consider, it is like a single night's lodging at a wayside inn. Should one forget that fact and seek some measure of worldly fame and profit? Though you may gain them, they will be mere prosperity in a dream, a delight scarcely to be prized. You would do better simply to leave such matters to the karma formed in your previous existences.
>
> Once you awaken to the uncertainty and transience of this world, you will find endless examples confronting your eyes and filling your ears. Vanished like clouds or rain, the people of past ages have left nothing

but their names. Fading away like dew, drifting far off like smoke, our friends of today too disappear from sight. Should you suppose that you alone can somehow remain forever like the clouds over Mount Mikasa?[14]

The spring blossoms depart with the wind; maple leaves turn red in autumn showers. All are proof that no living thing can stay for long in this world. Therefore, the Lotus Sutra counsels us: "Nothing in this world is lasting or firm but all are like bubbles, foam, heat shimmer." (WND-1, 63)

Saito: This means that we must not become attached to the world of heaven, which is as evanescent as foam on the water.

Ikeda: The Daishonin also states:

> Everywhere other than the Capital of Tranquil Light is a realm of suffering. Once you leave the haven of inherent enlightenment, what is there to bring you joy? I pray that you will embrace the Mystic Law, which guarantees that people "will enjoy peace and security in their present existence and good circumstances in future existences." This is the only glory that you need seek in your present lifetime, and is the action that will draw you toward Buddhahood in your next existence. Single-mindedly chant Nam-myoho-renge-kyo and urge others to do the same; that will remain as the only memory of your present life in this human world. (WND-1, 64)

DEVELOP INNER AFFLUENCE

Ikeda: Those in the world of heaven could be thought of, in the words of the Lotus Sutra, as wealthy persons who enjoy both material and spiritual abundance.

Nichiren Daishonin, citing the words of the Great Teacher

T'ien-t'ai of China, explains that there are three kinds of wealthy persons. These are the wealthy people of the secular world; world-renouncing wealthy people; and mind-observing wealthy people. I will not go into a detailed explanation here, but secular wealthy people could be thought of as millionaires who dwell in the world of heaven. For example, they may be people of outstanding character, great wealth, or tremendous knowledge. World-renouncing wealthy people means millionaires of Buddhism — Buddhas. Their lives are endowed with all manner of benefit and good fortune. Mind-observing wealthy people are ordinary people who realize that, just as they are, they can become such Buddhas.

Endo: In other words, those who uphold and practice to the true object of devotion, the Gohonzon, receive all the immeasurable practices and benefits of Buddhas.

Ikeda: Our aim is to become "mind-observing wealthy persons" whose lives shine throughout past, present and future; individuals who observe their own minds and perceive the world of Buddhahood, an inexhaustible ocean of good fortune. In other words, we are millionaires in the depth of our lives through the power of the Lotus Sutra.

Suda: I think that this points to the fundamental path for transcending the deadlock at which the present society of desire has arrived.

Ikeda: In the next chapter, we will be discussing the worlds of bodhisattva and Buddhahood. I propose that we base our discussion on the doctrine of the mutual possession of the Ten Worlds.

Saito: We are at long last going to embark on an essential journey in pursuit of the doctrine of the mutual possession of the Ten Worlds, which is the *sine qua non* of the Lotus Sutra.

NOTES

1. Four noble worlds: The four worlds of voice-hearers, cause-awakened ones, bodhisattva and Buddhahood.

2. Six paths: The six worlds of hell, hunger, animality, anger, humanity and heaven.

3. Five types of decay: Their (those in the world of heaven) robes become dirty, the flowers in their hair wither, their bodies smell bad, they sweat under their arms, and they lose their sense of security.

4. Six non-Buddhist teachers: Influential thinkers in India during Shakyamuni's lifetime who openly broke with the old Vedic tradition and challenged Brahman authority in the Indian social order.

5. Desdemona: Wife of Othello in the Shakespeare tragedy of the same name, she is smothered by her husband who wrongly suspects her of infidelity.

6. Aldous Huxley, *Proper Studies: The Proper Study of Mankind Is Man* (London: Chatto & Windus, 1957), pp. 283–99.

7. "Sei to Shi" (Life and Death), *Hideo Kishimoto shu* (Works of Hideo Kishimoto) (Tokyo: Keiseisha, 1976), vol. 6, pp. 252–53.

8. Hideo Kishimoto (1903–64): Professor at the University of Tokyo.

9. Ibid., p. 103.

10. Ibid., p. 171.

11. Ibid., p. 215.

12. Ibid., p. 208.

13. Translated from Japanese. *Nanden Daizokyo*, ed. Junjiro Takakusu (Tokyo: Taisho Shinshu Daizokyo Kanko-kai, 1971), vol. 11, part 2, p. 247. cf. *The Middle Length Sayings* (Majjhima- Nikaya), vol. 3, trans. I. B. Horner (Oxford: The Pali Text Society, 1993), p. 233.

14. Mikasa: A mountain located in the ancient Japanese capital of Nara. A place of great scenic beauty, it is a frequent theme in traditional poetry.

7   The Mutual Possession of the Ten Worlds

Ikeda: People need to grow. Leaders, especially, must not lull themselves into complacency, thinking, "Haven't I done enough already?" Rather, they should always reflect, asking such questions as "Am I truly going in the right direction?" "Is my present state of b   how it should be?" "Am I sure no one in the community is suffering?" We need to examine everything with clear eyes. Only when we can reflect seriously upon ourselves have we truly internalized the message of the Lotus Sutra, the "scripture of human revolution."

From a certain standpoint, nothing is as vulnerable and fragile as a human being. Nor, perhaps, is anything potentially as base or cruel. On the other hand, there is no limit to how strong or noble a person can become through cultivating the heart. One's spirit has no color, shape or dimension, but given the proper conditioning it can expand boundlessly.

Our present state of life, while it might seem stable, is in fact a fleeting phenomenon, an expression of the truth of temporary existence.[1] This means that our lives are changing constantly, never pausing for even a moment.

Endo: The view that all things are in a state of constant flux is termed the truth of nonsubstantiality.

Ikeda: Precisely because our lives are nonsubstantial, there are no limitations on the extent to which we can develop. We must not become attached to whatever aspect of the self appears at any one time; there is always change. The real issue, therefore, is the way in which we change—whether for better or for worse. It can only be one or the other.

Suda: Some people stop trying to develop, claiming they are incapable. But they are just spoiling themselves. If we are not moving forward in life, we are moving backwards.

Ikeda: Indeed, as Nichiren Daishonin says, to not advance is to retreat. In particular, there is nothing more deplorable than when the leaders of an organization stop growing. When this happens, everyone suffers.

This is precisely why human revolution is essential. The important point is to make a fresh start—to renew oneself—every day.

Leaders who have stopped seeking their own development tend to behave arrogantly. They are the ones you'll find needlessly scolding people. Such highhanded and arrogant conduct characterizes the worlds of animality and hunger. Praising others, on the other hand, is the hallmark of the world of bodhisattva. It is important to recognize greatness in others. SGI members throughout the world are like precious gems; we must respect and encourage one another to lead the best possible life. That is the whole purpose of the organization.

Now is the time for leaders to revolutionize their state of life. In light of the principles of three thousand realms in a single moment of life and the inseparable relationship between self and environment, when all members genuinely stand up in faith, a great current will be generated that cannot fail to change society.

Saito: Lack of direction and a sense of foreboding seem to pervade the world today. Only through a fundamental change in the lives of the people can the path to recovery be found.

Endo: In other words, it will no longer suffice to simply treat the superficial symptoms. The deep-rooted cause for the malady has to be addressed. For example, any attempt to effect educational reform that does not address issues of philosophy and views of humanity and life itself—which are the very starting point of education—will devolve into little more than clever arguments over teaching technique.

Suda: Moreover, if not approached properly, all such initiatives—however well intentioned—will simply become fodder for unscrupulous politicians.

THE BUDDHA UNDERSTANDS THE MYSTERIES OF THE HEART

Ikeda: Nichiren Daishonin says, "If you try to treat someone's illness without knowing its cause, you will only make the person sicker than before" (WND-1, 774). The key to revolutionizing our state of life is to revolutionize our hearts, our minds. That is most important. Where is the focus of our hearts? Are we striving to become healthier so that we can participate even more in activities for kosen-rufu? Or are we allowing ourselves to backslide, using illness, for example, as an excuse to slacken our efforts, consequently becoming more ill? Are we aspiring to grow and help those around us become happy? Or are we taking advantage of the organization and our position, lording it over others?

The results we produce are completely different depending on the focus of our hearts. Such subtle workings of the heart are the central theme of the doctrines of the Ten Worlds and their mutual possession. The Daishonin says: "This mind that is beyond comprehension constitutes the core teaching of the sutras and treatises. And one who is awakened to and understands this mind is called a Thus Come One" (WND-2, 844).

Saito: In other words, a Buddha is someone who thoroughly grasps the wonder of life.

Ikeda: That's right. Only through practice can we attain this state. A famous judo expert related the secret of his mastery. He recounted how he was thrown repeatedly by his teacher, becoming totally exhausted in the process, until suddenly his heart became one with his technique. From that point, he began to win. Likewise, in the process of reading a difficult book, even if at first we do not understand the ideas being expressed, if we continue making strenuous effort, in an unexpected moment of clarity we can grasp its meaning. Such flashes of insight come only after much steadfast and patient effort.

Everything depends on the heart. It is the same in our Buddhist practice. Only by studying and struggling to deepen our faith can we bring forth our Buddha nature. Simply talking on and on about revolutionizing one's state of life changes nothing. Someone who sits atop the organization and makes other people work hard while personally taking it easy is decadent. Such a person could never realize Buddhahood. Those who have agonized and endured the most on account of faith reveal their inherent Buddha nature.

BODHISATTVAS GO OUT OF THEIR WAY TO TAKE ON HARD WORK

Saito: That is the way of the bodhisattva.

Ikeda: Indeed. Bodhisattvas are those who willingly go out of their way to take on hard work; who possesses the spirit to eagerly undertake difficulties for the sake of the Law, for other people and society. This is the very antithesis of being self-centered.

Suda: Those dwelling in the six paths (hell, hunger, animality, anger, humanity, heaven) and the two vehicles of voice-hearers and cause-awakened ones are self-centered.

Endo: The world of bodhisattva is a realm in which people thoroughly dedicate themselves to other people and the Law. This is the exact opposite of what we find in the worlds up through the two vehicles. Reaching this stage entails fundamentally transforming our state of life. Nichiren Daishonin says, "The world of bodhisattvas, those who remain among the ordinary mortals of the six paths of existence, thinking little of their own lives but much of the lives of others, aiming always to take evil upon themselves and to dole out good to other beings" (WND-2, 201). Bodhisattvas treat themselves lightly while cherishing others, he says; and they take things that are difficult and painful on themselves while imparting joy to others. This is an ideal for all human beings and an unchanging code of conduct for leaders.

Suda: It's the exact opposite of a way of life based solely on instinct. In society today, many people think it natural to look out only for themselves without concern for others, some even going so far as to foist difficulties on others while jealously seeking comfort for themselves.

Ikeda: That's so true. From this we can really see the necessity of the SGI. The lives of SGI members illuminate the darkness of people's hearts with the light of happiness.

Endo: Dr. Linus Pauling remarked, "Number nine, the world of the bodhisattva—a state of compassion in which one seeks to save all people from suffering—this is a spirit that people would do well to accept."

CHANGING THE UNDERLYING CURRENT OF AN EGOISTIC SOCIETY

Ikeda: A self-centered heart is destined for the world of hell. This is true for individuals and society at large.

A heart directed "for the Law" and "for the people," on the other hand, is destined for the world of Buddhahood. In fact, in light of the principle of the simultaneity of cause and effect, Buddhahood already exists in such a heart.

Kosen-rufu is a struggle to change the underlying current of society from self-centered to altruistic, from egoistic to compassionate. Through our present activities, we are making the most necessary and fundamental contribution to this change. I hope you will take pride in this, and that you will have the confidence to defend the righteousness of our actions before any and all detractors.

The world of bodhisattva is not a special realm. The Daishonin says: "Even a heartless villain loves his wife and children. He too has a portion of the bodhisattva world within him" (WND-1, 358).

He is talking about the natural love a person has for family and the unabashed love parents have for their children. The world of bodhisattva emerges in a society where such heartfelt love and concern are not confined to families but extend to all people.

Endo: I am reminded of the Monument of Prayer for World Peace in Hiroshima.[2] One of the six bronze figures making up the monument symbolizes the spirit of continuity.

Ikeda: It's a statue of a mother holding a child.

Endo: Yes. The mother holds the child in her hands, raising it up above her. The expression on her face is striking; she seems to be saying, "I will bequeath to you a better world."

Saito: That spirit is a part of the world of bodhisattva.

A BETTER AGE FOR CHILDREN

Suda: It is now forty years since Josei Toda issued his famous Declaration for the Abolition of Nuclear Weapons.[3]

A little earlier it was said that a self-centered existence leads to the world of hell. I think that war and nuclear weapons are good symbols of this. This is a story of a mother who heroically battled this scourge of the modern age.

Her name was Asayo Yamashita, and she was a victim of the atomic-bombing of Hiroshima. Married in 1944, she was pregnant with her first child at the time of the explosion. She was only about 1.5 miles from the epicenter of the blast and narrowly managed to avoid being crushed by the buildings that collapsed around her. Running to a nearby school where she hoped to seek refuge, she was caught in a downpour of black rain[4] and drenched from head to toe.

Those who drank water from this rain, which contained high levels of radiation, within a few days lost their hair, became diarrhetic and eventually died. Of course at the time, Mrs. Yamashita had no way of knowing just how dangerous the rain was.

Four months later her first son was born, and three years later she gave birth to a second son. Mrs. Yamashita repeatedly taught her young children about the importance of peace. At meals, while doing the laundry or mending torn bedsheets, she would tell them, "Mommy will change the world so that when you become adults you won't have to go to war."

Around the time her eldest son was in fourth grade, Mrs. Yamashita began holding study meetings in her home with other mothers. They pursued a wide range of studies, including women's history, home education and history. In addition to engaging in impassioned discussion once a week, they also initiated and carried out a variety of grass-roots campaigns—a movement to ban atomic and hydrogen bombs, a petition drive to make available polio vaccines, and activities for peace, human rights and educational reform.

The study meetings steadily developed over time. Five years later, they had a regular participation of more than twenty mothers and were holding both daytime and night sessions.

Endo: It was a true grass-roots movement.

Suda: Yes, it was. Once, when her eldest son remarked on how busy she was with her activities, Mrs. Yamashita told him: "That's because these are activities to put an end to war. Even now the victims of the A-bomb continue to suffer. The people of Hiroshima who experienced the horror are the ones who must stand up in the forefront of this movement. No matter how arduous, this is something that has to be done."

Throughout this time, however, Mrs. Yamashita was gradually succumbing to the cancer she contracted from exposure to radiation. In the summer of 1962, she was hospitalized and underwent surgery. She was released from the hospital once but was sent back again the following February and underwent another operation in the summer of that year.

One day her eldest son, then a high school student, visited her in the hospital ward to find her neatly folding up some old pajamas. "What are you planning on doing with those?" he asked her. "You should just throw them away."

"When you get married and have children, they can be used to make diapers," she replied. Then, as if trying to gaze into the future, she said: "I wonder what the world will be like when your children are full grown. I would give anything to see that."

Jokingly her son responded, "You would doubtless be a meddling grandmother."

"I would like to tell the young people about how hard their grandmothers worked to create such a peaceful age," she said.

In May of the following year, 1964, she had a third operation. The results were not positive. On June 16, after thanking each of the family members and relatives who had gathered at her bedside—demonstrating concern for others to the very end—she died. She was thirty-nine The cancer had spread to her lungs, liver and uterus.

Saito: That must have been caused by the black rain.

Suda: The study meetings for mothers that she had pioneered continued over the next twenty years. This group's activities in promoting peace education and opposing war and nuclear arms shine to this day as a towering achievement.

At one point, Mrs. Yamashita's son, while helping her make a placard for use in a peace demonstration, asked, "Why do wars happen even though everyone knows that war is bad?"

"Before they realize what is happening, people get swept up in a current leading to war. That's human nature," she replied. "That's what's frightening." She recalled the very first words in the preamble to the UNESCO constitution and asked her son if he had learned them in school: "Since wars begin in the minds of men, it is in the minds of men that the defenses of peace must be constructed."

"What does it mean that war is born in people's minds?" he asked.

"The tendency for people to hate one another, to think: 'As long as I'm safe, nothing else matters,' to view others' suffering with indifference—such an attitude ultimately leads to war. The only way to guard against this is by constructing the 'defenses of peace' in people's minds."

"But how can war be eliminated?" he further probed.

Sighing a little, she replied, "I'm not sure."

Saito: It seems she clearly apprehended the deep-seated negativity that is part of the karma all people share. Because she was earnestly struggling to alter the reality of society, she keenly understood how enormously difficult it is to change people's hearts.

Suda: Two years after Mrs. Yamashita's death, her eldest son, Yoshinori, encountered Nichiren Buddhism and took faith. Having had to squarely face and overcome his own fear of death as a result of his exposure to the atomic bomb, he became a major force behind the series of antiwar publications produced by the youth division members of Hiroshima. Currently, he is vigorously participating in activities for kosen-rufu together with other Soka Gakkai members in Hiroshima. He is a central figure in the men's division.

Ikeda: I know him well. Your account illustrates the oneness of parent and child; he is certainly connected to his mother eternally. I think his mother must be really delighted by his continuing efforts for the cause of peace.

Saito: The prayer of Mrs. Yamashita and the other mothers to construct the "defenses of peace" in people's minds, I believe, is part of the great river of the popular movement for kosen-rufu.

The Oneness of Self and Others

Ikeda: There are countless people in the world whose hearts have been wounded for some reason. We need to extend a healing hand to them all. Through such efforts, we in fact heal ourselves.

When something untoward happens, people tend to imagine that no one could possibly be as unhappy and miserable as they. They wallow in self-pity and turn a blind eye to everyone and everything else. But dwelling on their own pain and stewing in feelings of discontent and hopelessness only cause their life force to wane even more. It seems to me that it is human bonds—the desire to live for the sake of others—that can give someone the strength to live on at such times. As long as one is holed up in egoism, there is no happiness. When we break out and take action for others, our lives spring with vitality.

Endo: In terms of psychology, we often hear that concern for others stimulates a person's own mental and emotional health. People laboring under stress or anxiety tend to brood endlessly over their own suffering. One treatment for such a condition is to bring such people together and guide them to put their energy into thinking about and coming to the assistance of one another.

Saito: Is that so they can learn to care about people suffering as they are?

Endo: Yes. An atmosphere is created where individuals can easily listen to one another and talk things over together. Researchers find that this kind of group therapy results in a marked rise in the strength and will to live of all involved.

Suda: When you encourage someone, you find your own spirits refreshed. This is something we often experience in our Buddhist activities.

Ikeda: The SGI is truly an oasis of rejuvenation.

When we look after and care for others — that is, help others draw forth the strength to live — our own strength to live increases. When we help people expand their state of life, our lives also expand. This is the marvel of the bodhisattva path; actions to benefit others cannot be separated from actions to benefit oneself.

To merely talk about benefiting others is arrogant. To only say the words "saving people" is hypocritical. Only when we realize that our efforts on others' behalf are also for our own sake are we practicing with true humility.

One's own life and the lives of others are ultimately inseparable. The bodhisattva path, therefore, is the correct path in life.

Endo: To put it another way, by helping others we help ourselves. A survivor of the concentration camps during the Holocaust attributed his survival to having lived based on one rule: "In our group we shared everything; and the moment one of the group ate something without sharing it, we knew it was the beginning of the end for him."[5]

Ikeda: That's a remarkable observation. This is a truth of life learned in the most extreme circumstances.

Saito: As soon as someone lost the spirit to share with others, they began to die. This is a chilling testimony.

Ikeda: It is of course impossible for those who were not there to casually discuss the concentration camp experience; it was such an overwhelming ordeal. For that very reason, this is a valuable lesson for humankind, as well as a stern reality.

Endo: Yes. While many survivors of the camps have labored under lifelong psychological scars, one survivor asserted that he did not suffer in the least over the experience in the years after the war. That's because, he explained, at Auschwitz he learned the true meaning of friendship. "When I was a child, strangers shielded me with their bodies from the blowing winds, for they had nothing else to offer but themselves."[6]

There were of course those who descended to the level of animals, only looking out for themselves. That's not unreasonable given the extreme hardships they faced. But there were also those who used themselves as shields to protect children from the harsh winds assailing them.

THE TRAP OF A "SOCIETY OF NARCISSISM"

Endo: The psychologist who shares these experiences, Julius Segal, warns that the modern age is caught in a trap of narcissism. He says: "Narcissism is becoming increasingly common and accepted in our culture. Thinking of others is out of fashion now."[7]

He then quotes the Viennese psychiatrist and Nazi death camp survivor Viktor Frankl who observed, "You're always forced—ordered—to feel joy, be happy, and experience pleasure." Dr. Segal adds, "Self-sacrifice and thinking about others are made to seem irrelevant, even unhealthy."[8]

Ikeda: He makes a good point. The question is have we realized a happier society as a result. I don't think so.

Endo: Indeed. Increasingly, people are becoming isolated, forgetting what it means to encourage one another. Consequently, they are losing their will to live to the fullest.

Saito: Then the desire to find something "still more fun" grows only more overwhelming. It's a vicious cycle.

Ikeda: It is the world of bodhisattva—the way of life of "number nine," as Dr. Pauling once called it—that cuts the dark chains of this trap. A well-known story clearly illustrates this point. Someone goes to hell and finds that everyone there is suffering because they cannot eat even though each has a sumptuous meal right in front of them. The reason they can't eat is that their chopsticks are longer than their arms, so they cannot put the food into their mouths. The person then goes to the Buddha land. There, again, the chopsticks are longer than people's arms. But everyone is content. Why? It's because they take turns feeding one another.

Saito: In other words, the difference between hell and Buddhahood is not one of environment. The difference lies solely in the hearts of those dwelling in these realms.

Suda: I think the story highlights why there is still a great deal of suffering in a time of so much abundance, as in Japan today.

Ikeda: In any event, society changes. It changes moment by moment. Politics, economics, fads—everything in the world undergoes change. The issue is whether, amid much change, one possesses an unchanging center. We have such a center in the Mystic Law.

The Mystic Law is the constant, unchanging core; and it is the fundamental power causing all things to go in a positive direction. People change, but the Law does not. People can be deceived, but the Law cannot. Trying to cheat the Law is of absolutely no avail. When we base ourselves on this absolute and unchanging Law, both our lives and society prosper eternally. Apart from the Law, everything else is, in a manner of speaking, an illusion.

After all is said and done, the supreme way of life is that of the Bodhisattvas of the Earth who thoroughly dedicate themselves to kosen-rufu. There is no more lofty or sublime way to live. Realizing this is a matter of faith.

A Courageous Heart of Faith Is Itself Buddhahood

Saito: It is said of bodhisattvas, "Seeking enlightenment above, saving sentient beings below."[9] From our standpoint, these correspond to practicing for oneself and practicing for others.

Ikeda: We become happy ourselves, and we help others do the same. This is analogous to the two motions of a planet, which rotates on its axis while revolving around the sun. It is a universal principle.

In a sense, bodhisattvas exert themselves to help people become happy, even if it means putting off their own happiness until later. This is the spirit of the Soka Gakkai. It is a most noble way of life.

Faith is a struggle. Life is a struggle. Buddhism is a struggle. By waging a courageous and high-spirited struggle against evil, we can draw forth the states of bodhisattva and Buddhahood from within.

This world is dominated by the devil king of the sixth heaven, which exerts a powerful force of misery over all people. That's why when a truly happy person appears, the devil king of the sixth heaven envies, hates and tries to destroy the person. Nichiren Daishonin vigorously battled this negative influence, as did Shakyamuni.

We must challenge and defeat this negativity in life, which causes people to resent and persecute one another, which seeks to keep them in a state of misery. Only when we win over the forces of evil can we achieve true happiness or Buddhahood. That's why Nichiren Daishonin urges us to "summon up the courage of a lion" (WND-1, 997).

Suda: Faith like the courage of a lion must be the hallmark of the

world of Buddhahood, which is also described as a state of indestructible happiness.

Ikeda: Yes. Such happiness is absolute, because a person in this state
of life can discern the significance of all affairs of life and society;
which is in itself wisdom. Also, no matter how things may change,
the person's heart remains calm and steady; this is inner strength.
Moreover, it's absolute because with it we can freely tap this wisdom and strength from the depths of our lives whenever necessary.

It certainly is not a state free of worry or suffering. Such a life, if
it existed, would be monotonous and dull. If everything were to
go smoothly—that in itself would be an illusion, a lie. Worries are
an integral part of the reality of life.

Nichiren Daishonin teaches the principle that earthly desires are
enlightenment. Because we have desires and worries, we can appreciate happiness. Because we face and overcome painful difficulties,
we can attain Buddhahood. The truth is that a life without any
suffering is not at all happy. That is the perspective of Buddhism.

What, then, is the world of Buddhahood? From our standpoint,
it is none other than faith.

President Toda said: "Attaining Buddhahood doesn't mean simply
becoming a Buddha or heading in that direction. Honestly believing in the Daishonin's teaching of the true entity of life and that
the ordinary person is most respectworthy, we are profoundly confident that we are Buddhas just as we are, from the eternal past into
the infinite future. This is what it means to become a Buddha."[10]

This comes down to faith, determination. It's a matter of our
internal awareness.

The Essential Teaching Is to "Return to the Original Life"

Ikeda: "The Life Span of the Thus Come One," the sixteenth
chapter of the Lotus Sutra, describes the Buddha enlightened since
the remote past, or the eternal Buddha. Just who is this Buddha?

Commenting on the passage in the Lotus Sutra that reads, "It has been immeasurable, boundless hundreds, thousands, ten thousands, millions of nayutas of kalpas since I in fact attained Buddhahood" (LSOC, 265–66), the Daishonin explains: "'I' represents the living beings of the Dharma realm. 'I' here refers to each and every being in the Ten Worlds" (OTT, 127).

The eternal Buddha of the "Life Span" chapter means all living beings. We are all "eternal Buddhas." Ordinary people are Buddhas just as they are.

There are no grades or distinctions among people. We are all equal; we are all equally Buddhas. The only difference among people has to do with whether, or the extent to which, we realize this in our hearts. From the standpoint of Buddhism, that is the only meaningful distinction.

A Buddha is not someone displaying the thirty-two features or eighty features.[11] Our lives, originally, are the Buddha. The universe itself is originally the Buddha. The appearance of the sun is a function of compassion. The illumination of the moon is also compassion, as is the beautiful respiration of green plants and trees. The entire universe is a great living entity carrying out activities of compassion from the beginningless past through the eternal future. This vast organism of compassion is the eternal Buddha. And the life of every being in the Ten Worlds is one with this Buddha of the "Life Span" chapter. Faith in the Mystic Law is the key enabling us to "return" to this original life.

Saito: Returning to the original life—that's the Lotus Sutra's essential teaching.

Ikeda: Exactly. The Daishonin clearly states in *The Record of the Orally Transmitted Teachings,* "The 'Life Span of the Thus Come One' chapter deals with the original life of the living beings of the Ten Worlds. This chapter is called the *hommon,* or essential teaching, because it is the gateway (*mon*), or teaching, by which one enters into what is essential or original (*hon*)" (OTT, 233).

Suda: The great life of the Buddha enlightened since the remote past is the "original life" of the beings of the Ten Worlds. The essential teaching is so called because it enables us to return to this original life.

Endo: Since this original life is fundamentally a property of one's own life, there is no limit to the extent to which we can tap the power of the original Buddha.

Ikeda: The entire universe is like our own personal bank account. The amount of fortune we can withdraw depends solely on our faith. Faith means battling life's negative functions. Justice means opposing evil. Buddhist practice means struggling against adversity.

At one point, the Daishonin's follower Shijo Kingo, who was known for his spirited practice, was so overwhelmed by difficulties that he unwittingly began complaining: "I thought that those who believe in the Lotus Sutra were supposed to enjoy peace and security in this life." When the Daishonin heard this, he instructed him as follows: "The pine tree lives for ten thousand years, and therefore its boughs become bent and twisted... The votary of the Lotus Sutra is the Thus Come One whose life span is immeasurable; no wonder his practice is hindered, just as the pine tree's branches are bent or broken" (WND-I, 471). Just as the pine tree stands up to wind and snow, showing proof of its immense longevity, practitioners of the Lotus Sutra, through enduring difficulties, manifest their true identity as Buddhas of eternal life. The Daishonin stresses to Shijo Kingo that now is the time to reveal the supreme world of Buddhahood. At this time when you are about to receive supreme benefit, he questions, what can you possibly have to complain about?

Saito: In the same writing, the Daishonin also says, "Those who uphold this sutra should be prepared to meet difficulties"; but he assures Shijo Kingo that "Buddhahood lies in continuing faith" (WND-I, 471).

Ikeda: It's a matter of embracing the Mystic Law. We need to steadfastly uphold the Mystic Law through every obstacle, confident that we truly have a mission for kosen-rufu.

WE ATTAIN ENLIGHTENMENT BY DEFEATING "DEVILS"

Ikeda: Shakyamuni constantly battled devilish functions. It would be no exaggeration to say that the definition of a Buddha is one who continuously fights these devilish functions.

Suda: It is clear from the sutras that Shakyamuni fought negative forces throughout his entire life. When devilish forces rose up against him, Shakyamuni dauntlessly put down their underhanded attempts to infiltrate his mind with illusion and lead him astray. His only defenses in this struggle were faith, tenacious effort and wisdom.

Ikeda: To begin with, the essence of Shakyamuni's enlightenment lay in this battle against negative influences. The words that Shakyamuni uttered immediately after attaining enlightenment beneath the bodhi tree are recorded in sutras.

Endo: There is a description of when Shakyamuni, after long years of earnest practice, awakened to the Law:

> *Routing the host of Mara doth he stand,*
> *Just as the sun when lighting up the sky.*[12]

Ikeda: When the Mystic Law blossoms in our hearts, our lives shine like the sun with perfect calm and composure and infinite strength. This is the world of Buddhahood.

Manifesting the world of Buddhahood and defeating the devilish functions are one and the same. Devils exist both within our lives and in our environment. But whether we defeat them or are defeated by them depends solely on our own spirit and determination.

The important thing is that we win over them and that we do so continually. Buddhist practice means never coming to a standstill. We have to cultivate a self that absolutely no negative influence can deter.

Suda: Not only at the time when he attained enlightenment, but thereafter as well, Shakyamuni continually fought against negative forces, driving back their insidious influence. The eminent Buddhologist Hajime Nakamura writes:

> It is not the case that the Buddha gained enlightenment after the devils had scattered in disarray. Rather, defeating devils and gaining enlightenment are two sides of the same feat.[13]
>
> Buddhahood can only be found within these very actions to drive off illusion. Continuous, spirited advancement is itself the activity of the Buddha. It is not that Shakyamuni became a different being because he attained enlightenment.[14]

Ikeda: Buddhahood is a state of life of oneness with the Mystic Law. A Buddha is someone who makes the Mystic Law his or her teacher. Thoroughly and steadfastly upholding the Mystic Law is itself the world of Buddhahood.

Immediately after attaining enlightenment, Shakyamuni vowed to "live always making the Law my teacher." He declared: "I have awakened to this Law. I will venerate and revere and base myself on this Law."[15] And that is precisely how he lived out the rest of his life.

Saito: When he was on the verge of death, Shakyamuni said, "I have succeeded in devoting my life to the self,"[16] meaning his complete devotion to the eternal Mystic Law within.

Endo: He also left behind words urging his disciples to likewise "rely on the Law and on your life."

Ikeda: The Six Paramitas Sutra[17] says "to become the master of your mind rather than let your mind master you" (WND-1, 486). It's not a matter of leading a self-centered existence but of living based on the Law, based on kosen-rufu. Faith means having such a spirit.

FAITH IS PROOF OF BUDDHAHOOD

Ikeda: Tremendous importance is attached to the Daishonin's statement in "The Object of Devotion for Observing the Mind": "That ordinary people born in the latter age can believe in the Lotus Sutra is due to the fact that the world of Buddhahood is present in the human world" (WND-1, 358). Our faith in the Lotus Sutra is proof that the world of Buddhahood exists in our lives.

Suda: I sense something very subtle and important in the proposition that it is possible to believe in the Lotus Sutra because we possess the world of Buddhahood. The usual assumption would probably be that because one believes in the Lotus Sutra, one can reach the world of Buddhahood. But it is just the opposite.

Ikeda: There are two ways of looking at it. Certainly, you can say that because we believe in the Lotus Sutra we will attain the world of Buddhahood. But it is because we ourselves are entities of the eternal Mystic Law, in other words, because the world of Buddhahood is inherent in our lives that it is possible for us to believe in the Lotus Sutra in the first place. Whether it is the revelation of the theoretical teaching that all people can become Buddhas, or the revelation of the essential teaching that the Buddha's life is eternal, we can believe in the teaching because we can sense something eternal in our lives.

Saito: I think that on some level—whether conscious or unconscious—everyone senses the existence of something eternal.

Ikeda: Everyone indeed can sense the eternal. That may be the most salient characteristic of human beings. That's probably why only humans have religion.

This inherent capacity could be described as an awareness of the sanctity of life or a connection to others or as the ability to harmonize with nature and the universe. This inner sense or capacity for goodness is itself the source of the faith to believe in the Lotus Sutra.

In any event, precisely because our lives are endowed with the world of Buddhahood, it is possible for us to believe in the Lotus Sutra. And when we summon forth the power of faith and believe in the Lotus Sutra, we can liberate the power of the world of Buddhahood inherent in our lives and channel that power to create value. Our continual practice then enables us to display the power of the world of Buddhahood all the stronger.

Suda: Because we possess the world of Buddhahood, we can manifest faith, and through faith we can open up the world of Buddhahood in our lives. This seems to be the correlation.

Saito: Exactly. Dwelling in the nine worlds could be compared to being shut inside a room. Dwelling in the world of Buddhahood, on the other hand, is like bathing in clear, bright sunshine. The beings of the nine worlds fundamentally dwell in the great macrocosm that is the world of Buddhahood. People vaguely sense this as some kind of eternal aspect of their lives, but because they are shut up in a room surrounded by dense walls of illusion, they fail to fully comprehend their true environment. When they break down these walls of illusion through faith, they can then freely enjoy the fresh air of the Mystic Law pervading the universe.

Endo: When you use the "key" of faith to open up the "window" of your heart, the "room" of your life is flooded with fresh air and brilliant light from outside. Then, there is no difference between being in the room and being outside.

Ikeda: Why don't we continue this discussion of the relation between the nine worlds and the world of Buddhahood in the next chapter?

A MIND THAT PERCEIVES THE BUDDHA IS THE BUDDHA

> *When living beings have become truly faithful,*
> *honest and upright, gentle in intent,*
> *single-mindedly desiring to see the Buddha,*
> *not hesitating even if it costs them their lives,*
> *then I and the assembly of monks*
> *appear together on Holy Eagle Peak.* (LSOC, 271)

Ikeda: This outpouring of inner strength is something we actually experience through faith. When we put our all into our activities for kosen-rufu, we feel a sense of unbounded freshness and exhilaration. We must not practice passively. When we practice with the spirit of not begrudging our lives, true power wells forth.

Nichiren Daishonin teaches that the world of Buddhahood appears in our heart, citing the passage, "single-mindedly desiring to see the Buddha, not hesitating even if it costs them their lives" (WND-1, 389). Single-mindedly striving to bring forth one's Buddha nature without begrudging one's own life is faith. This is the seeking spirit. The power of the original Buddha manifests in the heart of someone who earnestly seeks the life-state of the original Buddha.

The Daishonin's interpretation of the line "single-mindedly desiring to see the Buddha" is much more profound than the literal meaning.

Suda: Yes. In one place he says, "'Single-mindedly desiring to see the Buddha' may be read as follows: single-mindedly observing the Buddha, concentrating one's mind on seeing the Buddha, and when looking at one's own mind, perceiving that it is the Buddha" (WND-I, 389–90).

Ikeda: Exactly. While initially we start out "single-mindedly desiring to see the Buddha," he indicates that, in the end, we perceive that we are the Buddha. Our determination in faith, our spirit to practice without begrudging our lives, is itself the manifestation of the eternal world of Buddhahood. In short, faith itself is the world of Buddhahood. This is the true aspect of "the world of Buddhahood is present in the human world" (WND-I, 358).

Endo: Practicing without begrudging one's life—this is what is meant by the line: "If in a single moment of life we exhaust the pains and trials of millions of kalpas, then instant after instant there will arise in us the three Buddha bodies with which we are eternally endowed" (OTT, 214).

Saito: This is also what High Priest Nichikan indicated when he said, "What we call a strong mind of faith in the Lotus Sutra is the world of Buddhahood."[18]

Ikeda: The Daishonin and High Priest Nichikan were saying the same thing. We need to practice with the courageous spirit of a lion to protect Buddhism and the Buddha's children and to resolutely stand up to persecution. This is the secret to causing the world of Buddhahood to manifest in our lives.

Saito: I can really see the importance of the SGI spirit—that is, the spirit to spread the Law and practice selflessly without begrudging one's life, regardless of the cost.

Ikeda: Faith means carrying out a practice of dedicating one's entire being to realizing kosen-rufu. It means to abandon egoism and uphold one's principles no matter what.

President Makiguchi and President Toda lived entirely for the sake of kosen-rufu, for the sake of all others, for the sake of the members and for society, without giving any thought to themselves, putting everything off for later. And I have done the same.

One certainly cannot attain Buddhahood with a slovenly or lazy attitude. The Daishonin says, "On the path to attain Buddhahood it may invariably be when one has done something like lay down one's life that one becomes a Buddha" (WND-1, 202).

The Buddha is a human being—a person who struggles continuously. The Buddha is not some special being existing in another world. The Daishonin teaches that the ordinary person is the most respectworthy and noble being. This is the principle of the true entity of all life; the "true entity" manifests amid the reality of "all phenomena" of life and society. Therein exists the world of Buddhahood.

In the same way that people exert themselves in different fields, whether as a company employee, a teacher, a housewife or a farmer, so too does the world of Buddhahood pulse vibrantly in all spheres of activity. This is the perspective of the Lotus Sutra.

Suda: A high priest who wants to be revered as a Buddha while failing to take action to spread the Daishonin's teaching tramples on the heart of the Lotus Sutra.

Endo: Such fraud and deception are inexcusable.

Ikeda: Regarding the oneness of Buddhahood and the nine worlds, putting our palms together when we pray symbolizes this. It also represents the Mystic Law. In *The Record of the Orally Transmitted Teachings,* the Daishonin says, "(In the term *pressing palms together*) *pressing* means *myo* or wonderful, while *palms* refers to *ho* or the Law; . . . *pressing* is 'the world of Buddhahood' and *palms* are the nine worlds" (OTT, 45).

In other words, Buddhahood lies in chanting daimoku based on faith no matter what happens. Whatever sufferings of the nine worlds we may be undergoing, through strong faith we can lead lives in which the nine worlds manifest the world of Buddhahood, and the world of Buddhahood manifests the nine worlds.

While there may be instances when our prayers are answered immediately, there will also be times when that is not the case. Even so, we should continue offering prayer, chanting daimoku and taking action. Such resolute faith is itself the world of Buddhahood; it is victory. Maintaining such faith to the very end of our lives enables us to set out on a journey over the three existences at one with the eternal Buddha of the "Life Span" chapter.

NOTES

1. Truth of temporary existence: Along with the truth of nonsubstantiality and the truth of the Middle Way, one of the three truths formulated by the Great Teacher T'ien-t'ai of China to clarify the essential nature of phenomena. The truth of nonsubstantiality is that phenomena have no absolute or fixed existence of their own; the truth of temporary existence is that while all things are nonsubstantial in nature, they nevertheless possess a provisional or temporary reality that is in constant flux; and the truth of the Middle Way is that all phenomena are characterized by both nonsubstantiality and temporary existence yet are in essence neither nonsubstantiality nor temporary existence.

2. The Monument of Prayer for World Peace was commissioned by the Soka Gakkai and completed in June 1997. Sculpted by French artist Louis Derbré, the six-statue bronze monument pays tribute to the atomic bomb victims in Hiroshima and Nagasaki, as well as to all those throughout the world who have suffered at the hands of nuclear testing.

3. On September 8, 1957, at a youth festival held at the Mitsuzawa Athletic Stadium in Yokohama, President Toda proclaimed his absolute opposition to the testing of nuclear bombs, declaring, "It is my wish

to attack the problem at its root, that is, to rip out the claws that are hidden in the very depth of this issue." He further declared that anyone or anything that threatened the right of people to exist was a "devil incarnate," a "fiend" and a "beast."

4. Black rain: Following the atomic blast at Hiroshima, a wide area of the city and surrounding countryside was drenched in a heavy rain. The rain contained much soot caused by the destruction of the city, and was hence dubbed "black rain."

5. Julius Segal, *Winning Life's Toughest Battles—Roots of Human Resilience* (New York: McGraw-Hill Book Company, 1986), p. 103.

6. Ibid.

7. Ibid., p. 104.

8. Ibid., p. 105.

9. T'ien-t'ai's *Maka shikan* (Great Concentration and Insight).

10. *Toda Josei zenshu* (Collected Writings of Josei Toda) (Tokyo: Seikyo Shimbunsha, 1983), vol. 3, p. 175.

11. Thirty-two features or eighty features: Remarkable physical characteristics said to be possessed by Buddhas and bodhisattvas, symbolizing their superiority over ordinary people.

12. Hajime Nakamura, *Gotama Budda* (Gautama Buddha), bk. 1, *Nakamura Hajime senshu* (Selected Writings of Hajime Nakamura), vol. 11, (Tokyo: Shunshusha, 1992), p. 398.

13. Ibid., p. 401.

14. Ibid., p. 300.

15. Ibid., p. 420.

16. Hajime Nakamura, *Gotama Budda* (Gautama Buddha), bk. 2, *Nakamura Hajime senshu* (Selected Writings of Hajime Nakamura), vol. 12, (Tokyo: Shunshusha, 1992), p. 210.

17. Six Paramitas Sutra: A sutra translated into Chinese by Prajna of the T'ang dynasty. It explains in detail the six kinds of practices or "perfections" (Skt *paramita*) that bodhisattvas must carry out in order to attain enlightenment.

18. *Sanju hiden sho* (The Threefold Secret Teaching).

8 *Enacting the Drama of Kosen-rufu*

"I" in the passage "in truth the time since I attained Buddhahood is extremely long" (LSOC, 267) refers to Shakyamuni, who attained enlightenment in the remote past. According to the actual meaning of this ["Life Span"] chapter, however, "I" represents the living beings of the Dharma realm. Each and every one in the Ten Worlds is being referred to here in the word "I." (OTT, 126)

Non-existence of birth and death [from the passage "There is no ebb or flow of birth and death" (LSOC, 267)] means that all phenomena in the Dharma realm are simultaneously functions of Myoho-renge-kyo. "Existence" indicates that hell is just as it is, the total entity of the Wonderful Law originally endowed with the Ten Worlds. (OTT, 128)

Suda: We have discussed each of the Ten Worlds. Our focus here is the doctrine of the mutual possession of the Ten Worlds.

Ikeda: Nichiren Daishonin writes that while the doctrine of the Ten Worlds is found in sutras expounded before the Lotus Sutra, only the Lotus Sutra explains their mutual possession.

In one place he says: "This is nothing other than what is taught in the Lotus Sutra. The cause and effect of the Ten Worlds were clarified in the sutras preached prior to Lotus. By now [with the

Lotus Sutra] the fact that the cause and effect of the Ten Worlds are mutuallly possessed is set forth" (WND-2, 58).

It is the Lotus Sutra's most essential doctrine. For that reason, it cannot be adequately covered in a brief discussion. Therefore, why don't we first try to get at precisely what is meant by "mutual possession" and then talk about how understanding this principle can change our lives?

Suda: Mutual possession of the Ten Worlds literally means that each world from hell to Buddhahood contains all Ten Worlds. In other words, each of the Ten Worlds contains the other nine. This state of mutual possession is also described as the "hundred worlds," the product of multiplying ten times ten.

Endo: The doctrine of the Ten Worlds is often used to explain state of life. One of the most frequently asked questions is: "If the Ten Worlds mutually contain one another, giving us a hundred worlds, does this mean there are a hundred different states of life?" Within these hundred worlds we find, for example, the world of Buddhahood contained in the world of hell or the world of Buddhahood found in the world of humanity. This gives rise to the question, "If there are indeed a hundred worlds, then how does the world of hunger contained in the world of hell differ from the world of hell in the world of hunger?"

Suda: From one standpoint, to be born a human being is in and of itself to be in the world of humanity. Thus, the state of life of a person who (1) is born human, (2) experiences the suffering of hell on account of something like illness, and (3) subsequently awakens to his or her mission as a bodhisattva, could be described as the world of bodhisattva contained in the world of hell contained in the world of humanity. We would then have ten times ten times ten, or a thousand worlds.

Saito: That would mean that a single moment of life contains not three thousand realms, but thirty thousand!

Ikeda: Something is wrong here! We have so far tried to clarify each of the Ten Worlds using our own lives as a model. Though not explicitly stated, our talks have been naturally premised on the doctrine of the mutual possession of the Ten Worlds, in particular, the existence of the Ten Worlds within the world of humanity.

Suda: That's true.

Ikeda: In fact, such an approach to the Ten Worlds would be impossible without the teaching of the Lotus Sutra.

Saito: While the pre-Lotus Sutra teachings explain the Ten Worlds, they conceive of each as separate and independent. According to this understanding, those in the world of humanity cannot reach the world of Buddhahood until they have discarded the world of humanity. So according to these teachings one would have to practice for aeons, eradicating one lower state of life after another while being reborn into successively higher worlds, until one finally becomes a Buddha. Alternately, to make Buddhism more accessible, some schools taught that after death one could be reborn in another land far away from this strife-ridden saha world, such as the Pure Land of Perfect Bliss (of Amida Buddha).

Ikeda: We tend to take it for granted that the world of humanity contains the Ten Worlds, but this is in fact the key point of the teaching of the mutual possession of the Ten Worlds.

The Ten Worlds also exist in the universe. The entire universe is a great living entity endowed with the Ten Worlds, and it is there that we were born in the world of humanity. The world of humanity existing in the universe also contains the Ten Worlds, as do the worlds of animality, hunger and anger.

Endo: That is the mutual possession of the Ten Worlds in the life of the universe.

Ikeda: So why does the Lotus Sutra explain the mutual possession of the Ten Worlds? Ultimately, it is to reveal that the world of humanity contains the Ten Worlds, and, in particular, the world of Buddhahood. This means that ordinary people can reveal their Buddha nature just as they are—without having to be reborn in any other form or in another land.

Saito: To profoundly grasp this truth is called "observing one's mind." The Daishonin says that to "observe one's mind" means to perceive the Ten Worlds within it (WND-1, 356).

Suda: In "The Object of Devotion for Observing the Mind," Nichiren Daishonin emphasizes the concept of the Ten Worlds, and in particular the world of Buddhahood in the world of humanity.

Endo: Now that we have clarified the purpose of the doctrine of the mutual possession of the Ten Worlds, it seems that dwelling on the difference between the world of hunger existing in the world of hell and the world of hell existing in the world of hunger is actually missing the point.

Suda: What about the issue of the thousand worlds?

Saito: That's the question of the world of bodhisattva existing in the world of hell existing in the world of humanity, and so forth.

Suda: I think considerable confusion surrounds this point.

Saito: If we say that the Ten Worlds exist in the universe, and that people, who are born in one of these worlds, are entities of the mutual possession of the Ten Worlds (i.e., that they possess the hundred worlds), then the universe contains a thousand worlds. I think this interpretation reflects a basic misunderstanding about the Lotus Sutra's intention in setting forth the mutual possession of the Ten Worlds. This intention is primarily to elucidate the wondrous truth that all living beings, regardless of which world they happen to inhabit at any given moment, are endowed with the Ten Worlds.

Essentially, the Lotus Sutra explains the inscrutable, mystic truth of life—that the "part," or just one of the Ten Worlds, in fact contains the "whole," or all of the Ten Worlds; this is what is meant by "mutual possession." Given this reality, it can be said that one's life is endowed with a hundred worlds.

The Hundred Worlds Exist Both in the Universe and in Our Lives

Ikeda: Perhaps it is helpful to put it in these terms. The individual is a microcosm. The microcosm is itself the macrocosm; the two can never be separated, so the self is in fact the universe.

Since the entire universe is a living entity manifesting the mutual possession of the Ten Worlds, it possesses the hundred worlds. At the same time, since our lives, too, are one with the universe, we also possess the hundred worlds. We are entities of the mutual possession of the Ten Worlds just as the universe is.

Suda: Certainly, to say that we (the microcosm) are the hundred worlds and that the universe (the macrocosm) is the thousand worlds is contradictory, because then it could not be said that we are one with the universe. This is clear now.

Endo: The universe itself is a single great life; we, too, are a single life. Both are life and are in that sense equal. The doctrine of mutual possession explains the mystic true aspect of this single great life.

Ikeda: Whichever of the Ten Worlds we are in, the true aspect of our life at that moment is a perfect microcosm just as it is. This is what we learned from our discussion of the principle of the true entity of all phenomena.

Nichiren Daishonin says regarding the Lotus Sutra's teaching of the true entity of all phenomena, "All beings and environments in the Ten Worlds, from hell, the lowest, to Buddhahood, the highest, are, without exception the manifestations of Myoho-renge-kyo" (WND-1, 383). In this passage, "all beings and environments in the Ten Worlds, from hell, the lowest, to Buddhahood, the highest" refers to all phenomena in the universe, which are subsumed within the Ten Worlds. "All beings and environments" points to the inseparability of the entity of people's lives and the entity of the universe, meaning, for example, if a person is in the state of hell, then the person's environment will also be that of hell.

"All beings and environments in the Ten Worlds" indicates all phenomena in the universe. The Daishonin thus teaches that all phenomena without exception are "manifestations of Myoho-renge-kyo"; that is their true aspect. In other words, every phenomenon is an expression of the great life of the universe, which is Nam-myoho-renge-kyo.

Saito: From that perspective, the mutual possession of the Ten Worlds naturally follows from the principle of the true entity of all phenomena, since the teaching of the true entity of all phenomena reveals that all manifestations of life (all phenomena) are themselves expressions of the universal life (true entity).

Applying this to the Ten Worlds, we find that living beings in any world are endowed with the entire universe; that is to say, with the Ten Worlds. This is the relation between these two doctrines.

Ikeda: It's a truly remarkable view of life, the world and the universe. Nichiren Daishonin says, "Grass and trees, forests, mountains and rivers, the great earth or even one particle of dust all possess within themselves the full Ten Worlds" (WND-2, 840).

Suda: I am reminded of a poem by the famous English poet William Blake:

> *To see a World in a Grain of Sand*
> *And a Heaven in a Wild Flower,*
> *Hold Infinity in the palm of your hand*
> *And Eternity in an hour.*[1]

Ikeda: A grain of sand and a wild flower—these are both entities of the Mystic Law; they contain the life of the universe in its entirety.

Endo: Such a view transcends superficial distinctions between phenomena, like whether they are large or small.

With regard to the principle of three thousand realms in a single moment of life, Nichikan addresses the question: "How can we say that a single moment of life contains the vastness of three thousand realms?" In answer, he explains that the Lotus Sutra reveals the principle of "endowment and pervasiveness," saying: "The Dharma realm in its entirety is contained in each moment of life. And the moment of life in its entirety pervades the Dharma realm."[2]

The macroscopic exists in the microscopic. The microscopic encompasses the macroscopic. He continues: "To illustrate, a speck of dirt is endowed with all of the constituents making up the vast land that surrounds it. And when a drop of water is added to the ocean, it spreads out, pervading the entire ocean."[3]

Suda: Without understanding the truth of nonsubstantiality, it is probably impossible to make sense of such mysteries.

By the way, another question I am asked frequently is whether saying that the Ten Worlds exist in the universe means that there are specific parts of the universe that correspond to specific worlds. Some suggest that the vicinity of the earth, for example, would correspond to the world of humanity.

What Is "Nonsubstantiality"?

Ikeda: With regard to the Ten Worlds as they exist in the universe, President Toda would often use radio waves as a metaphor to explain the concept of nonsubstantiality. I imagine you may have heard this comparison before.

Endo: Yes. Radio waves transmitted from many different broadcast stations, including frequencies sent from overseas, all reach a single room. Despite the proliferation of radio waves, you cannot see them. Yet, if you doubt their presence, by setting up a radio and tuning the channel you can readily receive any one of them. The room is never too small to hold any number of frequencies, nor do they impinge on one another. Mr. Toda explained that the Ten Worlds in the universe are also in such a state.

Ikeda: That's right. But we need to remember that this is just a means of description. The condition in which radio waves exist does not itself signify nonsubstantiality. In the universe, each of the Ten Worlds neither pile up on one another nor are they lined up side by side or individually concentrated in any particular place. They are thoroughly diffused throughout the entire universe and manifest in accord with relations, or external causes. The same is true of the Ten Worlds extant in each person's life.

Saito: For instance, when our lives are manifesting the world of hell, no matter how we might search for a way out, all we find is hell. As we squirm about in hellish suffering, we cannot see the existence of any other state of life, such as heaven. Yet, it may happen that at the next moment our sufferings will disappear and the world of heaven will dominate. Where did this world of heaven come from? Certainly not from anywhere outside us.

While we were suffering in hell, the world of heaven was in a condition of nonsubstantiality. When any one of the Ten Worlds appears—and they appear only one at a time—then the other nine worlds all recede into nonsubstantiality. The worlds become manifest in our lives as "temporary existence" in response to external causes. This seems to be more or less how it works.

Ikeda: Nonsubstantiality is a difficult concept. Why don't we try to probe a little deeper?

Strictly speaking, the term *Ten Worlds* means "ten Dharma realms." What does "Dharma realm" signify?

Suda: "Dharma realm" means the world of all phenomena; that is, the entire universe. "Dharma" itself points to all phenomena, which are revealed through various chains of causality. There are ten different kinds of causality corresponding to each of the worlds from hell to Buddhahood.

"Realm" indicates the specific realm or domain as distinguished from the others. The ten Dharma realms, therefore, refer to the ten kinds of Dharma world—or universes—that appear according to ten kinds of causes.

Ikeda: Does that mean that there are ten different universes then?

Endo: There's only one universe. In terms of Dharma realm, "one Dharma realm" indicates the entire universe.

Ikeda: So "ten Dharma realms" does not suggest the existence of ten universes, which would be ten times as great as the space indicated by "one Dharma realm."

Endo: That's right. I guess there's no way to describe it except to state that one Dharma realm (one world) contains the ten Dharma realms (Ten Worlds) within it.

THREE WAYS OF INTERPRETING
THE TEN DHARMA REALMS

Ikeda: That's truly beyond our ordinary scope of thinking. The Daishonin says, "The Dharma realm is neither broad nor is it narrow" (OTT, 165). The Great Teacher T'ien-t'ai of China gives three ways of interpreting the term *ten Dharma realms*.[4]

Saito: Yes. These are "ten Dharma realms," "the realms of ten Dharmas" and "the ten [Dharma realms] are themselves the Dharma realm." These correspond to the three truths of nonsubstantiality, temporary existence and the Middle Way.

First, "ten Dharma realms" reflects the view that, differences in the Ten Worlds not withstanding, each of these worlds is a Dharma realm, a world of the true entity as perceived by the Buddha, which is identical with the entire universe. From this standpoint, every world, whether hell or humanity, is equally a "Dharma realm," an entity of the universal life or the Mystic Law.

Endo: This is the perspective of nonsubstantiality.

Saito: That's because, despite differences between the worlds of hell and humanity, for example, these differences are not viewed as substantial.

Ikeda: In other words, each world is seen as itself representing the totality of the universe. This is the perspective of "all phenomena are themselves the true entity," and "the part is itself the whole"; that a single grain of sand reveals the entire universe.

The corollary to this view is that since the true entity is all phenomena, the whole is the part. This is the standpoint that the life of the universe manifests through all phenomena with their myriad differences.

Suda: That is the idea of the truth of temporary existence. While all phenomena are equally manifestations of the Dharma realm, they still exhibit the differences of the Ten Worlds. This brings us to the interpretation, "the realms of ten Dharmas." In this case, "realm" is synonymous with "difference."

Ikeda: Why do such discrepancies exist?

Endo: It has to do with how the Dharma realm is perceived. Phenomena are perceived and sensed differently by different people. It would seem, therefore, that there are ten ways of seeing things, according to one's life-condition.

Ikeda: That sounds correct. In that sense, the ten Dharma realms (i.e., Ten Worlds), rather than being objective aspects of the universe, can be understood to express worlds of subjective perception—how we view things—or states of life.

While the ocean itself is the same, the amount of water people can draw from it will vary depending on the size of their ladles. The same is true of the "water" of wisdom.

Fundamentally, living beings, whichever of the Ten Worlds they inhabit, are themselves the entire universe. That is the true aspect of life and the universe that the Buddha perceives. But living beings, unable to realize this, suffer in hell and hunger, contend with one another in the world of anger, and once they reach the higher worlds of voice-hearers and cause-awakened ones, feel satisfied that they have achieved all that they need to achieve.

Even if one is in the world of hell, the world of hell is endowed with the Dharma realm in its entirety. This is the perspective of the truth of the Middle Way, the third interpretation that T'ien-t'ai provides.

Saito: Yes, that's the interpretation "the ten are themselves the Dharma realm." This means that the world of hell, just as it is, is the Dharma realm. There's no need to move from the world of hell to another world; hell contains all phenomena. Since "all phenomena" indicates all beings of the Ten Worlds and their environments, the world of hell contains the Ten Worlds. The same of course holds true for each of the Ten Worlds.

Endo: That's the principle of the mutual possession of the Ten Worlds. It seems very difficult to grasp this concept correctly, but I feel that it is gradually becoming clearer.

Suda: Probably what makes it hard to understand is that it is so far beyond our ordinary linear way of thinking where we assume that a collection of parts makes up a whole. But this assumption does not hold true in the profound Buddhist view of life, which holds that the part, or the individual fragment, is itself the whole.

KOSEN-RUFU LIES IN THE HAPPINESS OF THE INDIVIDUAL

Ikeda: That's why I'm always saying that the individual is so important. The life of one person is as large as the entire universe and is supremely worthy of respect. This is something that people have a hard time comprehending.

It's important that we go out of our way to encourage not only those in our immediate surroundings but those who are struggling inconspicuously behind the scenes. To only pay attention to those in the fore is no different than bureaucratism. A Buddhist first and foremost seeks to shed light on those who tend to go unnoticed. We need to make efforts to inspire all people and help them become happy. That is what is meant by kosen-rufu. To deviate from this fundamental path and try to run the organization top-down is completely counterproductive.

In any event, the concept of the true aspect of life, from the standpoint of which the part is itself the whole, certainly transcends our ordinary way of thinking. That's why it is called inscrutable or mystic.

Endo: T'ien-t'ai used the doctrine of the mutual possession of the Ten Worlds to express "the region of the unfathomable"[5] to which he had awakened. It may well be that it is impossible to fully comprehend the truth of life intellectually.

Ikeda: But this "region of the unfathomable" does not exist somewhere apart from the reality of people's lives. Rather, the lives of ordinary people are themselves mystic. The Lotus Sutra proclaims that the human being is sublime. We must never forget this. There isn't some "mystic place" or wondrous "mystic being" existing apart from the reality of our lives.

In terms of our Buddhist practice, we must decide that faith is the only way. We have to resolve: "I will win, basing my actions on faith!" "I will forge a path through faith!" The "region of the unfathomable" ultimately is none other than the Gohonzon and the realm of faith.

As the Daishonin says, "It is the heart that is important" (WND-1, 949). Someone who just goes through the motions of praying to the Gohonzon will eventually succumb to inertia or doubt; someone who merely complains or tries to avoid difficulties will not receive true benefit. The Daishonin says, "Whether or not your prayer is answered will depend on your faith; [if it is not] I will in no way be to blame" (WND-1, 1079).

There is no realm more wonderful than that of faith. The Gohonzon is the supreme storehouse of treasures. This is itself the inscrutable mystic realm; in our faith in the Gohonzon we have the most wonderful treasure. When we practice with such an overflowing sense of joy and conviction, we receive boundless benefit. If, however, we believe there may be a more wonderful place in some other world, or that there may be some method superior to that of faith in the Mystic Law, it will greatly undermine our ability to manifest the world of Buddhahood.

When we reveal the world of Buddhahood within our lives, we can truly validate the principle that Buddhahood contains the nine worlds and the nine worlds contain Buddhahood. Only then do we embody the principle of the mutual possession of the Ten Worlds.

Saito: Without faith, the doctrine of the mutual possession of the Ten Worlds is nothing but words.

Endo: A little earlier you cited the passage, "'Observing one's mind' means to observe one's own mind and to find the Ten Worlds within it." Nichikan explains that from the standpoint of the Daishonin's teaching, the phrase *observing one's mind means to observe one's own mind* indicates belief in the Gohonzon. That's why the Gohonzon is also called the "Gohonzon for observing one's mind." He further says that "to find the Ten Worlds within it" is to chant the Mystic Law.

Ikeda: That's right. We who invoke the Mystic Law correspond to the nine worlds, and the Mystic Law corresponds to the world of Buddhahood. Through chanting the Mystic Law of Nam-myoho-renge-kyo, the nine worlds and the world of Buddhahood become one; that is, we actualize the principle of the mutual possession of the Ten Worlds. This is what produces a great transformation in our state of life.

Unless we actually manifest the world of Buddhahood, the mutual possession of the Ten Worlds will remain nothing more than a theoretical potential. Through faith and practice, we can actualize this principle. In that sense, while the theory of the mutual possession of the Ten Worlds is very subtle and complex, there are countless people in the SGI who have demonstrated actual proof of it. I think we can go so far as to declare that only in the SGI are such people to be found.

Endo: The other day I heard the experience of a Ms. Chan Bok-soon of Hiroshima and was extremely moved. Ms. Chan is a Korean national living in Japan who was a victim of the atomic bomb. Having overcome anti-Korean discrimination from the

Japanese and the painful aftermath of the bombing, she is now active as a volunteer spokesperson for peace.

Ms. Chan, whose parents had immigrated to Japan, was born in Osaka. Her family had run an extensive agricultural operation in Korea. Militarist Japan invaded the country, however, and the family lost its land as a result of Japan's colonialist policies.

They had no choice but to come to Japan. In making their decision, they had placed their trust in advertisements promising that a wonderful life awaited them there. But after being sent to one dangerous construction site after another, they finally arrived in a small village deep in the mountains. They were put in a tiny room in the corner of a cocoonery that was partitioned off by only a straw mat, and they were made to work as assistants to a tenant farmer.

Moreover, they were assigned to work a swamplike field. There was no way they could get a satisfactory harvest from this poor piece of land. They reportedly lived in a constant state of hunger, surviving on a meager allowance and what plants and fruit they could collect.

Suda: That's terrible. At the time, a great many Koreans were similarly duped into coming to Japan.

Endo: They later moved near Hiroshima. A year later, on August 6, 1945, the rumor spread that the city had been totally destroyed by a new kind of bomb. Ms. Chan and her mother, concerned about the safety of relatives and friends, entered the city of Hiroshima immediately after the blast. As a result, Ms. Chan became a victim of secondary radiation from the bomb. She was twelve. When they finally located Ms. Chan's aunt and her son, they found them so badly burned that there was nothing they could do for them.

Her aunt cried: "There are too few doctors and too little medicine . . . not enough to go around for Koreans. All we can do is wait for death to come!"

At this, her mother wailed: "Our country was taken, and we

were brought all the way to Japan to be mercilessly worked like cows and horses. They don't even make death easy for us; instead they force us to die in excruciating flames. What offense did we commit? Will they continue to discriminate against us even after we are dead?" Even now Ms. Chan vividly recalls how her mother sobbed and lamented, pounding the ground with her fists.

Later, when she was sixteen, Ms. Chan married. She married so young because her family had limited means and there were too many mouths to feed. From around the time she gave birth to her first child, she was afflicted by severe anemia and various internal disorders—probably as a result of her exposure to the atomic bomb—and had to undergo many operations. She was told by her doctor that she had no chance of recovery, and when she was transferred to a hospital in Hiroshima, she was reportedly in a coma.

Her husband stopped coming to see her, and she and her two small children had to share her hospital meals. Since she had no money, she was forced to leave the hospital and wound up living in a tiny hut without running water or utilities. They had to go to a neighborhood park to use the toilet. It was a pitiful existence.

The local women of the Soka Gakkai extended a helping hand to Ms. Chan and her family. They would warmly encourage her, saying things like, "Let's become happy together!" and would sometimes bring over dishes of hot noodles for her and her children. What a profound impression this must have made on Ms. Chan, who had lost all trust in people!

In 1964, at age thirty-two, she began practicing Nichiren Buddhism. Through earnestly exerting herself in faith, she succeeded in recovering vibrant health. Upon witnessing this, her husband also took faith.

Ms. Chan had a question that had been on her mind for a long time. She wondered why she had to suffer so much. When she learned about the Buddhist concept of deliberately creating the appropriate karma, meaning that one undergoes suffering in order to help other people in similar circumstances, she found at last she could make sense of her predicament.

"I see," she exclaimed. "So I have a mission that only I can fulfill. My situation is my responsibility." Through reading President Toda's Declaration for the Abolition of Nuclear Weapons and studying your guidance, President Ikeda, Ms. Chan developed a strong determination: "There must be some unique way that I, as a Korean A-bomb victim living in Japan, can contribute to peace. I will put more effort into fulfilling my mission! I will study harder!"

At fifty-two, she enrolled in night middle-school classes. She later attended night high school, where she maintained a grade point average at the very top of her class. At fifty-seven, she was admitted to the night school of the University of Hiroshima.

Saito: To undertake one's education at that age is no small feat. It must have been very arduous.

Endo: She comments that she cannot recall having once gone to sleep in her bed while she was attending classes or being aware of when she fell asleep and when she awoke. Through such tenacious effort, in the spring of 1995, at sixty-two, she succeeded in getting her diploma.

Now, while teaching part-time in the night school she once attended, she is participating in lecture meetings and symposiums near and far as a spokesperson for peace. She has tirelessly given her support to schools for adult literacy and has carried out volunteer activities to promote education programs in many countries of Asia, including Nepal and the Philippines.

When she joined the Soka Gakkai, Ms. Chan was told by the person who first introduced her to Nichiren Buddhism, "You will become unimaginably happy." She recalls thinking at that time: "Rather than unimaginable happiness, I would be satisfied with happiness that I can readily imagine. It would be enough if my husband would just quit drinking and get a job." She has in fact constructed a state of life truly far beyond anything she could have then imagined.

Ms. Chan says emphatically, "Making the spirit of the 'Monument of Prayer for World Peace' that President Ikeda established in Hiroshima my own, I am determined to exert every ounce of strength I have to fulfill my mission for the peace and happiness of people throughout the world."

FREELY ENACTING THE TEN WORLDS

Ikeda: That's a wonderful experience. A wonderful life. A wonderful example of victory through faith.

In *The Record of the Orally Transmitted Teachings,* the Daishonin says of Bodhisattva Wonderful Sound (who appears in the twenty-fourth chapter of the Lotus Sutra): "He manifests thirty-four different bodily forms, illustrating the principle of the mutual possession of the Ten Worlds and preaching the Law so as to bring benefit to others" (OTT, 238).

To lead people to enlightenment, this bodhisattva appears in various guises (thirty-four bodily forms) and widely propagates the Lotus Sutra in accord with people's capacity and their worries. This, the Daishonin says, is "illustrating the principle of the mutual possession of the Ten Worlds."

Ms. Chan's life had sometimes revealed the suffering of the world of hell and, at other times, the sadness of the world of hunger. But through faith in the Mystic Law, she realized that these were the effects of karma she herself had willingly created in order to show actual proof of faith. She developed the confidence that, for the sake of kosen-rufu, a Bodhisattva of the Earth readily undergoes even the most abominable suffering. While revealing various states of life, in the end the bodhisattva demonstrates victory and so teaches others about the greatness of the Mystic Law. Those who do so are great actors in the drama of the Ten Worlds. Such a life could well be described as revealing "thirty-four different bodily forms" and "illustrating the principle of the mutual possession of the Ten Worlds."

Suda: "Illustrating the principle of the mutual possession of the Ten Worlds" refers to the idea that people, though originally Buddhas or bodhisattvas, manifest the various states of life of the Ten Worlds.

Saito: In "The Object of Devotion for Observing the Mind," Nichiren Daishonin, commenting on the passage in the "Life Span" chapter that reads, "Sometimes I speak of myself, sometimes of others; sometimes I present myself, sometimes others; sometimes I show my own actions, sometimes those of others" (LSOC, 267), says that it expresses the truth that "the world of Buddhahood contains the Ten Worlds" (WND-1, 357). Here, he interprets "myself" as pointing to the Buddha's life, or the world of Buddhahood, and "others" as meaning the various states of life that the beings of the Ten Worlds manifest.

Ikeda: The Daishonin elucidates that, since the remotest past, the Buddha, while appearing in various states among the nine worlds, had been continually taking action as the Buddha. This was possible because the nine worlds continued to exist in the Buddha's life even after the attainment of supreme enlightenment. This is the meaning of the passage, "All beings of the Ten Worlds are essentially Buddhas."

Also, in contrast to the "theoretical" mutual possession of the Ten Worlds found in the "Expedient Means" chapter, the "Life Span" chapter explains the "actual" mutual possession of the Ten Worlds. The Buddha revealed the mutual possession of the Ten Worlds through his own actual conduct. This is the meaning of "Sometimes I speak of myself, sometimes of others..."

Just as Bodhisattva Wonderful Sound leads people to enlightenment through freely manifesting thirty-four bodies, we advance kosen-rufu while carrying out various roles and activities, whether it be, for example, through education, business or taking care of the home. Whether revealing the pain-filled world of hell, the joyous world of heaven or the world of anger, through it all we continue progressing.

Based on our activities as SGI members to promote peace, education and culture and to reach people through words and actions grounded in Buddhism, we continue moving forward while revealing all aspects of life. This surely corresponds to the "thirty-four bodies" and represents the practice of the mutual possession of the Ten Worlds.

CHANGING LIFE ON A FUNDAMENTAL LEVEL

Suda: Here is one last point to confirm.

The purpose of the doctrine of the mutual possession of the Ten Worlds lies in helping people manifest the Ten Worlds inherent in the world of humanity, in particular, the world of Buddhahood. Human life is the entity of the one hundred worlds, just as the universe is. This much I can understand. But I'm still not completely clear on the significance of the hundred worlds contained within the world of humanity.

Saito: The Daishonin discussed the mutual possession of the Ten Worlds focusing on the Ten Worlds existing in the world of humanity. I think what you're asking is: What, exactly, does it mean to say that each person is an entity of the hundred worlds, or if there is even any sense in discussing it at all?

Ikeda: One way we can approach this problem is from the perspective of our basic life tendency. For example, while all people belong to the world of humanity, some, in terms of their basic life tendency, act mostly from the world of hell, for example, and others act mostly from the world of bodhisattva.

Saito: Someone whose life clings to the world of hell will become downcast and discouraged at the slightest setback. That is the kind of trend I think we're talking about.

Ikeda: We could term this the habitual tendency of a person's life.

This tendency has been built up by the cumulative causes that a person has made up until the present.

Saito: That would include one's personality.

Endo: It's the basic course of people's lives, the base or home to which they always retreat.

Ikeda: Just as a spring returns to its original shape after it has been extended, we return to our own basic tendency. Even if the world of hell is someone's base, that doesn't mean that the person remains in that state all the time. Rather, his or her state of life will shift from one world to another, sometimes entering the world of humanity and sometimes the world of anger.

Even a person who strives to be superior to others (a characteristic of the world of anger) will sometimes manifest the worlds of bodhisattva or heaven, for example.

Suda: Bodhisattva or heaven is contained in the world of anger.

Ikeda: But even if someone who has the world of anger as his or her fundamental tendency momentarily produces the world of bodhisattva, they will quickly revert to the world of anger. It is doing our human revolution, transforming our state of life at the deepest level, that enables us to change this basic tendency, to change our fundamental state of mind.

Your basic tendency in a sense determines your life. To illustrate, those who tend to act from the world of hunger are as though on board a ship called hunger. While navigating the course of hunger, they will sometimes experience joy and sometimes suffering. Though there are many changes and fluctuations, the boat unerringly continues to advance along that track. Consequently, these people's viewpoint is always colored in the hues of the world of hunger; after they die, their lives meld with the world of hunger existing in the universe.

Making the world of Buddhahood our basic life tendency is called "attaining Buddhahood." Of course, even if Buddhahood becomes our basic tendency, we still have the nine worlds; consequently, we still have worries and suffering. But the foundation of our lives becomes one of hope, and we acquire a rhythm of peace of mind and joy.

President Toda once explained this as follows:

> Even if we should become sick, we should have the attitude: "I'm all right. I know that if I chant to the Gohonzon, I will get well." Doesn't Buddhahood mean living with total peace of mind? Now, because the world of Buddhahood contains the nine worlds, we might still sometimes become angry or perplexed; enjoying total peace of mind doesn't mean that we cease to experience anger, for example. A worry is still a worry. Yet, underneath everything, we feel profound peace of mind. Someone in this state is a Buddha.

He also said:

> Isn't a Buddha someone for whom to be alive is itself an overwhelming joy? Isn't this what it means to attain the Daishonin's state of life? Even when facing the prospect of being beheaded, the Daishonin was calm and composed. In a similar situation, any one of us would be ready to give up. When he was exiled to Sado, the Daishonin continued instructing his disciples on various matters and produced such writings as "The Opening of the Eyes" and "The Object of Devotion for Observing the Mind." Without peace of mind, he could never have written such great treatises.[6]

Suda: Referring to what you said earlier, I can see how President

Toda enjoyed a state of life as vast as the Pacific Ocean even while facing great adversity. It seems that this is just the kind of peace of mind that he was talking about.

STRUGGLES IN THE NINE WORLDS
STRENGTHEN THE WORLD OF BUDDHAHOOD

Endo: The practice of reciting the sutra and chanting daimoku is the means for establishing the world of Buddhahood as our basic life tendency.

Ikeda: Reciting the sutra is a solemn ceremony in which we fuse our lives with the life state of the Buddha. By steadfastly and continually carrying out this practice and also chanting Nam-myoho-renge-kyo, the world of Buddhahood in our life becomes solidified, just as firmly packing together a pile of earth will produce a strong foundation. On this foundation, this stage, at each moment we freely enact the drama of the nine worlds.

Kosen-rufu is a struggle to make the world of Buddhahood the basic tendency of society. Fundamentally this comes down to forging ties of friendship with increasing numbers of people.

At any rate, when we base ourselves on Nichiren Buddhism, absolutely no effort is wasted. When we make the world of Buddhahood our basic life tendency, we can advance toward a future of hope while making the most of all our activities in the nine worlds, both past and present. In fact, our efforts in the nine worlds become the nourishment that fortifies the world of Buddhahood.

In light of the principle that earthly desires are themselves enlightenment, sufferings (i.e., earthly desires, or the nine worlds) all become the "firewood" or fuel for attaining enlightenment (the world of Buddhahood). This is similar to how our bodies digest food and turn it into energy.

Suda: Without wood there would be no flame, and without food our bodies would have no energy. Similarly, without the nine worlds, the world of Buddhahood would be diminished.

Ikeda: That's right. A Buddha who has no connection to the actual sufferings of the nine worlds is not a genuine Buddha—a Buddha of the mutual possession of the Ten Worlds. That is the essential message of the "Life Span" chapter.

In a sense, the world of Buddhahood is expressed in the inclination to take on even the hardships of hell. This is the world of hell contained in the world of Buddhahood. It is suffering for the sake of others, suffering willingly taken on as an expression of responsibility and compassion. Working to spread the Daishonin's teaching and encourage friends has the effect of strengthening the world of Buddhahood in our lives. Faith means gladly taking on hard work. Manipulating others to do things is not faith; that's organizationalism and authoritarianism.

Saito: To enthusiastically and joyfully go into the midst of suffering—that's analogous to the spirit of bodhisattvas to take on karmic suffering out of compassion for others.

Ikeda: We cannot grow as human beings without great effort. Those who avoid the struggle can neither manifest true faith nor carry out their human revolution.

President Toda once said:

> A sea bream of the Inland Sea is born in an inland body of water, grows up in the rough waves of the outlying Sea of Genkai, and then once again returns to the Inland Sea. Since it has withstood the fierce currents of the Sea of Genkai, its flesh is firm and its bones strong, and it has a wonderful taste. Similarly, battling the rough waves of the world enables young people to grow into outstanding individuals.[7]

According to a certain chef, the muscles that a fish has used most, such as those near the tail or the fins, taste best.

Suda: Those areas aren't usually eaten.

Endo: It seems that people leave the best parts behind!

Ikeda: In terms of people, those who have really struggled possess the "flavor" of profound character and humanity.

There are those who give up when things get tough and consequently fall into despair. This is comparable to how you will undermine your health if you eat too much at a time when your power to digest and assimilate food is weak. Therefore, having a strong life force is important. When our lives are strong, we can turn all of our toils into a source of spiritual nourishment.

On the other hand, no matter how much we may believe in the Mystic Law and carry out the practice of reciting the sutra and chanting Nam-myoho-renge-kyo, it is impossible to strengthen and solidify the world of Buddhahood in our lives if we avoid the hard work necessary for advancing kosen-rufu.

LIVE TRUE TO YOURSELF

Saito: In terms of the mutual possession of the Ten Worlds, attaining Buddhahood does not mean eradicating the nine worlds. Rather, it means making the best use of all of them. This gives us a sense of the broad-mindedness of this teaching.

Ikeda: To live based on the mutual possession of the Ten Worlds means to live thoroughly true to oneself based on faith.

Buddhist teachings that do not explain the mutual possession of the Ten Worlds treat the nine worlds with scorn, postulating that one can only enter the world of Buddhahood by eradicating the nine worlds. Their approach is essentially to try to carve away those parts of human existence that they regard as bad. They impose restrictions and condemn shortcomings. This ultimately leads to the idea of annihilating one's consciousness and reducing one's body to ashes, in other words, ridding oneself of earthly desires and attachments.

While self-reflection is of course important, if not done in a positive, growth-inspiring way, people's lives may become closed off and rigid, causing them to lose all sense of purpose.

A Japanese saying goes that trying to straighten the horns of a cow could kill the cow. Instead of nit-picking over others' weaknesses, it is far more valuable to encourage them, give them hope and enable them to find goals. Through doing so, we can help someone who is impatient, for example, become someone who can't wait to take positive action.

This applies to one's personal growth as well as that of others. We can be completely ourselves; there is no need to try to make ourselves appear to be what we are not.

Since we are human, there will be times when we want to cry, times when we want to laugh, times when we want to be angry, as well as times when we are confused. Though we are ordinary people subject to such frailties, when we make kosen-rufu our prime focus, the world of Buddhahood becomes our basic life tendency.

Once this happens, then when anger is appropriate we get angry. When suffering is needed, we suffer. When laughter is due, we laugh. We enjoy what there is to enjoy. The Daishonin says, "Suffer what there is to suffer, enjoy what there is to enjoy" (WND-1, 681). By leading such a vigorous and vibrant life, we can advance each day by leaps and bounds toward absolute happiness and help others do the same.

Suda: That must be what it means to live based on the mutual possession of the Ten Worlds.

Make Kosen-rufu the Prime Focus

Ikeda: It's vital that we possess a strong sense of responsibility for kosen-rufu. If we have the lackadaisical attitude that "Someone will take care of things" or "Somehow things will work out," then we do injury to the world of Buddhahood within our own lives. For instance, when the schedule for the month is decided, if we merely write down the dates in our appointment book, we may not be roused to action.

Our minds and energy should be concentrated on the tasks we must accomplish. Our prayer is then directed, and, through the principle of three thousand realms in a single moment of life, the entire universe will move toward our victory and success. We need to make kosen-rufu our prime focus. We need to fix our attention on our friends and fellow members. We need to pray wholeheartedly for kosen-rufu, for the prosperity of the SGI, and for the happiness of all; and we have to take action. This is what it means to be a true champion of kosen-rufu.

The Lotus Sutra says, the "evil demons will take possession of others" (LSOC, 233). We, however, must become people of whom the Buddha takes possession.

Kosen-rufu is what constantly occupies the thoughts[8] of the Buddha. When we are determined to accomplish this goal by working with our fellow members, Buddhahood will flow from our lives, and we will begin to actualize the principles of true mutual possession of the Ten Worlds and three thousand realms in a single moment of life.

The life of the Buddha wells forth in the nine worlds of an ordinary person. This is the mutual possession of the Ten Worlds.

The Daishonin says, "If in a single moment of life we exhaust the pains and trials of millions of kalpas, then instant after instant there will arise in us the three Buddha bodies with which we are eternally endowed" (OTT, 214). We need to "exhaust the pains and trials of millions of kalpas." When we work to the utmost for kosen-rufu, Buddhahood shines like the sun in our lives. This passage expresses the essence of the principle of the mutual possession of the Ten Worlds.

NOTES

1. *The Portable Blake*, ed. Alfred Kazin (New York: The Viking Press, 1946), p. 150.

2. *Sanju Hiden Sho* (The Threefold Secret Teaching).

3. Ibid.

4. *Hokke Gengi* (Profound Meaning of the Lotus Sutra).

5. *Maka Shikan* (Great Concentration and Insight).

6. *Toda Josei zenshu* (Collected Writings of Josei Toda) (Tokyo: Seikyo Shimbunsha, 1982), vol. 2, pp. 446–47.

7. Daisaku Ikeda, *Zuihitsu ningen kakumei* (Essay on the Human Revolution) (Tokyo: Seikyo Shimbunsha, 1978), p. 145.

8. This is a paraphrase of the line near the end of the "Life Span" chapter, "*mai ji sa ze nen*," which translates as, "At all times I think to myself ..." (LSOC, 273).

PART III:

"The Life Span of the Thus Come One" Chapter:

THE ETERNITY OF LIFE

9 Testimony to the Eternity of Life

"All that I preach is true and not false.

"Why do I do this? The Thus Come One perceives the true aspect of the threefold world exactly as it is. There is no ebb or flow of birth and death, and there is no existing in this world and later entering extinction. It is neither substantial nor empty, neither consistent nor diverse. Nor is it what those who dwell in the threefold world perceive it to be. All such things the Thus Come One sees clearly and without error."
(LSOC, 267)

To conceive of life and death as separate realities is to be caught in the illusion of birth and death. It is deluded and inverted thinking. When we examine the nature of life with perfect enlightenment, we find that there is no beginning marking birth and, therefore, no end signifying death. Doesn't life as thus conceived already transcend birth and death? (OTT, 843)

Suda: I heard about the experience of Richard Yoshimachi, a vice general director of the SGI-USA. On April 10, 1993, Mr. Yoshimachi suffered a myocardial infarction while at the SGI-USA Headquarters in Los Angeles and was immediately taken to a nearby hospital. He complained of a tightness in his chest. Told that they would draw some blood, he responded, "OK," and then immediately blacked out. When he came to, he found himself surrounded by doctors and nurses. The head nurse was holding his hand. While he was unconscious, his heart had stopped beating for about twenty seconds.

In that time, Mr. Yoshimachi had a remarkable experience. He explained that he found himself surrounded by total darkness in a world of complete silence. He felt no pain and sensed nothing unusual about his heart, nor was he aware of having fallen down. He recalls wondering to himself, "How did I get here?" Looking down, he could see his bare feet, but could discern no surface on which he was standing.

He surveyed the scene around him. To the right he could see nothing, but when he turned to the left, he could make out a faint light coming from somewhere behind his left shoulder. It was far away. It seemed to him as though this faint light was filtering through an opening in a wall.

He immediately walked toward the light. As he did so, it increased in intensity. The light was a tunnel. Following it, he came out in the main auditorium at the SGI-USA Headquarters. The auditorium was a place he had been on many occasions, attending to matters on stage. He now saw himself there. A meeting was going on.

Looking to his right, he saw the smiling faces of members who were seated. On stage, he saw you, President Ikeda, giving a speech. You also wore a bright smile. It then occurred to him that this was the SGI-USA general meeting held three months earlier on January 27, 1993. At that moment he opened his eyes to find everyone staring down at him as he lay in bed.

Ikeda: I recall that general meeting well. At the time, Mr. Yoshimachi was the SGI-USA youth division leader. Just before that, his mother, who was living in Japan, had passed away. But rather than return immediately to Japan for the funeral, he resolutely stood at the head of the youth division, saying, "I feel that to work for kosen-rufu together with President Ikeda in America is the greatest memorial I can give my mother."

Endo: Mr. Yoshimachi's experience sounds like a dream. But seeing light in darkness and observing things from outside one's body are in fact typical of the experiences of people who have been close to death.

Suda: That's true. After undergoing a week of intensive therapy, Mr. Yoshimachi told the attending physician, who was a heart specialist, what he had felt while he was unconscious. The doctor responded that he knew of a number of cases where people recounted similar experiences.

Ikeda: In recent years, quite a bit of research has been done on near-death encounters. I understand that full-fledged statistical surveys are being conducted.

Saito: Yes. A United States survey revealed that 15 percent of Americans sampled reported having had a narrow brush with death. Of these, one in three, or as many as eight million people in the U.S. population, reported having had some kind of "otherworldly experience" at that time.[1]

Endo: Eight million people—that's a phenomenal number.

Ikeda: It would be a waste to let such experiences simply go unnoticed. In the future, I hope to see a similarly rigorous survey conducted worldwide.

In a sense, whether there is an afterlife and, if so, what kind of place it is, is of far greater importance than space exploration. It is one of humankind's greatest issues, for an answer to this question could completely change the thinking and way of life of people everywhere.

I seem to recall that the Swiss psychologist Carl Jung describes his encounter with death in his autobiography.

Endo: Yes. In 1944, Jung suffered a myocardial infarction and collapsed, consequently breaking a leg. He writes that, as he lost consciousness, he had an incredible experience:

> It seemed to me that I was high up in space. Far below I saw the globe of the earth, bathed in a gloriously blue light. I saw the deep blue sea and the continents. Far below my feet lay Ceylon, and in the distance ahead of me the subcontinent of India. My field of vision did not include the whole earth, but its global shape was plainly distinguishable and its outlines shone with a silvery gleam through that wonderful blue light. In many places the globe seemed colored, or spotted dark green like oxidized silver...
>
> Later I discovered how high in space one would have to be to have so extensive a view—approximately a thousand miles! The sight of the earth from this height was the most glorious thing I had ever seen.[2]

Ikeda: He remarks that the earth appeared blue. That was before the time of the Soviet cosmonaut Yury Gagarin, wasn't it?

Saito: Gagarin [the first person to travel in space] orbited the earth in 1961, so it was seventeen years before that. In 1944, when Jung wrote this, no one had ever seen the earth from outer space.

Endo: Jung says that after viewing the earth, he began to drift through space with the Indian Ocean behind him. He saw a large black boulder. The middle of the boulder was hollowed out, and it became a Hindu temple. Jung entered. While there, he describes feeling as though he had discarded all he ever knew and thought, and everything existing on the earth.

Ikeda: It must have been a very vivid experience. This became a major impetus behind Jung's broad-ranging investigations into the world of the spirit.

Endo: In fact, it seems that Jung was convinced that there is life after death.

THE LAST MOMENT: A SETTLING OF LIFE'S ACCOUNTS

Ikeda: Being close to death is of course not the same as being dead. Still, it is doubtless an instant in which we powerfully sense the reality of death. As a result, for many people, having a near-death experience completely changes the way they live the remainder of their lives.

Endo: Certainly it seems there are many cases where such people became more tolerant toward and actively concerned about the well-being of others.

Suda: Mr. Yoshimachi describes having wondered, "Can it be that we really have so little control over ourselves at the time of death?" He recalls saying to himself, "Life is so fleeting and fragile," and being left with a powerful awareness of the need to spend each day so that if he were to die at any moment he would have no regrets.

Saito: That's the spirit Nichiren Daishonin described as regarding the present as the last moment of one's life.

Though different from what's been termed a near-death experience, it seems that many people who live through major disasters also find their view of life greatly changed by the ordeal. I have heard of a number of such accounts from survivors of the Great Kobe Earthquake (January 1995), many of whom reported that they realized there is something far more precious than material possessions, status, fame and honor—namely, life. Some said that, though intellectually they had understood this before, surviving the disaster left them with a profound understanding of this truth.

Ikeda: Confronting death enables us to clearly see what is most important. I heard the following account of a mother in the United States. She had suffered a stroke and spent several weeks in a coma. Just before dying, she suddenly opened her eyes and, smiling, reached out to something that was invisible to everyone else. With her gaze downward, she made a gesture with her arms as though cradling a baby. Her face at that moment shone with genuine joy and happiness. She then passed away.

It turned out that her first child had died shortly after birth. She later gave birth to five children and raised them all into fine adults. She would never talk about the baby she lost when she was young. Her surviving children were all convinced that at the moment of death, their mother had met that child and had died with that child in her arms.[3]

Suda: That's very moving.

Ikeda: People who have had near-death experiences often report seeing their entire life flash before them in a succession of panoramic scenes. In terms of Buddhist doctrine, we could say that this is equivalent to all of one's karma (consisting of one's thoughts, words and deeds) that has been etched into the *alaya* consciousness—the eighth of the nine consciousnesses, which is likened to a storehouse—appearing before one's eyes in an instant. At any rate, the moment of death is a final settlement of accounts for one's life.

Saito: I think there is deep significance in the Daishonin's conclusion that one should "first of all learn about death, and then about other things" (WND-2, 759).

Ikeda: Shakyamuni lost his mother shortly after he was born and consequently turned his thoughts to death at a very early age. The Daishonin, too, thought about death from the time he was a child. He writes:

> From childhood, I, Nichiren, studied Buddhism with one thought in mind. Life as a human being is fleeting. An outgoing breath does not wait for an incoming one. Not even dewdrops on the verge of being blown off by the wind suffice to describe this transience. No one, wise or foolish, young or old, can escape death. Therefore I thought that I should first learn about death, and then learn about other matters. (WND-2, 759)

The instant before we die could perhaps be compared to the summit of a mountain. Having completed our climb of the mountain of life, it is from that vantage point that we can look back and for the first time take in the whole of our life. We can survey our accomplishments, what we are leaving behind, how much good or harm we caused, and whether we were kind to others or hurt them. And we can assess which of these was greater. We may also ask ourselves to what did we attach the greatest importance in our lives. At that crucial moment one's mind is bombarded with such questions.

This is one aspect of the last moment of our lives.

Endo: While someone on the brink of death may be lying still, a tumultuous drama may well be unfolding in that person's heart. The only reason it does not appear externally is the lack of physical vigor to express it.

Ikeda: Though there are of course cases where people meet their end peacefully, one prisoner reports having had quite a different near-death experience. Because he wanted to get transferred to the hospital ward within the prison, he swallowed a large amount of soap to make himself sick. His plan was successful, but he became a lot sicker than he would have liked. Writhing in excruciating pain, he saw his entire life spread out before his eyes in successive images. He said he relived in minute detail his long criminal career and felt every pang of suffering he had inflicted on others.[4]

Endo: It sounds like a frightening experience. This illustrates the strictness of the principle of cause and effect.

Ikeda: Opinions may vary as to how such experiences should be interpreted, but I believe that, if we set aside all our preconceived ideas regarding life and death and then closely examine actual near-death experiences through surveys and research, we will learn that there are essential elements that simply cannot be explained by the current view that life ends with death. But research in this area has only just begun.

NEAR-DEATH EXPERIENCES HAVE A UNIVERSAL CONTENT

Saito: Yes. Dating from ancient times, there have been a number of instances in Japan of people nearly dying and then regaining consciousness who have reported various mysterious phenomena. These include seeing the River of Three Crossings,[5] having an out-of-body experience, and meeting deceased parents. While there have been similar accounts from people in all parts of the world, it is only with the pioneering work of psychiatrist Elisabeth Kübler-Ross that this subject has become a focus of scholarly investigation. In her 1969 work *On Death and Dying*, Dr. Kübler-Ross details a number of actual examples of near-death experiences that she encountered in the course of providing care to the dying.

Endo: Dr. Kübler-Ross herself had a near-death experience. Describing the incident, she recounts feeling the pain of death and immediately thereafter going through a kind of rebirth. She says that her second self watched as her body approached a light and became engulfed in it, and that the instant it became one with the light, she enjoyed a state of profound peace and tranquillity. When she opened her eyes, she says, she could sense the pulse of life in all living beings, even in insentient things such as rocks.

> I was in total love and awe of all life around me. I was in love with every leaf, every cloud, every grass, every little creature. I felt the pulsation of the pebbles on the path and I literally walked above the pebbles, conveying to them, "I cannot step on you. I cannot hurt you."[6]

Suda: After Dr. Kübler-Ross had broken ground in this area, Dr. Raymond Moody, a specialist in internal medicine, collected a number of accounts of people who had been declared clinically dead and then came back to life (which he published in 1976).[7] This had a major impact, causing scholarly research to get under way in earnest. Today there is an international research body devoted to studying the issue.

Ikeda: Up until then, near-death experiences had been written off as simply dreams or fantasies. But as more data was accumulated, the scientific community began to think that perhaps it could not be taken so lightly.

Saito: Yes. Near-death experiences have a number of features that seem to be universal, transcending any cultural and religious differences. Moreover, it seems there were quite a few cases in which people underwent something that directly contradicted religious beliefs they'd held for a lifetime.

What could account for the high degree of similarity in the experiences of people from totally different cultures? From that standpoint, it is logical to infer that there is some universal facts that all people encounter upon death. Furthermore, there are things about these experiences that disciplines such as psychology, pharmacology and neurology cannot adequately explain.

Ikeda: At this stage, researchers have not yet come to any definite conclusion as to the meaning of near-death experiences.

Endo: That's right. Broadly speaking, there are two schools of thought. One postulates that some form of consciousness continues after death. The other holds that all near-death experiences can be explained as neurological phenomena. Scientists who adopt this latter position argue that near-death experiences do not point to the existence of an afterlife.

Ikeda: Certainly, any discussion of the hereafter can amount to nothing more than speculation since the existence of such a realm cannot be proven empirically—it is but a theory. Conversely, there are no grounds to assert that a materialist view of life is any more scientific or less speculative than a view that holds that life continues after death. Both views are essentially on the same level, in that neither can be fully substantiated.

The Claim That There Is Nothing After Death Cannot Be Proven

Saito: It is a fact that many who receive a modern education blindly accept the tenet that belief in the afterlife is superstitious and nonscientific. In that it cannot be proven, this assumption itself is a superstition.

Ikeda: The question then becomes which of these theories is the more logical and persuasive. The answer can only be found through investigation of the many examples of near-death experiences or the accounts of people who claim to remember their past lives, and see which theory can more adequately explain these phenomena.

As was mentioned a little earlier, it seems that the core content of people's experiences at the time of death is not greatly influenced by culture or religion or personal factors. On the contrary, there appears to be a surprisingly high degree of similarity, such as reports of out-of-body experiences. This in itself is rather mysterious.

Suda: An extraordinary number of people who have been close to death have recounted leaving their bodies, hovering in the air, and gazing down on themselves and the people gathered around their bedside. This is of course not to say that everyone has such an experience.

Endo: What happens to people at the moment of death may vary considerably depending on their state of life.

Suda: In that light, keeping in mind that this is the personal account of one individual, I would like to introduce the experience of a Soka Gakkai member. Suffering a recurrence of meningitis, she lost consciousness, developed a high fever and a very irregular pulse, and finally her pupils dilated, indicating that she was about to die. Those around her evidently began discussing funeral arrangements, going so far as to talk about what photo of her to use at the funeral.

She later came to, saying:

> At that time, I felt a cone-shaped object emerge from my head and my mind went completely blank. The object attached itself to a corner of the ceiling of the room and watched the scene below. The part of me looking down from above had left the self that was lying

on the bed. And I could see the forms of everyone in the room moving back and forth. The moment I thought, "I am dying," I was reminded of the Daishonin's passage: "When one dies, if one is destined to fall into hell, one's appearance will darken, and one's body will become as heavy as a stone that requires the strength of a thousand men to move. But in the case of a good person, even if she should be a woman seven or eight feet tall and of dark complexion, at the hour of death, her countenance will become pure and white, and her body will be as light as a goose feather and as soft and pliable as cotton." (WND-I, 288)

She continues: "Then I was not afraid to die, but I was very much afraid of not attaining Buddhahood. Thinking over and over, 'I have to attain Buddhahood!' in this dreamlike state I began trying to chant daimoku, although I could not produce any sound."

Her mother and others chanted much earnest daimoku, and three days later she regained consciousness.

Saito: Her experience indicates that people in a near-death state can see things that we wouldn't expect them to if they were actually in a coma. In a number of cases, "unconscious" people have later proven that they could "see" by identifying, for example, the clothing worn by relatives and people who had come to visit them.

Endo: Stranger still, there are instances of blind people relating that they saw the people around them perfectly well. Dr. Kübler-Ross reports on the case of a blind person who could explain in detail the clothing of all the people gathered at his bedside.

Ikeda: Although these occurrences would be extremely difficult to explain from a physiological standpoint, I think a great many such examples could be cited. Once people make up their mind that life after death is superstition, however, they often close themselves off to any such evidence.

Endo: Even in the SGI, there are many people who, prior to taking faith, would have discounted as irrational the notion that through practicing Nichiren Buddhism you can, for one, strengthen your life force and heal illness. Probably all attempts at explanation, however reasonable, would have at one time been lost on them.

Saito: Dr. Kübler-Ross notes that people will make countless arguments to refute something they are not prepared to accept. But when it comes to the question of dying, she adds, "If you are not interested in knowing about it, it doesn't make any difference because once you have died you will know it anyway."[8]

Ikeda: Certainly, the only way to really know is to actually die. At that point, however, it may be too late! In any event, from a logical standpoint, it is clear that as of yet there is no explanation with a decisive claim to truth. In this connection, I am always reminded of the argument put forward by Blaise Pascal.

Suda: Pascal was the French thinker and mathematician who described human beings as "thinking reeds."

Ikeda: Yes. He is well known for his work in probability theory. True to his intellectual proclivities, Pascal discusses the matter of life after death in terms of a wagering theory.

He asserts that intelligence cannot provide an answer to the question of whether there is an afterlife. This was also the conclusion reached by the German philosopher Immanuel Kant. On this premise, Pascal says that if people gamble their lives on the chance that there is life after death, then, even if they are wrong and the reality is that there isn't, they haven't lost anything. On the other hand, if they gamble their life on the chance that there is no after-life, and it turns out that in fact there is, then they are powerless to do anything to alter the course they have taken. Even if at that point they wish to have done more good things while alive for the sake of the hereafter, it is too late.

Therefore, Pascal reasons that gambling on a belief in the after-life brings fortune if you win and costs nothing if you lose. Losing a wager on the opposite belief, however, leaves you helpless and empty-handed. He therefore concludes that it makes the most sense to lay one's stakes on the belief that there is life after death, i.e., to accept religion; and that this is the choice that any rational person would make.[9]

This argument may be controversial, but I nevertheless find Pascal's reasoning persuasive.

Endo: His view of this issue as a gamble is interesting. I suppose that no important life decisions would be made if we insisted on always knowing how things were going to turn out; there simply are no guarantees.

Ikeda: No one can avoid death—this is the only thing of which we can be absolutely certain. But it's also true that there are few people who give any earnest thought to this most fundamental issue of life and death. Nichiren Daishonin writes:

> Having received life, one cannot escape death. Yet though everyone, from the noblest, the emperor, on down to the lowliest commoner, recognizes this as a fact, not even one person in a thousand or ten thousand truly takes the matter seriously or grieves over it. (WND-I, 99)

These days, in particular, it seems that people increasingly adhere to the position on the matter that Buddhism describes as the doctrine of annihilation.

Saito: The doctrine of annihilation refers to the view that upon death life reverts to nonexistence. Perhaps it can be said that modern hedonism and intemperance, as well as the underlying sense of unease and pessimism that accompany these conditions, have their roots in this doctrine.

Suda: If you believe that life finishes with death, then the idea of merely seeking to enjoy oneself in the present would be quite seductive. There are of course those who resolve, "Since I only have one life, I will strive to live it to the fullest," but I think that in reality there are very few people who can truly face death without a sense of foreboding.

Overcoming the "Suffering of Death"

Ikeda: This is an extremely important theme in the field of terminal care. The way we spend our final days when confronted with the prospect of our imminent demise will differ dramatically depending on our view of life and death.

Endo: That's right. A book on this subject titled *After Death* was recently released. The book was written by the American psychotherapist Dr. Sukie Miller. Over the course of many years of caring for patients facing death, she apparently pursued research on the theme of life after death. In the book, the author chronicles her work as one of the first researchers to study the cross-cultural dimensions of life and death issues, and what happens after death.

Ikeda: Her keen sense of responsibility in helping patients grapple with the prospect of their own death is probably what started her thinking seriously about the issue.

Endo: That's right. Through observing many such patients, she understood that a patient's attitude toward death differs dramatically depending on his or her view of life and death.

Ikeda: When confronted with death, a person's vanity and pretensions are stripped away. Status, honor, wealth—these all count for nothing. We have no choice but to face death with nothing but our naked, unadorned selves.

The Buddhist scriptures describe demons who take one's clothing after death. I think this symbolizes the idea that worldly trappings and adornments lose all meaning when we die. Buddhism therefore urges that we polish and develop our lives through faith while we're healthy.

Endo: Dr. Miller talks about the death at age forty-five of a friend of hers of some twenty years. She writes that he thought much of intellectual achievement and viewed matters of the spirit and the like as childish fantasies. And she explains how he came to doubt any explanation not based on logic and empirical proof:

> When death became inevitable for James, he found—to the surprise of all who cared for him—that he had no tools, no comforts, no healing thoughts. Far from wondering what he faced, what aspect of reality he was entering, James trembled and shied away. Regarding death, he had no access to meaning and certainly none to comfort or reassurance.

Dr. Miller writes that "the idea of his inevitable demise inspired nothing but sheer terror in his heart."[10]

Ikeda: That is the stern reality of death. There may be some who live out their lives convinced that death is the absolute end of their existence. But what kind of comfort could such a person give to a close relative or family member who is suffering in the face of imminent death? Would such a conviction and view of life and death ultimately provide any hope?

The Buddhist perspective of life as existing eternally over the three existences of past, present and future not only brings hope to oneself, it can also encourage and give strength and hope to others.

Endo: It may well be that people seek some kind of immortality. In the United States, the process of cryogenics is being applied to preserve the human body in a frozen state. There are reportedly a number of facilities that offer this service.

When a person who has contracted in advance with one of the facilities dies, his or her body is frozen, the idea being that future scientific advances might some day bring that person back to life.

Saito: That sounds incredible, but I wonder if it is really possible to revive a human body that has been frozen. The entire scheme depends on future developments in medicine.

Endo: That's true. At present, experiments on animals haven't been successful. Even so, despite the considerable contract fee, there is a steady stream of applicants.

A procedure also exists where just the brain is removed and preserved in a frozen state. It attracted a lot of attention recently when a big-name celebrity signed up for this service.

Ikeda: This suggests just how deep-seated is the desire for immortality. I recall, incidentally, that the first Chinese emperor Shih Huang Ti of the Ch'in dynasty sought an elixir of perennial youth and eternal life.

Removing just the brain and preserving it is a thoroughly modern approach, in that it reflects the assumption that the brain is the storehouse of the mind and personality.

Endo: This is the notion that we took up in our first discussion on the "Life Span" chapter, that the mind is solely a neurological phenomenon.

THE BRAIN IS THE MIND'S "VENUE OF MANIFESTATION"

Ikeda: It is clear that the mind is closely related to the body and to the brain in particular. But it is debatable whether the mind exists only within the brain.

The British biologist Rupert Sheldrake uses a simple analogy to explain the relationship between memory and the brain. He likens it to the connection between televised images and sounds and the television receiver. You might, for instance, view something impressive on television; but once it passes you cannot find the same scene anywhere in the television. The television merely receives radio waves. An image will not appear without a receiver, but that doesn't mean that the image exists inside the television.

Saito: This analogy suggests that the mind, even if it functions through the mediation of the brain, is not housed in the brain itself.

Ikeda: That's correct. The mind and the brain cannot be separated. In that sense, there is a oneness. This is not to say, however, that they are the same or identical.

The relationship is perhaps best characterized as "two but not two." The spiritual aspect, which is the mind, and the physical aspect, which is the neurological phenomena, while distinct ("two"), function together as one ("not two"). This is the viewpoint of Buddhism. It could be said that the brain is the venue where the activity of the mind becomes manifest.

Endo: If a television set isn't in good working condition, the picture will not appear clearly. Likewise, someone whose brain is damaged will experience abnormal psychological phenomena. If a television set is completely broken, there will be no image at all. In the same way, when the brain cells are destroyed upon death, the venue where one's psychological and spiritual activity takes place is also destroyed. I think it can nevertheless be postulated that this merely represents the disappearance of their venue of manifestation, and that the functions of the mind actually continue even after death.

Suda: People with unflagging belief in the advancement of science seem to think that with further advances in research on the brain it will eventually become possible to explain all spiritual functions in terms of the neurological activities of the brain, even in areas that at this point defy explanation. But no matter how meticulously brain cells are studied, I don't think it will ever be possible to pinpoint the mind.

Ikeda: Take, for example, the case of someone thinking about the melody of Beethoven's "Ode to Joy." This psychological state would probably be accompanied by some kind of neurological phenomena. But even if that neurological activity were examined in great detail, one would not discover in it the melody itself of "Ode to Joy."

Suda: Still, there are many scientists who believe that this will someday become possible. Such belief is part and parcel of modern science. Often termed elementalism, this is the idea that you can get to the heart of anything by analyzing its minute constituent parts.

But, regardless of how closely the matter is probed, human life cannot be explained by analyzing the human body, just as simply combining all the necessary organs and tissues will not produce a human being.

Endo: One scholar criticizes this approach of science, saying, "Who could understand music only from an analysis of the composition of the instruments of an orchestra?"[11]

Neither Annihilation nor Eternity

Saito: It seems that many people view life and death based on this doctrine of annihilation, or what we might call "annihilationism." At the same time, the concept of an immortal soul is also prevalent in many different forms. This is the doctrine of eternity, the idea that there is an unchanging "soul" distinct from the body and that continues on forever. Both concepts, however, are rejected by Buddhism.

Ikeda: Yes. There is no such thing as a spiritlike entity that flutters through the air. All that really exists is the oneness of body and mind. When we die, our life, in a state of nonsubstantiality, becomes one with the universe. Both the doctrine of annihilation and the doctrine of eternity are flawed. Each is a biased view that accounts for only one side of the truth.

What, then, is the "eternal life" that the "Life Span" chapter explains? Let us take up that question in the next chapter.

Nichiren Daishonin says, "Only in the Life Span chapter of the essential teaching is to be found the vital doctrine needed to free one from the sufferings of birth and death" (WND-2, 985).

How we perceive the meaning of death and the meaning of life hinges completely on whether we are able to establish a correct view of life and death. Goethe says, "those who have no hope of another life are already dead in this one."[12]

We study Buddhism to live vibrantly and with eternal hope. Will death, which inevitably comes to each of us, be a time of dignity and honor? Or will we end in pitiful demise? This is completely reliant on how we live our lives right now, today. In that sense, the moment of death truly exists in the present.

NOTES

1. Karlis Osis and Erlendur Haraldsson, *At the Hour of Death*, third edition (New York: Hastings House, 1997), p. 15.

2. C. G. Jung, *Memories, Dreams, Reflections*, ed. Aniela Jaffé (New York: Pantheon Books, 1961), pp. 289–90.

3. Maggie Callanan and Patricia Kelley, *Final Gifts* (New York: Poseidon Press, 1992).

4. Susan Blackmore, *Dying To Live: Near-Death Experiences* (Buffalo, NY: Prometheus Books, 1993), p. 190.

5. River of Three Crossings: A river that the dead are said to cross after their demise. It has three points of crossing, shallow, deeper and deepest, and the place where a person crosses depends on the individual's karma.

6. Elisabeth Kübler-Ross, *Death Is of Vital Importance: On Life, Death and Life after Death* (Barrytown, NY: Station Hill Press, 1995), p. 103.

7. Raymond A. Moody, Jr., *Life after Life* (New York: Stackpole Books, 1976).

8. Elisabeth Kübler-Ross, *On Life after Death* (Berkeley, CA: Celestial Arts, 1991), p. 10.

9. Blaise Pascal, *Pensées,* trans. H. F. Stewart (New York: Pantheon Books, 1950), pp. 117–21.

10. Sukie Miller, *After Death* (New York: Simon and Schuster, 1997), p. 29.

11. Erwin Chargaff, *Heraclitean Fire: Sketches from a Life before Nature* (New York: The Rockefeller University Press, 1978), p. 170.

12. J. P. Eckermann, *Conversations with Goethe*, trans. Gisela C. O'Brien (New York: Fredcrick Ungar Publishing Co., 1964), p. 33.

10 The Meaning of Eternal Life

Saito: The more I think about the eternity of life, the more questions I find myself confronted with. Take for example, the concept of life after death. We know that once dead, the physical body starts to decompose. So what is it that remains? What is eternal? What continues on after death?

Endo: In the previous chapter, we pointed out that no evidence exists to support the view that once we die nothing remains of our existence. That is, we refuted the doctrine of annihilation. But neither is there evidence of an unchanging soul, distinct from our physical body, which continues on eternally.

Suda: In other words, as the rebuttal to the doctrine of eternity points out, there is no spiritlike substance that flits about hither and yon after death.

Saito: Nonetheless, it seems many people think that Buddhism ascribes to this idea of an eternal soul in its view of life after death. It often comes as quite a surprise to them to hear that Buddhism in fact rejects this view.

Suda: If not a soul, then just what continues on after death? This is a difficult question.

Ikeda: Josei Toda would often say that upon death our lives fuse with the universe. It's not a matter of there being a soul; rather, one's life, as an entity of the oneness of body and mind, returns to the universe. The universe itself is one great living entity. It is a vast ocean of life. It nurtures all things, gives all things life and enables them to function. When things die, they return again to its embrace and receive new vitality.

There is a boundless and overflowing ocean of life always in motion. As it moves and changes, it enacts the rhythm of life and death. Our individual lives are like waves produced from the great ocean that is the universe; the emergence of a wave is "life," and its abatement is "death." This rhythm repeats eternally.

This is not only true of the lives of people. Nichiren Daishonin says, "No phenomena—either heaven or earth, yin or yang,[1] the sun or the moon, the five planets,[2] or any of the worlds from hell to Buddhahood—are free from the two phases of life and death" (WND-1, 216). "heaven or earth, yin or yang, the sun or the moon, the five planets" refers to the realm of celestial bodies. Stars also experience birth and death. They have a life span. The Milky Way was born and it, too, will die; its life is limited. The laws of birth and death dictate this. The same holds true in the realm of the microscopic world. Each of the Ten Worlds from hell to Buddhahood, in all phenomena, experiences birth and death. For example, the state of hell may manifest in life at one time and in death at another.

The Daishonin writes to his follower Nanjo Tokimitsu about his late father, "When he was alive, he was a Buddha in life, and now he is a Buddha in death. He is a Buddha in both life and death" (WND-1, 456), indicating that the effect of Buddhahood he had attained in his life would continue even after death.

All things in the universe weave an eternal rhythm of life and death. What, then, is the state after death in which one fuses with the universe? Let's try to investigate this further. Why don't we first consider the moment of death, which is the transition from life to death.

The Disintegration
of the Five Components

Suda: Perhaps we could start by looking at the "Cautions on the Moment of Death."[3] As the title suggests, this document, which is a record of sermons delivered by Nichikan, the twenty-sixth high priest of Taiseki-ji, contains several things to bear in mind at the time of one's death.

Endo: These include, for example, "People who are intoxicated should not come near the ailing person," and "The person should not be surrounded by large numbers of boisterous people."[4] What this basically means is that one must take care not to interrupt the dying person's tranquillity.

Ikeda: Our frame of mind, at the moment of death is a major determinant in which of the Ten Worlds in the universe we will enter. Therefore, Nichikan warns that every precaution should be taken to ensure that the dying person can single-mindedly focus on the Mystic Law.

Saito: To enable the person to concentrate on the Mystic Law, he advises against such things as placing items of sentimental value nearby to which the sick person might feel a strong attachment or engaging in discussion that may arouse feelings of anxiety or causing them to become excited.[5]

Suda: He also says, "Even after the person has stopped breathing, you should continue chanting daimoku near the deceased." That's because, he explains, "even after death the fundamental mind remains."[6] Even though in Nichikan's day the cessation of breathing was held to constitute the moment of death, he asserts that for a while thereafter the "fundamental mind" remains. He says that one should allow that mind to hear the sound of daimoku.

Endo: This suggests that the transition from life to death does not take place in a single instant but occurs gradually.

Ikeda: Yes. Death is seen as a process that continues over a certain period of time.

Saito: In terms of the physical body, that process involves a transformation from "sentience" to "insentience." In the course of this process, the possibility exists that, due to some circumstance, the person may return to life. But it seems that once a certain stage is passed, that is no longer possible. The near-death experiences that we have discussed earlier of course involve people who were at the stage when it was still possible to return.

Suda: After passing the point at which return to life is no longer possible, the person finally proceeds toward complete death. This may be the point that has since ancient times been described in Buddhism as the "river of three crossings."[7]

Ikeda: Just what takes place when a living entity makes the transition from life to death? Buddhism after all views the physical and spiritual functions of a living entity as a temporary union.

Endo: That's what's referred to as the "temporary union of the five components."

Ikeda: Of the five components, form indicates the physical dimension of life. Perception, conception, volition and consciousness indicate life's spiritual functions.

[Perception is the spiritual function that enables one to take in stimuli from the external world via the "six sense organs"—the five sense organs plus mind, which integrates the impressions of the five senses. Conception is the function of creating mental ideas about what has been perceived. Volition is the spiritual function to take some action based on conception. And consciousness is the fundamental spiritual activity that integrates the functions of perception, conception and volition.]

Life has the power to harmoniously fuse these physical and spiritual functions. It harmonizes them, unifies them, and enables proactive engagement with respect to the external world.

Endo: Certainly, viewed strictly in terms of the physical aspect, our bodies are an amalgam of materials existing in the universe.

Ikeda: According to one source, the cells of the human body number sixty trillion. As they age, old cells are constantly being replaced by new ones. In other words, the life and death process is taking place constantly on the cellular level. Here we see once again the laws of birth and death at work.

At the same time, a single living entity strictly integrates and governs these cells, allowing itself to carry out activity. When death approaches, the integrative power of life is lost and the five components, which have hitherto been held in a state of temporary union, disintegrate. Life's physical and spiritual functions subsequently recede into latency, and the union of the five elements[8] is also lost.

Suda: Nichikan's "Cautions on the Moment of Death" reads, "When the wind of the 'devil of extinction' enters the body, the bone and flesh separate."[9] This seems to suggest that the dying person senses a wind passing through the body as the five elements all go their separate ways. The annals of near-death experiences in fact include such accounts. The distress that one experiences at that time is termed the suffering of death. Nichikan says of the suffering of death, "If people have accumulated good karma, they will not suffer a great deal."

Ikeda: Even if the only benefit of faith in the Mystic Law was to be free of suffering at the time of death, it would still be wonderful.

CHANGES IN APPEARANCE AT THE TIME OF DEATH CORROBORATED BY MEDICINE

Saito: In the SGI, there are countless reports of people who have died with a look of peace and ease at the final moment. You frequently hear about people who, though they may have died of illness, experienced no pain; or who, although they died due to some untoward accident, breathed their last with a peaceful look as though simply dozing off.

Suda: I once heard someone who worked for a funeral home remark: "No matter how you might try to improve the appearance of a corpse with cosmetics, you cannot fundamentally alter the person's visage at death. No amount of money or status can acquire a good appearance at that time. Having seen a great many people in life and in death, it seems to me that, ultimately, how a person looks at death reflects how he or she has lived."

At funerals for SGI members, there is definitely something different about the general atmosphere, too. Observers note the heartfelt mourning of other members and are often left with the sense that the deceased must have truly treasured others.

Endo: In particular, the funerals for individuals who have worked hard to help others are attended by endless streams of mourners. You often hear about how family members or people in the community who are not SGI members gain a new understanding of the great achievements of the deceased by the large numbers of people who come to pay their last respects, even though the deceased may not have had any special standing in society.

Ikeda: Such people propagate the Daishonin's teaching even in death. This is truly wonderful. They are genuine champions of the people. A passage in the "Encouragements of the Bodhisattva Universal Worthy" chapter of the Lotus Sutra indicates just this when it says: "When the lives of these persons come to an end, they will be received into the hands of a thousand Buddhas, who will free them from all fear and keep them from falling into the evil paths of existence" (LSOC, 363).

A thousand Buddhas applaud those champions of the people who have fought hard for kosen-rufu. Here, a "thousand Buddhas" could be said to point to the many people who chant daimoku for the sake of the deceased.

Of course, the important thing is not how many see a person off but that the deceased be embraced by sincere daimoku. There is no greater way to embark on the journey for Eagle Peak than to be sent off from this life by the sincere daimoku of one's fellow members.

Suda: I heard the experience of Harue Yamaguchi of Hachioji, Tokyo, who died in 1996. The funeral of Mrs. Yamaguchi, who had fought for many years for kosen-rufu in her community, was attended by an extraordinary number of people.

She was sixty-five when she died, but the look on her face was so peaceful that it became the talk of the community. During the five days her body lay at home while funeral ceremonies were under way, she reportedly grew lovelier by the day. The wrinkles on her forehead vanished, and she looked as though she had actually grown younger. On viewing her, one person even remarked in surprise: "She is smiling like a child. That's truly how she looks."

Mrs. Yamaguchi, who joined the Soka Gakkai in 1955, had undergone surgery to remove a tumor from her lung eight years before her death. But even after that, she continued energetically carrying out activities in the Hachioji area.

Ikeda: I have heard a great deal about her. She was deeply trusted by many people not only in Hachioji but throughout western Tokyo.

Suda: Whenever she had a moment, she would talk with local members or call someone to offer encouragement. She was so lively and high-spirited, people sometimes would ask her, "How do you manage to always be so bright and cheerful?" To which she would reply: "It's because I chant daimoku to help people overcome their problems. It seems to me that the more I encourage others, the more abundant my own life force becomes."

Because she was always brightly encouraging other members, people were surprised at her sudden death. While alive, she had often said, "Life is eternal. I would like to die quickly, the way the petals of a flower scatter after it has bloomed. I don't want to become a burden for others."

When she died, she quickly lost consciousness and experienced no suffering. As has already been noted, she also had a truly peaceful countenance—with the same look on her face she had when encouraging someone.

Saito: Her appearance in death was indeed a source of great encouragement for everyone.

Endo: Nichiren Daishonin indicates that our appearance at the moment of death reveals our condition of life. He says, for example, that the expression of a virtuous person at the time of death will be "pure and white" and that person's body will be "as light as a goose feather and as soft and pliable as cotton"(WND-1, 949).

A specialist in terminal care once explained to me the circumstances in which a person's facial color improves upon death. When a person dies with a sense of satisfaction and peace of mind, generally the blood vessels will be dilated and unconstricted. The formation of blood clots and hardening of the muscles take comparatively longer to occur. As a result, the person's face brightens while the body remains supple.

On the other hand, when someone dies with feelings of chagrin and regret, in a state of suffering, the body becomes like a clenched fist and consequently the blood vessels are constricted. Then the clotting of the blood and hardening of the muscles begin sooner, so that the person's appearance darkens as the body stiffens.

While on a different level from attaining Buddhahood, it seems that, in general, the state of a person's mind upon encountering death is reflected in his or her appearance.

Ikeda: This suggests that, to some extent, medicine can explain the differences in people's appearance at death.

Of course, since the benefit of the Mystic Law purifies our lives, those who really exert themselves in faith have absolutely no need to fear death. Even if someone should die in an accident, as long as the person has maintained strong faith in life, he or she will attain Buddhahood without fail.

THE ENERGY OF KARMA CONTINUES AFTER DEATH

Saito: We still haven't answered the question of what it is that continues after death. Specifically, Buddhism explains the concept of selflessness, denying the existence of a soul after death. It teaches that there is no "self" that lives as an eternally unchanging entity. At the same time, it teaches that life continues after death, and in a qualified sense recognizes the concept of transmigration. We need to consider whether these two views are contradictory.

Ikeda: This is a very old question posed since the dawn of Buddhism. While it would be very interesting to explore the historical development of thought on the matter, I think that because of the complexity, we should perhaps pass over this discussion for now. I would just like to note that the concept of nonsubstantiality and the investigations of the Consciousness-Only school[10] involve a close awareness of this issue.

What continues after death? Shakyamuni's conclusion is that karma continues. Our circumstances in this present life are the effect of our past actions (karma), and our actions in the present determine the circumstances of our lives in the future. In other words, the influence of our actions carries on from one existence to the next transcending life and death.

Saito: Karma, as indicated by the concept of the three categories of action—thoughts, words and deeds—means both physical and spiritual activity. What we have done, what we have said, what we have thought—the consequences of all these actions continue into the future unabated. When you think about it, this is an extremely strict perspective on causality.

Ikeda: That's right. Essentially, it is the energy of karma that continues beyond birth and death.

Endo: The mention of energy calls to mind the principle of the conservation of energy, a law of physics that holds that energy can be neither created nor destroyed. While thermal energy may change into kinetic energy, and potential energy may turn into electrical energy, energy cannot suddenly be produced from nothing. Nor can existing energy simply disappear. It only changes form.

Suda: Even matter is nothing more than a stable form of energy. From that standpoint, some claim that energy is the ultimate reality.

Ikeda: the French art historian René Huyghe discusses this in his important work *Formes et forces* (Forms and Forces).[11]

According to Huyghe, there is a dynamic of form and energy operating on all levels of existence, from the atomic to the universal. The high-level spiritual activity of artistic creation is no exception.

He proposes that, through some function, force produces a stable form. Should the energy contained in the form remain active, it will eventually take another form or will return to a state of pure force. In terms of the Buddhist concept of the three truths, force represents the truth of nonsubstantiality, and form the truth of temporary existence

Saito: So with respect to life and death, we can say that life is when the energy of karma temporarily assumes a fixed form, and death is when the form breaks down and becomes one with the life current of the universe as a flow of pure energy.

Ikeda: Generally speaking, that comparison is probably appropriate. Of course, form changes continually from moment to moment.

Endo: Speaking of the principle of conservation of energy, we can speak loosely of a principle of conservation of karma.

Ikeda: I find it deeply intriguing that Huyghe identifies wave motion as an important factor in energy's transformation into form. He postulates that form is determined by the various wave, vibratory and rhythmic attributes of force. This is based on well-known experiments in cymatics.

Saito: Cymatic experiments involve imparting a fixed vibration to liquids, or to dust or metal shavings spread over a disc-shaped surface. When a certain frequency is reached, the particles describe a particular pattern on the surface. The patterns include those of helices, snails, dendriforms or tree-like patterns, hexagons and scales.

Ikeda: They also often manifest the shapes of such organic substances as sprigs of coral, broad beans, shells, fish skeletons, turtle shells, and the hexagonal loculi of a beehive. Based on these experiments, Huyghe speculates that all matter is made up of energy and a particular vibration or rhythm. His insight is that each living entity may have a particular "vibratory reality." [12]

Of course, the energy of karma is different from physical energy. It is latent life energy that influences both physical and spiritual aspects of our being. So we should always remember that this is merely an analogy for helping us understand the true nature of life and death.

THE ALAYA-CONSCIOUSNESS: A VEHICLE FOR THE CONTINUATION OF KARMA

Suda: This karmic energy is said to continue on, transcending life and death. Since there is both positive karma and negative karma, each living being's present circumstances are determined by its karmic energy of both good and evil from previous existences.

Ikeda: That's right. One's present form of life is determined by a balance of positive and negative energies.

Endo: As an effect of this karmic energy a person might, for example, be born with superior intelligence or good looks. Because this is an effect that appears in the subject, it is termed a "life effect." By contrast, to be born, for example, in a home that is the scene of constant fighting is an "environmental effect."
President Toda once said:

> All of our actions in past existences are contained in their entirety in our lives. This is why Buddhism is so important. While we might want to say, "What I did in the past is irrelevant. I was born with a clean slate," we cannot get away from our past so easily.
> "Why was I born poor?" "Why aren't I smarter?" "Why is my business failing even though I am working as hard as I can?" The answer to all of these questions is to be found in our past lives. Although the cause is in our past lives, Nichiren Buddhism teaches how we can break through such obstacles.
> Looking at our lives from a physiological standpoint, in the course of several years every cell in our body, from the center of our eyeballs to the marrow of our

bones, is replaced. This is recognized by medical science. On that basis, you could perhaps argue that you are not liable for a debt incurred five years earlier. But while we might like to be absolved of our debts, the debt collector will come without fail. Similarly, we have no choice but to take responsibility for our past actions.

While we can readily understand this from a logical standpoint, when we are faced with it as an actual problem we find ourselves at a loss. In this connection, Nichiren Daishonin says that those who worship the Gohonzon, though they may be people of little virtue or people who committed great offenses in the past, will be completely absolved, and will receive the same effects as they would if they had made many good causes in the past (OTT, 129). That's why faith is so important.[13]

Saito: The karmic energy that sustains our lives does not all become manifest at once in the present. But sooner or later that energy will produce some kind of effect, though it may not be until a future lifetime. In terms of the theme of our discussion this time, the question is how this karmic energy continues on after death.

Ikeda: I think the doctrine of the nine consciousnesses speaks most aptly to this subject.

Saito: Indeed. The Consciousness-Only doctrine clarifies the interior dimension of human life to such an extent that it has had an important influence on modern psychology. In the first place, it resolves the seeming contradiction between the view of the self as empty and the concept of transmigration.

Suda: Of the nine consciousnesses, the first five are based on the senses of sight, hearing, smell, taste and touch. These are functions of perception and awareness. The sixth consciousness integrates these five consciousnesses into coherent images; it is the function of intelligence to make inferences and judgments about things. It is primarily with these six functions of life that we perform our daily activities.

Endo: Going further, we come to the seventh or *mano*-consciousness and the eighth or *alaya*-consciousness, which we refer to as the realm of the subconscious.

Ikeda: The eighth consciousness ensures the continuity of karma from one lifetime to the next.

Saito: The functions of all the consciousnesses up through the seventh consciousness cease upon death. But the *alaya*-consciousness continues to function throughout past, present and future. The original meaning of the Sanskrit term *alaya* is storehouse or repository. Since it is where karma is stored, it is also known as the storehouse consciousness.

Ikeda: Incidentally, it is said that the word *Himalaya* is a combination of *hima* or "snow" and *alaya* or "storehouse."

All of our karma accumulates in the *alaya*-consciousness as though in a storehouse. Both good karma and bad karma are stored there like seeds in a granary. The term *storehouse* conjures the image of an actual structure into which things of substance can be placed. But in fact it may be more accurate to say that the life-current of karmic energy itself constitutes the eighth consciousness.

Saito: A Buddhist text likens the eighth consciousness to a rushing stream.

Ikeda: Moreover, the eighth consciousness transcends the boundaries of the individual and interacts with the karmic energy of others. On the inner dimension of life, this latent karmic energy merges with the latent energy of one's family, one's ethnic group, and humankind, and also with that of animals and plants.

Suda: That's a magnificent image. That's why the human revolution of one person also changes the destiny of the person's family and society. A positive change in the karmic energy in the depths of one person's life becomes a cogwheel for change in the karma in the lives of others.

Ikeda: There are methods for changing the karmic energy in one's life from negative to positive through steadily accumulating good causes. But in reality that is not practical; sooner or later we are liable to do something that erases the good causes we have made, just as in piling up stones we can only get so high before we upset what we have worked to create. That is particularly so in an age when society to its very depths is swirling with negative energy.

By contrast, the Lotus Sutra teaches how, by activating the ninth consciousness, which lies at the utmost depths of our beings and is fundamentally free of impurity, we can at once change both the negative and positive karmic energy in our lives into supremely positive energy. The ninth consciousness is the universal life that underlies the eighth consciousness and every other facet of our lives.

The eternal Buddha of "Life Span," the sixteenth chapter, could be called an expression in human form of this pure consciousness that has no limits in time and space. When we activate this fundamentally pure consciousness, the energy of all life's good and evil karma is directed toward value creation; and the mind or consciousness of our ethnic group and of humankind is infused with the life current of compassion and wisdom.

Saito: The Daishonin calls this fundamentally pure consciousness the "unchanging reality that reigns over all of life's functions" (WND-1, 832). It is the Gohonzon, which exists "only within the mortal flesh of us ordinary people who embrace the Lotus Sutra and chant Nam-myoho-renge-kyo" (WND-1, 832).

Endo: The Daishonin also says, "The five characters of Myoho-renge-kyo represent the ninth consciousness" (OTT, 223). This is saying that Myoho-renge-kyo itself is the universal life.

THE TEN WORLDS ARE "LIFE WAVELENGTHS"

Ikeda: So, life after death means that the life current of karma, in a state of nonsubstantiality, merges with the universal life.

Since it is nonsubstantial, it is neither existence nor nonexistence. Nor can it be said to exist in any particular place in the universe. Rather, it becomes one with the life of the universe in its entirety.

Suda: President Toda humorously put it this way: "The lives of your grandfather and your grandmother exist in the universe but that doesn't mean that they are out there somewhere holding hands. They're there. It's just that there's no way of pinpointing a single location for them."[14]

Ikeda: Since they are in no particular place in the universe, you cannot simply say that they exist. On the other hand, they will be born again in response to the appropriate causes; so you cannot say that they do not exist either. Life after death transcends the concepts of both existence and nonexistence.

This might seem to defy common sense, but we in fact find similar concepts in areas of physics such as quantum mechanics. The fact that light has properties both of a wave and of a particle seems to fly in the face of common sense.

Suda: It does seem contradictory to say that something is both a wave and a particle. That light has the properties of both—

sometimes displaying those of a wave and sometimes those of a particle—confounds ordinary logic.

Saito: President Toda used the analogy of radio waves to explain life in the state of nonsubstantiality. In this day and age, it may make more sense to use the example of televisions.

Ikeda: Yes. Broadcast waves of various wavelengths from stations in many different countries crisscross the world. When you take a television receiver and tune it to the wavelength of the broadcast you want to receive, you hear sound and see images. Through the *relation* or *external cause* of the receiver, the silent and invisible waves become audible sounds and visible images. It could be said that this represents the transformation of wavelengths from death to life.

Suda: The broadcaster breaks down sounds and images into various streams of data and transmits them as radio waves. Through the television receiver they are reconstituted and the original sounds and images reappear. Although the sound and image are broken down into unintelligible signals, the original composite is later reconstituted and reappears. This seems analogous to the temporary union of the five components.

Ikeda: We are born with a body and mind (a life effect) and in an environment (an environmental effect) that matches our own karmic energy. Of course, life and environment are in fact inseparable. For they both are manifestations (effects) of our own karmic energy.

President Toda often used the example of the Japanese board game *go* to explain the transition from death to life. In an important title match between two masters, a single game can take as long as two days to complete. If on the first day there is no winner, the play is suspended. This corresponds to the moment of death. But on the following day, the match is resumed with the stones laid out exactly as they had been at the end of play the day before. This corresponds to the next life. There is continuity. We aren't born with a blank slate; rather, we continue where we left off. That's why the expression "to be born anew"[15] is something of a misnomer.

President Toda emphasized this point, saying: "We don't say that a partially used stick of incense or a cigarette is reborn when we relight it. They simply resume burning from the point where they had stopped before. When we die and are reborn, our lives, just as they are, continue."[16]

"This very body continues on," he added, thumping his chest for emphasis. In other words, he was saying that the continuity of our lives, consisting of entities of body and mind, is not impeded by our going through death and rebirth.

At any given moment our lives are in one of the Ten Worlds. President Toda compared the differences between the Ten Worlds to the differences between various wavelengths, calling them differences in life wavelength.

The Ten Worlds also exist in the great life of the universe. If your state of life at the last moment is that of the world of hell, then your life fuses with the world of hell in the universal life; if you are in rapture, your life fuses with the world of rapture (heaven).

Endo: In other words, it merges with the world in the universal life whose wavelength matches that of your own life.

Saito: Life wavelength — that reminds me of Huyghe's comment that all matter ultimately is composed of energy and a particular rhythm.

Suda: As to the manner in which our lives fuse with the universe, even though we speak of the Ten Worlds inherent in the universal life, they do not, as we have discussed previously, exist as actual places somewhere in the universe. It's not the case, for example, that the eight cold hells lie beyond Pluto, or that the world of rapture is next to Venus. Rather, they permeate the entirety of the universal life.

Ikeda: Whether we are speaking of the world of hell, the world of rapture or the world of Buddhahood, each pervades the entire universe. This is a point we covered in discussing the principle of the mutual possession of the Ten Worlds.

When our lives become one with the world corresponding to our state of life at the moment of death, we become one with the entire universe. For precisely this reason, as long as the appropriate external cause exists, there is no restriction on when and where in the universe we can reappear. We are reborn with the body and mind and in the environment most suited to us.

Endo: President Toda said of this life that pervades the entire universe: "At some stage, life comes to concentrate in one part of the universe. It is then that it is born as a living being." Isn't he saying that when the proper external cause is present, our lives, which pervade the universe, instantaneously become concentrated in one particular place and manifest as distinct living entities?

Ikeda: That is one explanation.

At the same time, we should bear in mind that "pervading the entire universe" does not indicate that life is expansive, nor does existing in a life form as tiny as the head of a pin mean that life is small and narrow.

Saito: In his writing, "The Unanimous Declaration by the Buddhas," the Daishonin says: "One may put it inside a mustard seed and the mustard seed will not be stretched nor will the mind be cramped thereby. One may put it in the vast heavens and the heavens will not be too broad for it nor the mind too narrow to fill them" (WND-2, 843).

Ikeda: In other words, it's not a matter of something widely spread out over infinite space suddenly concentrating together in a discrete location. After death and before rebirth, life is in a state of latency; it is not dispersed. Since the entire universe is one living entity, a life that is one with the universe is never distant and can manifest anywhere in an instant. We must be clear on this point.

Endo: It's a rather difficult concept.

CAN THE DECEASED FEEL SUFFERING OR JOY?

> *When living beings witness the end of a kalpa*
> *and all is consumed in a great fire,*
> *this, my land, remains safe and tranquil,*
> *constantly filled with heavenly and human beings.*
> *The halls and pavilions in its gardens and groves*
> *are adorned with various kinds of gems.*
> *Jeweled trees abound in flowers and fruit*
> *where living beings enjoy themselves at ease.*
> *The gods strike heavenly drums,*
> *constantly making many kinds of music.*
> *Mandarava blossoms rain down,*
> *scattering over the Buddha and the great assembly.*
> (LSOC, 272)

Suda: If the life of someone who has died is in a state of latency and has neither physical nor spiritual properties, then is it possible that the deceased feel suffering or joy?

Ikeda: Indeed, they do.

President Toda once said that it would be interesting if a device were invented that could make it possible to see life after death. He elaborated: "If it were possible to see the life of a deceased father or sibling that had become one with the universe, you would find some there shrieking in agony and some filled with joy. But the deceased entity, which abides in a state of suffering or joy depending on its karma, is not visible, having neither form nor color. Unless you understand this view of nonsubstantiality, you cannot grasp the essence of the Buddhist doctrine of life."[17]

Saito: It's been said that the great inventor Thomas Edison had a keen interest in life after death. Drawing inferences based on the scientific principle that energy continues to exist eternally, he speculated that an "indestructible and undying personality" continued to exist after death. In 1920, he reportedly announced that "he was working on a sensitive apparatus with which to detect and record the myriad infinitesimal, immortal monads 'prowling through the ether of space.'"[18]

Ikeda: That's very interesting. If the king of invention had succeeded in building such a device, that would have been the greatest invention in human history.

Saito: He wrote: "The reason why you are you and I am Edison is because we have different swarms or groups or whatever you wish to call them, of entities."[19] From the standpoint of Buddhism, this view could perhaps be expressed as follows: The individuality of each living entity is due to differences in the composition of the five components, reflecting its karmic energy.

Incidentally, Edison's last words were, "It is very beautiful over there."[20] Edison, who had been in a coma state, suddenly opened his eyes and uttered these words to his wife.

Ikeda: These words are very suggestive. At any rate, if such a device as Edison described were built, then we would probably find that the deceased experience good and bad life feelings according to their respective karma.

Suda: What would be doing the experiencing?

Ikeda: That would be the life current itself of the individual, which had been colored by the person's good or bad karma. Apart from this life current, which changes from moment to moment, there is no self.

Moreover, this current is constantly interacting with other life currents in a relation of dependent origination. The life current therefore has no self, no fixed substance. But at the same time, the individual self definitely has its own life current.

Saito: In light of the concepts of nonsubstantiality and "no self," which try to clarify the true aspect of our lives, perhaps we could say that this life current is the self.

Ikeda: While activity is the main characteristic of one's life current while alive, one's life current after death is passive. From that standpoint, we cannot independently change our state of life after we have died. For instance, while we are alive, even if our underlying tendency is that of the world of hell, through contact with other people and the influence of the environment, we may experience a variety of different worlds—heaven, humanity and so on. But in the state of death we lose touch with external stimuli, reverting to the underlying state of our own lives.

Upon death, a life that has the world of hell as its underlying tendency becomes one with the world of hell existing in the universe and is filled with unmitigated pain and suffering. A life that has the world of hunger as its underlying tendency will be tormented by a sense of hunger even more overwhelming than any experienced while alive.

The self of a life that has the world of heaven or humanity as its fundamental tendency will, after passing through the suffering of death, regain its peace and tranquillity and be gently embraced, experiencing a sense of fulfillment and satisfaction.

Lives that have Buddhahood as their fundamental tendency will upon death instantaneously become one with the world of Buddhahood in the universe and be infused with a sense of great and brilliant joy. Perceiving that the entire universe is the Buddha land, they will enjoy the state of life described by the passages: "This, my land, remains safe and tranquil, constantly filled with heavenly and human beings" and "living beings enjoy themselves at ease. The gods strike heavenly drums" (LSOC, 272). In accord with their sworn prayer, their lives will function as one with the eternal Buddha in both life and death. Let's talk further about life and death in regards to the world of Buddhahood in the next chapter when we sum up the "Life Span" chapter.

CAN YOU CHANGE YOUR STATE OF LIFE AFTER DEATH?

> The countless entities in the three thousand realms which are undergoing the process of birth, duration, change and extinction are all in themselves embodiments of [the Thus Come One's] transcendental powers.
>
> But in the view of Nichiren and his followers, the realization and understanding of the concept of attainment of Buddhahood in one's present form is what is meant by the words "the Thus Come One's secret and his transcendental powers." For outside of the attainment of Buddhahood, there is no "secret" and no "transcendental powers." (OTT, 125)

Endo: Since life after death is devoid of activity, can nothing change the state of a person who dies and fuses with the world of hell?

Ikeda: That's why we need to struggle to do our human revolution in this life. If you spend your life in vain, then, even though you may regret it for all eternity, it will be too late to do anything about it.

But the power of the Mystic Law is enormous. The daimoku that we chant reaches the lives of the deceased latent in the universal life. President Toda said: "The power of daimoku is immense. It can cause a life laboring under painful karma to experience a peaceful and dreamlike state as though frolicking in a garden of flowers."[21] The sound of our voices chanting daimoku resonates throughout the entire universe.

Endo: Daimoku chanted by those who are alive reaches the lives of those who have died. If that is true, do the lives of those who have died then come to function on behalf of those who are living?

Saito: Life after death is in a state of latency; it has lost all activity. Accordingly, it would seem to follow that the lives of those who have died could not function in any active capacity.

Suda: That's indeed so. There are religions that solicit money from their adherents by telling them, for example, that the spirit of their ancestor wants this or that. That is reprehensible.

Endo: Yes. But many people have reported actually hearing the voice of a deceased person or seeing a ghost. It would seem that we cannot deny all such accounts as illusions or hoaxes.

Ikeda: President Toda once told someone who claimed to have heard the voice of a dead person: "Living people have the Ten Worlds in their lives. So it may happen that someone will sense the 'life wavelength' of someone who has died and whose life has become one with the universe. I think that you sensed this as audible words."

With a weak life force, a person will simply become a receiver like a radio or television, passively picking up such life wavelengths from beyond. On the other hand, as President Toda pointed out to the person, if he developed his life force through strong faith, then he could broadcast the wavelength of his own world of Buddhahood and bring the deceased person peace and repose. He further declared: "Up to now you were deceived into thinking that your deceased wife or your deceased ancestors were spirits. You must not be fooled by such deceptions. If this were in fact the case, then the whole world would be full of ghosts, and it would be so crowded you could not move."[22]

At any rate, the universe eternally enacts the rhythm of life and death. The infinite currents of the ocean of life surge high one moment and quiet down the next, never stopping for an instant, repeating the drama of life and death. The "Life Span" chapter explains that the driving force behind this is the "transcendental power" of the Thus Come One.

In *The Record of the Orally Transmitted Teachings,* the Daishonin says, "The countless things in the three thousand realms that undergo the process of birth, abiding, change, and extinction, are all in themselves embodiments of transcendental powers" (OTT, 125).

In essence, the "Life Span" chapter exhorts us to develop these transcendental powers, this great, fundamental vitality, in ourselves. The important thing—whether we are speaking about transcendental powers or the universal life—is that we can only attain this through wholeheartedly taking action for kosen-rufu. It's a matter of practicing with the spirit of "single-mindedly desiring to see the Buddha, not hesitating even if it costs them their lives" (LSOC, 271).

President Toda battled difficulties head-on and was imprisoned. It was there that he attained enlightenment. Based on a sense of mission transcending life and death, he vowed to give his life for the sake of kosen-rufu and as a result awakened to the true aspect of life and death.

The faith to continue tirelessly struggling for kosen-rufu throughout past, present and future is itself the great ship for embarking on an eternal voyage across the ocean of life and death.

Notes

1. Yin and yang: Two complementary principles of ancient Chinese philosophy that make up all aspects and phenomena of life. Yin is seen as earth, female, dark and absorbing; yang is heaven, male, light and penetrating. Their interaction was thought to affect the destiny of all things.

2. Five planets: Mercury, Venus, Mars, Jupiter and Saturn. The more distant planets were undetected in thirteenth-century Japan.

3. *Fuji Shugaku yoshu* (Essential Writings of the Fuji School), ed. Hori Nichiko (Tokyo: Seikyo Shimbunsha, 1977), vol. 3.

4. Ibid., p. 264.

5. Ibid.

6. Ibid., p. 265.

7. River of three crossings: A river that the dead are said to cross after their demise. It has three points of crossing, shallow, deeper and deepest, and the place where a person crosses depends on the individual's karma.

8. Five elements: The five constituents of all things in the universe, according to ancient Indian belief; earth, water, fire, wind and space. The first four correspond respectively to the physical states of solid, liquid, heat and gas. Space, here, is interpreted as integrating the other four elements.

9. *Fuji Shugaku yoshu*, ibid., p. 265.

10. Consciousness-Only school: (Skt *Vijnanavada*) Also called the Yogachara school, one of the two major Mahayana schools in India, along with the Madhyamika school. Maitreya, around 270–350, is regarded as the founder. Maitreya's doctrine, the Consciousness-Only doctrine, was expounded in his one-hundred-fascicle "Yugashiji Ron" ("Treatise on the Stages of Yoga Practice") and was further developed by his disciples Asanga and Vasubandhu in the fifth century. This school upholds the concept that all phenomena arise from the *vijnana* or consciousness and that the basis of all functions of consciousness is the *alaya-vijnana* or *alaya*-consciousness.

11. René Huyghe, *Formes et forces: de l'atome à rembrant* (Forms and Forces: From the Atom to Rembrandt) (Paris: Flammarion, 1971).

12. Ibid., p. 356.

13. *Toda Josei zenshu* (Collected Writings of Josei Toda) (Tokyo: Seikyo Shimbunsha, 1985), vol. 5, p. 412.

14. *Toda Josei zenshu* (Tokyo: Seikyo Shimbunsha, 1982), vol. 2, p. 190.

15. Born anew: This is the literal translation of the Japanese term commonly used to mean rebirth.

16. *Toda Josei zenshu*, vol. 5, p. 411.

17. *Toda Josei zenshu* (Tokyo: Seikyo Shimbunsha, 1984), vol. 4, pp. 253–54.

18. Neil Baldwin, *Edison: Inventing the Century* (New York: Hyperion, 1995), p. 377.

19. Ibid.

20. Ibid., p. 407.

21. *Toda Josei zenshu*, vol. 4, pp. 261–62.

22. *Toda Josei zenshu*, vol. 2, pp. 169–70.

11   Eternally Advancing
With Great Life Force

Ikeda: Let's continue to explore eternal life. I hope that in this lifetime, we can firmly grasp this principle.

Endo: There recently appeared in Japan a rather unusual book titled *The Truth About the Dead: The World of English Epitaphs* (*Shisha no Honne: Eikoku Bohimei no Sekai*). The author discusses numerous epitaphs on the gravestones in British cemeteries.

Saito: Could you give some examples?

Endo: Well, one epitaph for instance reads, "Here lies my wife. / Here let her lie! / Now she's at rest / And so am I."[1]

Ikeda: What brutal honesty!

Suda: From the sound of it, she must have been quite hard on him!

Endo: There are also epitaphs expressing a wife's feelings of bitterness at having been preceded in death by her husband. "To follow you I'm not content. / How do I know which way you went?"[2]

Saito: That's very blunt.

Ikeda: Just because people are married doesn't guarantee that they will be together in the afterlife. The fact remains that we are born alone and we have to die alone. It's harsh, but true.

Buddhism, however, teaches that through the power of the Mystic Law we can be born along with our loved ones in lifetime after lifetime, over eternity.

Suda: Surely there are also many epitaphs expressing endearing sentiments.

Endo: Yes, of course.

Ikeda: What kind of epitaph is most common?

Endo: I don't know the exact statistics, but according to the book, the following is typical of many of the epitaphs found on English graves over the last more than two hundred years: "As I was so are you and as I am so shall you be."[3]

Saito: That's quite philosophical. It says to the person viewing the headstone: "Someday you too will be dead."

Endo: Along the same general lines, another epitaph reads: "Don't stare, / Pass me by. / You'll soon lie here, / Same as I."[4]

NOTHING IS AS CERTAIN AS DEATH

Suda: That epitaph is really a *memento mori*, a reminder of mortality. It calls to mind the oft-cited passage in the "Heritage of the Ultimate Law of Life" where the Daishonin urges us to exert ourselves in faith "with the profound insight that now is the last moment" of our life (WND-I, 216). It would make more sense to me if he said "with the *determination* that now is the last moment of our life." What is the significance of the words *profound insight?*

Ikeda: That's a very important point. Everyone knows that they will die "sometime." But we tend to imagine that death is always a long way off, an event that will occur in the indefinite future. That young people should think this way is only to be expected, but the same is true of those getting on in years. In fact, people's tendency to ignore death's imminence may actually increase with age.

What is the true aspect of life? The reality is that a person may be alive one moment and dead the next. The possibility of death—from earthquakes, accidents, sudden illness or other causes—exists at all times. People simply forget this.

Saito: That's very true. Even if one should flee to the ends of the earth or the furthest reaches of the universe, death cannot be avoided.

Ikeda: Someone once described the approach of death, saying, "Death who is not in front of us, but comes up on us from behind." Years and years can slip by while you say to yourself, "I'll start practicing in earnest someday," or "I'll work harder once I get through my present difficulties." Then, finally, it dawns on you that you will have to face death without having accumulated any real fortune in your life. I don't think this is an uncommon human experience. Once you realize what has happened, though you may wish you had acted differently, it is too late to do anything about it.

Suda: Certainly, if you were told that you would be dead in three days, you wouldn't just sit around idly watching TV.

Ikeda: But if you really think about it, whether it's three days or three years or three decades, the issue is essentially the same. The only way, then, is to live in the present—so that no matter when we might die, we will have no regrets.

Also, from the standpoint of eternity, even a hundred years is but an instant. It is literally the case that "now is the last moment" of our lives. Josei Toda used to say, "In truth, we practice faith for the time of our death."

If we're looking for certainty, nothing is more certain than death. Therefore, the important thing is that right now, without hesitation, we do our best to accumulate "treasures of the heart" that will endure eternally.

Most people, however, live out their lives putting off this most important issue of all, spending their time in pursuit of momentary pleasure. Nothing is more important than the issue of life and death itself. Everything else is of little consequence by comparison. We will absolutely understand this at the time of death.

Someone who works as a caregiver to the terminally ill commented: "At the end of life, it's as if all at once your entire existence comes back to you in a vast panorama. At that point, it's not superficial matters like whether you were a company president or how much success you achieved in business that take precedence, but how you lived, how you regarded others. Did you show them love and kindness, or did you treat them with contempt? You feel a sense of satisfaction for having maintained your convictions, or know the pain and regret of having betrayed them. It is these human aspects of our lives that confront us all at once and with intensity as we face death. That is death's true nature."

Saito: What that person refers to as "the human aspects of our lives" can be viewed in light of the doctrine of the Ten Worlds as our fundamental or underlying life tendency. Hearing such accounts really drives home the need for all of us to strive wholeheartedly to elevate our basic life tendencies.

Ikeda: In that sense, having an awareness and understanding of death actually raises our life-condition. For it is when we are mindful of death that we begin to earnestly seek "something eternal" and resolve to make the most valuable use of each moment of life.

Endo: It's like having a deadline for a manuscript you are writing. It can be stressful, but the fact of the matter is that without a deadline it's really hard to get it done; I would probably never get around to writing anything.

Suda: The same could be said for exams. As far as Buddhist study goes, if there were no exams, then it would be easy to let time slip by without making any progress, thinking all the while, "I'll get around to studying eventually."

Ikeda: What would happen if there was no death? Presumably life would just go on and on and might even become boring.

Saito: Without any sense of pressure or urgency, people would probably just while away their time.

Endo: Then we'd really have a serious problem with overpopulation!

Suda: Even if you were three hundred years old and totally infirm, you could not die. The first Chinese emperor Shih Huang Ti of the Chin dynasty is said to have sought an elixir of eternal youth and immortality. Under such circumstances, however, people might begin actively seeking an "elixir of death."

Looking Toward the Eternal

Ikeda: Because we know we are going to die, we strive to make the most of the present. Modern civilization has been described as a "civilization that has forgotten death." It's no coincidence that it has at the same time become a civilization of unbridled greed.

Just as with any individual, when a society or civilization tries to avoid the fundamental issue of death, its people become decadent, seeking only immediate gratification.

It is awareness of death that distinguishes people from animals and that in fact makes us human. This point has been made in many scholarly writings, such as Edgar Morin's *L'homme et la mort* (Man and Death [Paris: Éditions du Seuil, 1970]). To ignore death is to lead a shallow, animalistic existence.

Saito: This means that for both the individual and humankind as a whole, death is not something to dread or think of negatively; rather, it has positive value in that it prompts us to search for something eternal.

Ikeda: That's right. This is part of what is signified by the important doctrine of the "Life Span" chapter indicated by the line, "as an expedient means I appear to enter nirvana" (LSOC, 271).[5]

Suda: Simply put, death is an expedient.

Endo: It is a means for causing people to seek the eternal Buddha.

Ikeda: The Buddha, out of compassion, uses even his death as a means to lead his disciples to enlightenment. We should probably reconfirm this point from the standpoint of the text of the sutra.

Saito: Yes, in the "Life Span" chapter, Shakyamuni explains that although his life is in fact infinite, through the power of expedient means he appears to enter nirvana in order to lead people to enlightenment. The rationale, here, is that if the Buddha were to continue to abide in the world indefinitely, then people would cease to seek out his teaching.

Endo: One passage of the sutra reads:

If the Buddha remains in the world for a long time, those persons with shallow virtue will fail to plant good roots but, living in poverty and lowliness, will become attached to the five desires and be caught in the net of deluded thoughts and imaginings. If they see that the Thus Come One is constantly in the world and never enters extinction, they will grow arrogant and selfish, or become discouraged and neglectful. They will fail to realize how difficult it is to encounter the Buddha and will not approach him with a respectful and reverent mind. (LSOC, 268)

Suda: I think in my case this is definitely true!

Endo: Even a person with strong faith would probably grow lazy, thinking, "In the end the Buddha will somehow lend me a hand."

THE PARABLE OF THE EXCELLENT PHYSICIAN AND HIS SICK CHILDREN

Ikeda: The significance of the passage "as an expedient means I appear to enter nirvana" will probably become more clear if we view it in terms of the parable of the excellent physician and his sick children.

Endo: To summarize the parable: There is an excellent physician who has many children. While the physician is away on a journey, the children drink poison. When he returns, he finds them in great suffering. And so he prepares highly effective medicine to cure them.

Suda: The excellent physician represents the Buddha, and the children represent the people. The highly effective medicine corresponds to the Lotus Sutra and to the "eternal Mystic Law," which is also Shakyamuni's teacher. In the Latter Day of the Law, it is the Gohonzon.

Endo: Although their father has given them the best medicine, some of the children, because the poison has penetrated deeply do not drink it.

Those who take the medicine are immediately restored to health. But nothing can be done for those who refuse it, and they continue to writhe in agony.

Ikeda: These children represent befuddled people. They are called befuddled because, even though they are sick and desire to be cured, they refuse to take the medicine. The poison has penetrated so deeply that they have lost their ability to reason. They refuse the great beneficial medicine because they think it will taste bad. The "Life Span" chapter says that their "minds no longer function as before" (LSOC, 269). They cannot think rationally. This is the state the Lotus Sutra is describing when it states, "their heads will split into seven pieces" (LSOC, 351).

Saito: Broadly speaking, it seems to me that most people today are befuddled. While many talk about how society is ill and something must be done to rectify the situation, when it comes to the issue of fundamental change in people's lives—which offers the only genuine cure for society's problems—they do not pursue this path in earnest. Confining themselves to abstract arguments or superficial approaches, they make no effort to understand the principle of human revolution. As a result, nothing really changes.

Ikeda: That's probably a fair statement. Tsunesaburo Makiguchi, the first Soka Gakkai president, was very strict in his stance toward such social ills.

Suda: He concluded that human society was afflicted by what he called "symptoms of higher psychosis."

Endo: Taking pity on such befuddled people, the excellent physician, representing the Buddha, causes them to think that he has died in order to show them the way.

Suda: After setting out again, he dispatches a messenger with instructions to tell the children that their father has died in a distant land. When they hear this, the children are filled with grief and sadness, and agonize at the thought that they now have no one on whom they can depend. They can finally open their eyes.

"That's right!" they think, "We have the medicine that our father left behind for us." They decide to drink it and are immediately cured. When the father receives word that his children are all well, he immediately comes back and appears before them. That is the substance of the parable.

Single-mindedly Seeking the Teacher

Ikeda: When we have access to something all the time, then, no matter how lofty and sublime it may be, we tend to forget our sense of appreciation. It isn't until we lose it that we begin to truly appreciate how important it was and the extent to which it had benefited us.

Saito: When the children hear of their father's death, the sutra says, "All harbor thoughts of yearning and in their minds thirst to gaze at me [the Buddha]." It further describes them as "single-mindedly desiring to see the Buddha, not hesitating even if it costs them their lives" (LSOC, 271). In response to this "single-minded" seeking spirit, the eternal Buddha appears before them.

Ikeda: That's another way of saying that they awaken to the eternal world of Buddhahood within their own lives. And single-mindedly seeking the Buddha is the key to this awakening.

Nichiren Daishonin says that he manifested the world of Buddhahood in his own heart and became enlightened to the

Three Great Secret Laws through reading with his life the passage "single-mindedly desiring to see the Buddha, not hesitating even if it costs them their lives" (WND-1, 389).

As we have noted before, regarding the term "single-mindedly," the Daishonin remarks, "'Single-mindedly desiring to see the Buddha' may be read as follows: single-mindedly observing the Buddha, concentrating one's mind on seeing the Buddha, and when looking at one's own mind, perceiving that it is the Buddha" (WND-1, 389-90). In other words, the mind of an ordinary person who seeks the Buddha becomes the mind of the Buddha itself.

The heart is what really matters. One simply cannot understand Buddhism without a pure seeking spirit stemming from the depths of one's heart. When we practice with the awareness that we might only encounter the Gohonzon once in a hundred million or ten billion years, a profound sense of appreciation fills our heart each time we perform gongyo.

Nichiren Daishonin, the Buddha of the Latter Day of the Law, manifested the world of Buddhahood in his own heart through living the passage "single-mindedly desiring to see the Buddha, not hesitating even if it costs them their lives." We should deeply reflect on what this means.

The only way for us to attain Buddhahood is to manifest a spirit of utter selfless devotion, of "not hesitating even if it costs us our lives." Without this spirit, there can be no Buddhism. To arouse such a spirit in people, the Buddha leaves this existence. This is what is meant by "as an expedient means I appear to enter nirvana."

WHAT IS THE "MOMENT OF DEATH"

Ikeda: President Toda once remarked: "Whose 'last moment' do you suppose the line 'now is the last moment of this life' refers to? It's the last moment of the Buddha's life. How forlorn we would feel if the Buddha ceased to exist. We should summon resolute faith and practice with the sense that we now have to part with the Buddha."[5]

After President Toda died, those who had not listened carefully to these words were filled with regret, wishing that they had done more while he was still alive.

"Now is the last moment of this life" is an exhortation to struggle intensely for kosen-rufu with the thought that now is the last moment of the mentor's life. It is a truly fortunate thing to work for kosen-rufu together with and supported by a mentor. Someone who doesn't understand this point cannot be called a true disciple.

Those who realize this and devote themselves in earnest while the mentor is alive correspond to the children in the parable who have not lost their senses. Those who fail to realize this correspond to the children in whom the poison has penetrated deeply.

Saito: I see now that I hadn't fully grasped the significance of this parable. The principle of mentor and disciple is indeed the very soul of the "Life Span" chapter.

Ikeda: The "Life Span" chapter is the crystallization of the Buddha's immense compassion to try to teach us about the oneness of mentor and disciple. The mentor is the Buddha enlightened since the remote past. The disciples, made up of all people, are also Buddhas from the remote past. How can people be made to realize this? That is the Buddha's constant thought as expressed in the chapter's closing lines, *Mai ji sa ze nen*.[6]

There is no such thing as a mentor who does not wish for his disciples to become truly outstanding in their own right. But it is difficult for the disciples to grasp the mentor's spirit. No matter how much a parent is concerned about a child, the child rarely shares the same degree of concern for the parent. They become one only when they share mutual concern.

President Toda's spirit of concern for Mr. Makiguchi was truly awesome. Though strong and bold as a lion, near the end of his life when his long years of exertion had finally taken their toll, Mr. Toda would often say, "Without President Makiguchi I feel lonely. I would really like to return to his side." Whenever his thoughts turned to President Makiguchi, Mr. Toda was very solemn. When he talked about his mentor's death in prison, he would burn with intense indignation. He would sometimes cry bitterly from the depths of his heart and other times lash out in anger. He constantly reminisced about his mentor.

I believe it was when President Toda learned from one of his interrogators in prison of Mr. Makiguchi's death that he determined to struggle relentlessly against the devilish nature of power that had driven his mentor to his death.

In that sense, we can say that President Makiguchi's death in prison functioned as the expedient means that set the stage for the kosen-rufu movement in the postwar era. It could not by any means have been possible without the single-minded seeking spirit of the disciple for the mentor.

Myo (or Mystic) corresponds to death, and *ho* (or Law) to life. The mentor corresponds to death and the disciple to life. Mentor and disciple are themselves the Mystic Law, and the Mystic Law is itself life and death. This is truly the oneness of life and death and the oneness of mentor and disciple.

President Toda composed a poem:

> *My mentor has left this world*
> *making the offering*
> *of Bodhisattva Medicine King.*
> *Left behind,*
> *what offering can I make*
> *to the Buddha?*

He is saying that since his mentor had the spirit of "single-mindedly desiring to see the Buddha, not hesitating even if it cost him his life," he, too, would live with this spirit. This is the spirit of the "Life Span" chapter. Without this continuity of mentor and disciple, discussion of "eternal life" would be little more than abstract theory.

Another important point in the "Life Span" chapter is that the mentor appears differently depending on the state of life of the disciple. It explains that disciples understand the greatness of the mentor only to the extent that they themselves grow.

THE MEANING OF THE VERSE SECTION:
THE "SELF" IS THE "ETERNAL BUDDHA"

Endo: The passage "as an expedient means I appear to enter nirvana" probably reflects the situation at the time Shakyamuni died. His disciples, bewildered at the loss of their great mentor, were probably thrown into utter confusion, not knowing where they would turn for support as they lived out their lives.

Suda: According to a sutra, they were so afraid that their hair stood on end. It describes the scene, saying that disciples "tear their hair and weep, and stretch forth their arms and weep, fall prostrate on the ground, and roll to and fro."[7]

Saito: I think the adherents of Buddhism in later generations must have also felt a profound sense of loss at the fact that Shakyamuni was no longer in the world. In that context, the passage "as an expedient means I appear to enter nirvana" taught that one must not become attached to Shakyamuni's outward life and death. It urged them to open their eyes to the eternal life of the Buddha that transcends this dimension.

Ikeda: That's right. Moreover, when we awaken to the eternal and boundless life of the Buddha, we simultaneously realize that the Buddha's life constitutes the foundation of our own lives. This is the dawn of our lives.

Therefore, the verse section of the "Life Span" chapter begins with the character *ji*, meaning "one," and ends with the character *shin*, meaning "self." In other words, the verse section in its entirety is concerned with elucidating the enlightened self totally free of all impediments.

Suda: The verse section is the essence of the "Life Span" chapter, and the "Life Span" chapter is the soul of all Buddhism. The call to open one's eyes to the greater self is therefore the quintessential message of Buddhism.

Endo: The "Life Span" chapter says, "The Thus Come One perceives the true aspect of the threefold world exactly as it is. There is no ebb or flow of birth and death, and there is no existing in this world and later entering extinction" (LSOC, 267). In summary, this means that there is neither life nor death.

Ikeda: But in reality there is both life and death. So why does it say this?

Endo: I imagine that it's because the Lotus Sutra seeks to direct people's attention toward something that transcends the appearance of life and death.

Saito: That seems correct. The Great Teacher Dengyo of Japan says, "The two distinct phenomena of life and death are mystic functions of the one mind."[8] I think that the purpose of Buddhism is to awaken us to this "one mind."

Ikeda: That sounds true enough. But when we awaken to this "one mind," or the universal life of Nam-myoho-renge-kyo, we understand that "life" is the life of the Mystic Law, and "death" is the death of the Mystic Law. Therefore, saying there is no life and death is meaningless, and asserting so is an escapist approach, representing an illusory attachment.

The Eternally Unchanging Entity of Life

Suda: Yes. The Daishonin says:

> To look on birth and death with repulsion and try to escape from them is termed delusion, or a viewpoint of acquired enlightenment. Seeing and understanding the originally inherent nature of birth and death is termed awakening, or original enlightenment. Now when Nichiren and his followers chant Nam-myoho-renge-kyo, they realize the originally inherent nature of birth and death, and the originally inherent nature of ebb and flow. (OTT, 127)

Ikeda: This is the correct Buddhist view of life and death. In the case of the Buddhism of Shakyamuni, it could be said that the teaching so encourages people to seek the "eternal great life" of the Buddha that it creates the tendency to try to avoid actual life and death.

When we practice Nichiren Buddhism, however, we can experience the "eternally unchanging entity of life" and actualize the principle that "the sufferings of life and death are nirvana" based on this eternal great life.

Saito: It seems that in the West, many people have the image of Buddhism as a teaching aimed at attaining a "nirvana of tranquillity," a state in which there is neither life nor death.

Suda: That is the way of thinking of the Hinayana teachings, which promote an image of nirvana as a state free of the transmigration of life and death.

Ikeda: But the "Life Span" chapter rejects this view, explaining that such a "nirvana" is nothing more than an expedient means for pointing people in the right direction. Its strong point, nonetheless, is that it still emphasizes a realm that transcends life and death.

By contrast, Nichiren Buddhism teaches that we can quickly awaken to the "eternally unchanging entity of life."

Both Life and Death Are the Buddha

Ikeda: What, then, does it mean to experience life and death based on the cosmic Law of Nam-myoho-renge-kyo? The Daishonin says, "Passing through the round of births and deaths, one makes one's way on the land of the Dharma nature, or enlightenment, that is inherent within oneself" (OTT, 52). He is talking about a state of life of absolute freedom that exists eternally over past, present and future.

"Birth and death secure upon the ground of our intrinsically enlightened nature" means undergoing life and death based on the supreme life of the Mystic Law. When we embrace the Gohonzon, we can advance with our lives rooted in the "great earth of Buddhahood," which is one with the life of the universe.

Undergoing the cycle of life and death in the nine worlds means awkwardly navigating one's way through difficulties and hardships. It is like veering along a path strewn with potholes; sometimes we fall in and cannot get back on track; sometimes we have accidents and get injured.

On the other hand, experiencing life and death in the world of Buddhahood is like driving along on a smooth highway in a high-performance car; while enjoying the brilliant scenery around us, we take action with infinite life force to help others become happy.

Endo: We are traveling through life and death with the world of Buddhahood as our foundation.

In Japan, many people believe that you become a Buddha only after death. But that's not correct.

Suda: The Daishonin says to one of his followers, "When he was alive, he was a Buddha in life, and now he is a Buddha in death. He is a Buddha in both life and death. This is what is meant by that most important doctrine called attaining Buddhahood in one's present form" (WND-1, 456).

Saito: This truly signifies the oneness of life and death.

Ikeda: We therefore have to be victorious in our present lifetime. Victory in this life translates into victory after death, in future lives, and over eternity. President Toda said, "If we can become happy in this life, then we will definitely be happy in our future lives, too."

Endo: There are religions that teach that happiness only comes with death, without even attempting to offer people solutions to misfortunes and trials in this life. Nichiren Buddhism, however, teaches that actual proof of happiness in this life is itself actual proof of happiness after death and in lives to come.

Ikeda: We cannot verify eternal life with our eyes; nor can it be proven empirically. In that sense, it belongs to the realm of belief rather than to the ordinary world of knowledge. This means that anyone can fabricate stories about the afterlife.

Suda: It seems to me many religions do just that.

Ikeda: Nichiren Buddhism is different in that it teaches the inseparability of life and death, indicating that we can see the state of one's afterlife in the state of his or her present life.

If we could not become happy in the present through practicing this Buddhism, we would have a hard time believing in promises of happiness after death. On the other hand, experiencing actual proof of happiness in this life gives us complete confidence that we will also enjoy happiness in the next. If the Daishonin's teaching about happiness throughout eternity was in fact mistaken, then it stands to reason we couldn't receive immeasurable benefit in the present life through its practice.

Saito: That seems indisputable.

Ikeda: What about life and death based on the world of Buddhahood? What happens to a person who dies having maintained faith in the Mystic Law? Why don't we begin by seeing what the Daishonin says about this?

Endo: In one place he says, "If he were he to go right now to Eagle Peak, he would be as delighted as if the sun had come out and he were able to see in all ten directions. He would rejoice, wondering how an early death could be so happy a thing" (WND-1, 938).

Suda: That's a remarkable passage. There's not even the tiniest speck of doubt. He is saying that death, rather than being something to fear, is something we might even look forward to.

Saito: The Daishonin also says:

> At that time, hasten to the summit of perfect enlightenment, and look around you in all directions. The entire realm of phenomena will have changed into the Land of Tranquil Light, with the ground made of lapis lazuli, the eight paths marked off by golden ropes, the four kinds of flowers raining down from the heavens, music resounding in the air, and Buddhas and bodhisattvas all being caressed by breezes of eternity, happiness, true self, and purity. We, too, will surely be among their number. (WND-1, 843)

Ikeda: It's a state of being where life is joyful, and death is joyful, too.

The Daishonin also says, "Because he has the wings of the single vehicle to rely upon, he can soar into the sky of Tranquil Light" (WND-1, 821). With eternity and the entire universe as our venue of activity, we soar gracefully into the great sky of happiness.

Therefore, it is not death that we need to fear but the strict law of cause and effect. A person who lives well also dies well and will be reborn well.

A person who lives poorly, dies poorly, and will be reborn in the same way. The ancient Greek philosopher Antisthenes poses the question, "What is the best thing you can do as a human being?" His answer: "Die well."

The Spirit of the "Life Span" Chapter Is To Live Out Our Lives Based on the Mystic Law

Suda: Juryo, in the title of the chapter, *"Nyorai Juryo-hon"* (Life Span of the Thus Come One), means to measure or fathom the life and wonderful virtues of the Buddha.

As we learned in our first discussion on the "Life Span" chapter, to practice the "Life Span" chapter is to live our lives filled with the great life force of the Buddha.

Endo: I guess this means that longevity is important.

Ikeda: Someone once said, "Longevity is the art of life." To live long is itself a kind of victory. A passage in the chapter says, "Let us live out our lives!" (LSOC, 269). Every day, morning and evening, I pray that all SGI members will enjoy excellent health and long lives.

At the same time, our success or failure in living based on the world of Buddhahood is not determined simply by our life-span in years. Nichiren Daishonin was only sixty at his death.

In Japan, someone who is sixty years old is said to have completed one round of the calendar, because on the lunar calendar it marks the completion of five twelve-year cycles. This suggests that a person who reaches this age has lived completely. Nikko Shonin, the Daishonin's successor, died at eighty-eight.

Saito: At that time, especially, he would have been extremely long-lived.

Ikeda: He was hale and hearty, reportedly attesting that his ears and eyes were as sharp and clear as ever. He took to bed early in February 1333 and died in the middle of the night on the seventh. Accounts describe how to the very last moment he never suffered from senility or illness.

Nichimoku, the third high priest, died at seventy-four while on a journey to urge the imperial court to accept the Daishonin's teaching.

Endo: He died at a place called Tarui in Mino Province, which is part of what is now Gifu Prefecture.

Ikeda: The circumstances of his death reflect his total dedication to the Law. Rather than peacefully living out his life, he died engaging in a fierce struggle to uphold and spread his mentor's teaching.

Suda: Nichimoku's death in the middle of a journey must have come as quite a surprise to all.

Ikeda: I think that each of the three teachers[9] dying in such a different manner is quite significant; although each of them embodied the eternal life of the Buddha achieved by thoroughly dedicating oneself in the struggle for kosen-rufu, the circumstances surrounding their deaths vary greatly. I believe there is profound meaning in this.

Saito: The Daishonin says, "Your mother [Toki Jonin's mother], obeying the principle of birth and death, set out on her journey to the Yellow Springs" (WND-2, 658). The Daishonin teaches that life and death take many forms.

Ikeda: Nichiren Buddhism is flawless. It comprehends all aspects of life and is entirely free of contradiction. If, for instance, it expounded an ideal age for people to live to, then not reaching the desired age would cause unhappiness and suffering.

Saito: President Toda died at fifty-eight. He cannot be said to have lived long. President Makiguchi was seventy-three when he died in prison. Had he not been subjected to the harsh conditions of prison life, he would have surely lived longer.

Ikeda: However long you may live and whatever the place and circumstances of your death, if you have steadfastly dedicated yourself to kosen-rufu, then you are certain to experience life and death based on the world of Buddhahood.

From a young age, I was told that with my frail health I would not live past thirty. But I have lived long and vigorously in President Toda's stead. Mr. Toda once told me: "You'll become the Takayama Chogyu of the Mystic Law.[10] The real Chogyu died at thirty-one. You have to live on. You have to live on as my successor." Another time he went so far as to say he would "give his life" to me so that I could carry on. Now I have reached seventy [in 1998], and I am healthy. I believe I still have many good years ahead of me.

Endo: It seems to me that this is truly the essence of the "Life Span" chapter.

Ikeda: Longevity itself is a treasure. But how you live is more important still. The Daishonin says, "It is better to live a single day with honor than to live to 120 and die in disgrace" (WND-1, 851).

Suda: We find similar statements even in early Buddhist texts. One passage reads, "Better than a hundred years not seeing one's own immortality is one single day of life if one sees one's own immortality."[11]

Saito: Immortality, here, means the state of life in which one has awakened to the eternal life of the Buddha.

Suda: Yes. The same text contains the following description: "Watchfulness is the path of immortality: unwatchfulness is the path of death. Those who are watchful never die: those who do not watch are already as dead."[12]

IMMORTALITY THROUGH EFFORTS FOR KOSEN-RUFU

Ikeda: For us, to be ever watchful, to dedicate our life and work to actualize the great wish of kosen-rufu, is to attain a state of "immortality." This is what it means to read the "Life Span" chapter with one's life. We become one with the eternal Buddha, the Thus Come One, only through making continuous efforts for kosen-rufu. Then the infinite life of the Thus Come One manifests through our own finite life. This was certainly true of President Toda. Even when he was sick in bed, if someone raised a question relating to Buddhism, he would prop himself up and provide an answer. "No matter how bad a mood I may be in," he would often say, "being asked a question about the Daishonin's teachings always cheers me up." This was his attitude until the very last moment of his life.

There was a certain chapter leader who, by struggling very hard, had gone from being a poor laborer to a successful businessman. On the day before we were to set out for the historic March 16 pilgrimage [in 1958], President Toda called up the man on the telephone. After explaining that he would be gone for a few days, President Toda, despite his very weak condition, proceeded to energetically and politely instruct the man for thirty minutes on how to conduct his business.

Several days later, the man called President Toda at the head temple to tell him how things were going. At the time, Mr. Toda was severely ill. Even so, as soon as he heard that the chapter chief was on the line wishing to speak with him, he asked for the phone. Then, leaning on the person next to him for support and having someone else hold the receiver for him, he talked to the chapter leader. He was truly a remarkable teacher.

Saito: I understand that President Toda had a premonition of his own death. According to the notes of his attendant, the year before he died, Mr. Toda remarked: "I should have died long ago. I'm trying to see just how long I can go in this life . . . Here's the truth: I will die in April of next year. Yes, I will die."

I cannot begin to comprehend President Toda's state of life. But I am moved to hear accounts of how to the very end of his days, having awakened to life's eternity, Mr. Toda always treated people with the most profound compassion.

Ikeda: When we grasp the eternity of life, compassionate action naturally wells forth. Otherwise our understanding is not genuine.

Those who perceive that all people's lives are the same as the Buddha's life will freely expend their own lives to convey that understanding to others. Whether we call it the Buddha's state of life or enlightenment, only in such concrete action can we envision what it means to be enlightened. The same was certainly true of President Makiguchi.

The following is the experience of a woman who had only just taken faith. She was trying sincerely to introduce other people to the Daishonin's teaching. One day she brought a friend who was worried about the illness of a parent to see Mr. Makiguchi. President Makiguchi advised her, "To enable your parent to take faith is an act of the highest filial devotion." The friend immediately decided to practice.

The woman joined her friend in earnestly chanting daimoku, and half a year later the friend's parent passed away with a truly beautiful and peaceful look. The friend was glad to have done everything she could for her parent's eternal happiness.

Next the woman introduced her friend's younger brother to

the practice. But the very night that the brother decided to take faith he was killed in an accident. The woman, shaken by this turn of events, rushed to see President Makiguchi at his home. She asked him, "Why did he die so suddenly after deciding to take faith?"

Although it was late at night, out of concern for the woman's friend, Mr. Makiguchi said, "Let's go see her together," and they set out. As soon as they arrived, he suggested that they all chant daimoku together earnestly. With him leading, they continued chanting for a long time. Some people who were not members joined in the chanting, and later they reportedly also joined the Soka Gakkai.

Questions of life and death cannot be addressed by pat answers or simple logic. It is by really expending our life and mustering the utmost sincerity that we can open and revive the hardened hearts of people overwhelmed with grief and sorrow. It is through such conduct that we can show actual proof of the teaching that "*Myo* means to revive, that is, to return to life" (WND-1, 149).

Saito: I see.

For the benefit of our readers, let's discuss the death of the twenty-sixth high priest, Nichikan. I receive many questions about Nichikan. It seems that many members want to learn more about him, as they are praying daily before the Gohonzon that he transcribed.

Ikeda: Leaders should always give immediate responses to the questions that are on people's minds. Let's take that up right now.

NICHIKAN'S LAST MOMENTS

Endo: There's a famous episode concerning Nichikan's final moments that involves Japanese *soba*, or buckwheat noodles. He died in the early morning hours of August 19, 1726. He was sixty-two.

It seems that Nichikan knew that death was upon him. A day or two before, he dressed in his robes and emerged from his sickbed. Boarding a litter, he went around the temple grounds to make his farewells. First he recited the sutra and chanted daimoku at the main temple. Then he went to pay homage at the graves of the three teachers in the cemetery. He then went around to see the former high priest and the new high priest. Passing through the commercial area at the foot of the temple, he returned to the Dai-bo lodging complex. It is said that the path was lined with well-wishers.

Suda: As soon as he was back in his quarters, he had workers begin preparations for the funeral, and he personally wrote a few lines of verse on the lid of what would be his coffin.

Saito: He was completely self-composed.

Suda: Late at night on the eighteenth day of that month, he had those around him enshrine a Gohonzon nearby and instructed them about chanting daimoku when he died and about other matters. He then asked them to prepare some buckwheat noodles, which was a favorite dish of his.

Consuming the noodles in seven mouthfuls, he smiled brightly and remarked, "It's magnificent—the Palace of Tranquil Light." He then rinsed his mouth and held his hands together in prayer facing the Gohonzon. Around 8:00 A.M. on the morning of the nineteenth, he passed away peacefully, with his eyes and mouth slightly opened.

Saito: The fact that there are such detailed records probably shows just how moved people were.

Ikeda: He ate the noodles to fulfill a promise he had made. About half a year before his death, he remarked, "Upon his death, the great translator and scholar Kumarajiva said, 'After my death, if my tongue does not burn, you will know that all that I have said is true.' And, indeed, his tongue was not consumed in flames. Likewise, since I have always been fond of buckwheat noodles, at the time of my death I think I will eat buckwheat noodles, give a big smile and chant daimoku. If this is indeed how it turns out, then you must not doubt a single word that I have spoken."

Endo: And his final moments were indeed just as he had said.

Ikeda: Also two months before his death, in June of that same year, Nichikan remarked: "Taiseki-ji is now flourishing. The number of people chanting daimoku is increasing. The three powerful enemies are therefore sure to arise. Since this past spring I have been praying to dispel calamity. Therefore the Buddhas and heavenly deities in response have assumed the form of... the devil of illness that has afflicted me personally. Since this is certainly the principle of lessening karmic retribution, there is no need to be saddened by it in the least."

Endo: It was around that year that the Kanazawa persecution[13] came to a head.

Reborn in the Time and Place We Desire

Ikeda: He had the dauntless attitude of a leader of kosen-rufu. I think that Nichikan could retain such calm and dignity in the face of death because of his profound sense of responsibility.

At any rate, to experience birth and death from the standpoint of the world of Buddhahood means that death is something we absolutely need not fear. It's the same as going to sleep one day and waking up the next. Just when you think you are dead, before you know it, you've entered your next existence!

Suda: I feel much better now!

Ikeda: Moreover, we are born in the place and at the time and in the form that we desire. And this is not limited to this world. If you've grown tired of earth, you can go and work on some other planet!

The Daishonin speaks of attaining the "mysterious power of perfect freedom of action" through faith in the Mystic Law (WND-1, 423). And in "The Unanimous Declaration by the Buddhas," he says that those who embrace the Mystic Law will be reborn "in the space of a moment."

Endo: Yes. The passage reads:

> Then in no time one will return to the dream realm of the nine worlds, the realm of birth and death, will cause one's body to pervade the lands of the entire phenomenal realm of the ten directions, and will cause one's wind to enter into the bodies of all sentient beings, encouraging them from within, leading and guiding them from without, inner and outer complimenting one another, causes and conditions functioning in harmony, and in this way will utilize the pity and compassion of one's freely exercised transcendental powers to bestow unhindered benefit upon living beings far and wide. (WND-2, 860)

Saito: This is what is meant by life and death based on the world of Buddhahood.

Endo: Some people probably would much rather take a break than be reborn right away!

Ikeda: They should definitely rest then! To rest after a life of hard exertion is only natural. Death is rest. It is a time when, embraced by the healing sea of the universal life, we recharge our worn-out lives and prepare for the explosion of vitality that is birth.

At the same time, when we base ourselves on the world of

Buddhahood, compassion becomes the very foundation of our lives. Therefore, we want to be born again quickly so we can help more people become happy.

The expression "in the space of a moment" is better thought of in terms of "life-time" as opposed to "physical time." Just as the sufferings of hell for even a brief time can seem like an eternity, time passes quickly when one is experiencing the great joy of the world of Buddhahood. "In the space of a moment" refers then to experiential time.

A WARNING TO MODERN SOCIETY

Saito: This will conclude our discussion of the "Life Span" chapter. There are still many points that we could discuss, but now let's turn to the remaining chapters, beginning with the "Distinctions in Benefits" chapter.

Ikeda: Here I would like to comment on the passage from "The Opening of the Eyes" that reads, "If one fails to become acquainted with the Buddha of the 'Life Span' chapter, one is no more than a talented animal who does not even know what lands one's father presides over" (WND-1, 258).

While this passage can be interpreted in various ways, I think it is a warning to people of the modern age who are confused about the foundation of their own lives.

In summation, the "Life Span" chapter seeks to change "talented animals" into genuine human beings who are awakened to the Law of life. The sun of the true "century of the human being" will rise when people learn and put into practice the spirit of the "Life Span" chapter, the great philosophy of Nichiren Buddhism.

Kosen-rufu is a magnificent movement to create a society in which all fields of endeavor—economics and politics, education and science, industry and agriculture, the home and life itself—are illuminated by the brilliant light of the Mystic Law.

NOTES

1. Motohiro Umemori, *Shisha no honne: Eikoku bohimei no sekai* (The The Truth about the Dead: The World of English Epitaphs), (Tokyo: Shufunotomosha, 1997), p. 21. This Japanese book includes original English epitaphs.

2. Ibid., p. 6.

3. Ibid., p. 161.

4. Ibid., p. 162.

5. From the April 1960 edition of the *Daibyakurenge*, the Soka Gakkai study journal.

6. "At all times I think to myself: / How can I cause living beings / to gain entry into the unsurpassed way / and quickly acquire the body of a Buddha?" (LSOC, 273).

7. *Dialogues of the Buddha*, part 2, trans. T. W. and C. A. F. Rhys Davids (Oxford: The Pali Text Society, 1995), pp. 178–79.

8. "Tendai Hokkeshu Gozuhomon Yosan," cf. *Gosho zenshu*, p. 1543.

9. Three teachers: Nichiren Daishonin, Nikko Shonin, the second high priest, and Nichimoku, the third high priest.

10. Takayama Chogyu (1871–1902): Japanese aesthetician, moralist, literary critic and essayist who led the literary and philosophical world of the Meiji era (1868–1912).

11. *The Dhammapada: The Path of Perfection*, trans. Juan Mascaró (London: Penguin Books, 1973), p. 51.

12. Ibid., p. 38.

13. Kanazawa persecution: The persecution of those who had converted to Nichiren Buddhism by the sixth feudal lord of the Kanazawa area in what is known today as Ishikawa Prefecture. The persecution began with the oppression of samurai believers but soon spread to believers among the general public. While many gave up, many others persisted in their faith despite the harsh treatment, which lasted for some seventy years beginning in the early eighteenth century. (See November 1998 *Living Buddhism*, p. 14)

Glossary

benefit   (Jpn *kudoku*) *Ku* means to extinguish evil and *doku* means to bring forth good.

bodhisattva   A being who aspires to attain Buddhahood and carries out altruistic practices to achieve that goal. Compassion predominates in bodhisattvas, who postpone their own entry into nirvana in order to lead others toward enlightenment.

Bodhisattvas of the Earth   Those who chant and propagate Nam-myoho-renge-kyo. *Earth* indicates the enlightened nature of all people. The term describes the innumerable bodhisattvas who appear in the "Emerging from the Earth" chapter of the Lotus Sutra and are entrusted by Shakyamuni with the task of propagating the Law after his passing. In several of his writings, Nichiren Daishonin identifies his own role with that of their leader, Bodhisattva Superior Practices.

Buddhahood   The state a Buddha has attained. The ultimate goal of Buddhist practice. The highest of the Ten Worlds. The word *enlightenment* is often interchangeable with Buddhahood.

Consciousness-Only school   Also known as the Yogachara school, one of the two major Mahayana schools in India, the other being the Madhyamika school. This school upholds the concept that all phenomena arise from the *vijnana,* or consciousness, and that the basis of all functions of consciousness is the *alaya*-consciousness.

daimoku   Literally, 'title.' (1) The title of a sutra, in particular the title of the Lotus Sutra, Myoho-renge-kyo. (2) The invocation of Nam-myoho-renge-kyo in Nichiren Buddhism.

Daishonin   Literally, 'great sage.' In particular, this honorific title is applied to Nichiren to show reverence for him as the Buddha who appears in the Latter Day of the Law to save all humankind.

dependent origination   Also, dependent causation or conditioned co-arising. A Buddhist doctrine expressing the interdependence of all things. It teaches that no being or phenomenon exists on its own, but exists or occurs because of its relationship with other beings or phenomena. Everything in the world comes into existence in response to causes and conditions. In other words, nothing can exist independent of other things or arise in isolation.

devil king of the sixth heaven The king of devils, who dwells in the highest of the six heavens of the world of desire. He works to obstruct Buddhist practice and delights in sapping the life force of other beings. He is also regarded as the manifestation of the fundamental darkness inherent in life. Also called the heavenly devil.

dharma   A term fundamental to Buddhism that derives from a verbal root *dhri,* which means to preserve, maintain, keep, or uphold. *Dharma* has a wide variety of meanings, such as law, truth, doctrine, the Buddha's teaching, decree, observance, conduct, duty, virtue, morality, religion, justice, nature, quality, character, characteristic, essence, elements of existence, and phenomena. Some of the more common usages are: (1) (Often capitalized) The Law, or ultimate truth. For example, Kumarajiva translated *saddharma,* the Sanskrit word that literally means correct Law, as Wonderful Law or Mystic Law, indicating the unfathomable truth or Law that governs all phenomena. (2) The teaching of the Buddha that reveals the Law. The *Dharma* of *abhidharma* means the Buddha's doctrine, or the sutras. (3) (Often plural) Manifestations of the Law, i.e., phenomena, things, facts, or existences. The word "phenomena" in "the true aspect of all phenomena" is the translation of *dharmas.* (4) The elements of existence, which, according to the Hinayana schools, are the most basic constituents of the individual and his or her reality. (5) Norms of conduct leading to the accumulation of good karma.

Eagle Peak   (Skt Gridhrakuta) Also, Vulture Peak. A mountain located to the northeast of Rajagriha, the capital of Magadha in ancient India, where Shakyamuni is said to have expounded the Lotus Sutra. Eagle Peak also symbolizes the Buddha land or the state of Buddhahood. In this sense, the 'pure land of Eagle Peak' is often used.

earthly desires   Also, illusions, defilements, impurities, earthly passions, or simply desires. A generic term for all the workings of life, including desires and illusions in the general sense, that cause one psychological and physical suffering and impede the quest for enlightenment.

earthly desires are enlightenment   (Jpn *bonno-sokubodai*) Mahayana principle based on the view that earthly desires cannot exist independently on their own; therefore one can attain enlightenment without eliminating earthly desires. This is in contrast with the Hinayana view that extinguishing earthly desires is a prerequisite for enlightenment. Mahayana teachings reveal that earthly desires are one with and inseparable from enlightenment.

essential teachings   (1) The teaching expounded by Shakyamuni from the perspective of his true identity as the Buddha who attained enlightenment numberless major world system dust particle kalpas ago. T'ien-t'ai classifies the last fourteen chapters of the Lotus Sutra as the essential teaching. (2) The essential teaching of the Latter Day of the Law, that is, the teaching of Nam-myoho-renge-kyo.

expedient means   The methods adopted to instruct people and lead them to enlightenment. The concept of expedient means is highly regarded in Mahayana Buddhism, especially in the Lotus Sutra, as represented by its second chapter entitled "Expedient Means." This is because expedient means are skillfully devised and employed by Buddhas and bodhisattvas to lead the people to salvation.

five components   Also, the five components of life and the five aggregates. The constituent elements of form, perception, conception, volition, and consciousness that unite temporarily to form an individual living being. The five components also constitute the first of the three realms of existence.

four sufferings   The four universal sufferings of birth, aging, sickness and death. Shakyamuni's quest for enlightenment is said to have been motivated by a desire to find a solution to these four sufferings.

fundamental darkness   Also, fundamental ignorance. The most deeply rooted illusion inherent in life, which gives rise to all other illusions and earthly desires.

Gohonzon   *Go* means 'worthy of honor' and *honzon* means 'object of fundamental respect.' The object of devotion in Nichiren Buddhism and the embodiment of the Mystic Law permeating all phenomena. It takes the form of a mandala inscribed on paper or on wood with characters representing the Mystic Law as well as the Ten Worlds, including Buddhahood. Nichiren Buddhism holds that all people possess the Buddha nature and can attain Buddhahood through faith in the Gohonzon.

gongyo   Literally, 'assiduous practice.' In Nichiren Buddhism, it means to chant Nam-myoho-renge-kyo and recite portions of the "Expedient Means" and "Life Span" chapters of the Lotus Sutra. It is performed morning and evening.

Gosho   Literally, 'honored writings.' The individual and collected writings of Nichiren Daishonin.

Hinayana   The teaching that aims at attaining the state of *arhat*. Hinayana, literally "lesser vehicle," was originally a pejorative term used by Mahayana Buddhists, who regarded the practitioners of these teachings as preoccupied solely with achieving personal emancipation and indifferent to the salvation of others. Hinayana teachings are represented by the doctrines of the four noble truths and the twelve-linked chain of causation. They regard earthly desires as the cause of suffering and assert that suffering is eliminated only by eradicating earthly desires.

human revolution   A concept coined by the Soka Gakkai's second president, Josei Toda, to indicate the self-reformation of an individual — the strengthening of life force and the establishment of Buddhahood — that is the goal of Buddhist practice.

inconspicuous benefit   Benefit that accumulates over a period of time and is not immediately recognizable.

kalpa   An extremely long period of time. Sutras and treatises di er in their definitions, but kalpas fall into two major categories, those of measurable and immeasurable duration. There are three kinds of measurable kalpas: small, medium and major. One explanation sets the length of a small kalpa at approximately sixteen million years. According to Buddhist cosmology, a world repeatedly undergoes four stages: formation, continuance, decline and disintegration. Each of these four stages lasts for twenty small kalpas and is equal to one medium kalpa. Finally, one complete cycle forms a major kalpa.

karma   Potential energies residing in the inner realm of life, which manifest themselves as various results in the future. In Buddhism, karma is interpreted as meaning mental, verbal and physical action, that is, thoughts, words and deeds.

kosen-rufu   Literally, to 'widely declare and spread [Buddhism].' Nichiren Daishonin defines Nam-myoho-renge-kyo of the Three Great Secret Laws as the law to be widely declared and spread during the Latter Day. There are two aspects of kosen-rufu: the kosen-rufu of the entity of the Law, or the establishment of the Dai-Gohonzon, which is the basis of the Three Great Secret Laws; and the kosen-rufu of substantiation, the widespread acceptance of faith in the Dai-Gohonzon among the people.

ku   A fundamental Buddhist concept, variously translated as nonsubstantiality, emptiness, void, latency, relativity, etc. The concept that entities have no fixed or independent nature.

Latter Day of the Law   Also, the Latter Day. The last of the three periods following Shakyamuni Buddha's death when Buddhism falls into confusion and Shakyamuni's teachings lose the power to lead people to enlightenment. A time when the essence of the Lotus Sutra will be propagated to save all humankind.

Lotus Sutra   The highest teaching of Shakyamuni Buddha, it reveals that all people can attain enlightenment and declares that his former teachings should be regarded as preparatory.

Mahayana Buddhism   The teachings which expound the bodhisattva practice as the means toward the enlightenment of both oneself and others, in contrast to Hinayana Buddhism, or the teaching of the Agon period, which aims only at personal salvation. Mahayana literally means 'greater vehicle.'

mentor-and-disciple relationship   See *oneness of mentor and disciple*.

Miao-lo   The sixth patriarch in the lineage of the T'ien-t'ai school in China, counting from the Great Teacher T'ien-t'ai. Miao-lo reasserted the supremacy of the Lotus Sutra and wrote commentaries on T'ien-t'ai's three major works, thus bringing about a revival of interest in T'ien-t'ai Buddhism. He is revered as the restorer of the school.

Middle Day of the Law   Also, the period of the Counterfeit Law. The second of the three periods following a Buddha's death. During this time the Buddha's teaching gradually becomes formalized, the people's connection to it weakens, and progressively fewer people are able to gain enlightenment through its practice. Some sources define the Middle Day of the Law of Shakyamuni as lasting a thousand years, while others define it as five hundred years.

mutual possession of the Ten Worlds   The principle that each of the Ten Worlds contains all the other nine as potential within itself. This is taken to mean that an individual's state of life can be changed, and that all beings of the nine worlds possess the potential for Buddhahood. See also *Ten Worlds*.

Mystic Law   The ultimate law of life and the universe. The law of Nam-myoho-renge-kyo.

Nam-myoho-renge-kyo   The ultimate law of the true aspect of life permeating all phenomena in the universe. The invocation established by Nichiren Daishonin on April 28, 1253. Nichiren Daishonin teaches that this phrase encompasses all laws and teachings within itself, and that the benefit of chanting Nam-myoho-renge-kyo includes the benefit of conducting all virtuous practices. *Nam* means 'devotion to'; *myoho* means 'Mystic Law'; *renge* refers to the lotus flower, which simultaneously blooms and seeds, indicating the simultaneity of cause and effect; *kyo* means sutra, the teaching of a Buddha.

Nichiren Daishonin   The thirteenth-century Japanese Buddhist teacher and reformer who taught that all people have the potential for enlightenment. He defined the universal law as Nam-myoho-renge-kyo and established the Gohonzon as the object of devotion for all people to attain Buddhahood. Daishonin is an honorific title that means 'great sage.'

nonsubstantiality   One of the three truths. The truth of nonsubstantiality means that all phenomena are nonsubstantial and in a state transcending the concepts of existence and nonexistence.

oneness of body and mind   A principle explaining that the two seemingly distinct phenomena of body, or the physical aspect of life, and mind, or its spiritual aspect, are two integral phases of the same entity.

oneness of life and environment   The principle stating that the self and its environment are two integral phases of the same entity.

oneness of mentor and disciple   This is a philosophical as well as a practical concept. Disciples reach the same state of Buddhahood as their mentor by practicing the teachings of the latter. In Nichiren Buddhism, this is the direct way to enlightenment, that is, to believe in the Gohonzon and practice according to the Daishonin's teachings.

shakubuku   A method of propagating Buddhism by refuting another's attachment to heretical views and thus leading him or her to the correct Buddhist teaching.

Shakyamuni   Also, Siddhartha Gautama. Born in India (present-day southern Nepal) about three thousand years ago, he is the first recorded Buddha and founder of Buddhism. For fifty years, he expounded various sutras (teachings), culminating in the Lotus Sutra.

Soka   Literally, 'value creating.'

Ten Worlds   Ten life-conditions that a single entity of life manifests. Originally the Ten Worlds were viewed as distinct physical places, each with its own particular inhabitants. In light of the Lotus Sutra, they are interpreted as potential conditions of life inherent in each individual. the ten are: (1) hell, (2) hunger, (3) animality, (4) anger, (5) humanity or tranquillity, (6) rapture, (7) voice-hearers, (8) cause-awakened ones, (9) bodhisattva and (10) Buddhahood.

theoretical teachings   The first fourteen chapters of the twenty-eight chapter Lotus Sutra, as classified by T'ien-t'ai. In contrast to the essential teaching—the latter fourteen chapters of the sutra, which represent preaching by Shakyamuni as the Buddha who attained enlightenment in the remote past, the theoretical teaching represents preaching by the historical Shakyamuni, who first attained enlightenment during his lifetime in India. The core of the theoretical teaching is the "Expedient Means" chapter, which teaches that all phenomena manifest the true aspect and that all phenomena are endowed with the ten factors.

three existences   Past, present and future. The dimension of time. The three aspects of the eternity of life, linked inseparably by the law of cause and effect. "Throughout the three existences" means throughout eternity.

Three Great Secret Laws   The object of devotion of Buddhism, the invocation or daimoku of Buddhism and the high sanctuary of Buddhism. These three constitute the core of Nichiren Buddhism.

three obstacles and four devils   Various obstacles and hindrances to the practice of Buddhism. The three obstacles are: 1) the obstacle of earthly desires; 2) the obstacle of karma, which may also refer to opposition from one's spouse or children; and 3) the obstacle of retribution, also obstacles caused by one's superiors, such as rulers or parents. The four devils are: 1) the hindrance of the five components; 2) the hindrance of earthly desires; 3) the hindrance of death, because untimely death obstructs one's practice of Buddhism or because the premature death of another practitioner causes doubts; and 4) the hindrance of the devil king.

three poisons   Greed, anger and foolishness. The fundamental evils inherent in life that give rise to human suffering.

three powerful enemies   Also, the three types of enemies. Three types of people who persecute those who propagate the Lotus Sutra after the Buddha's passing, as described in the "Encouraging Devotion" chapter of the sutra. They are: (1) lay people ignorant of Buddhism who denounce the votaries of the Lotus Sutra and attack them with swords or staves; (2) arrogant and cunning priests who slander the votaries; and (3) priests respected by the general public who, fearing the loss of fame or profit, induce the secular authorities to persecute the sutra's votaries.

three thousand realms in a single moment of life   A philosophical system set forth by T'ien-t'ai in his *Great Concentration and Insight,* clarifying the mutually inclusive relationship of the ultimate truth and the phenomenal world. This means that the life of Buddhahood is universally inherent in all beings, and the distinction between a common person and a Buddha is a phenomenal one.

Thus Come One   One of the ten honorable titles for a Buddha, meaning one who has arrived from the world of truth. That is, the Buddha appears from the world of enlightenment and, as a person who embodies wisdom and compassion, leads other beings to enlightenment.

T'ien-t'ai   Also called Chih-i. The founder of the T'ien-t'ai school, commonly referred to as the Great Teacher T'ien-t'ai.

treasure tower   A tower adorned with treasures. A treasure tower often appears in Buddhist scriptures. In Nichiren Daishonin's writings, the treasure tower primarily indicates the tower of the Buddha Many Treasures that appears from beneath the earth in the "Treasure Tower" chapter of the Lotus Sutra. He also equated this with the Gohonzon and human life.

Index

absolute happiness, 80–81
action, failing to take, 79
"actual attainment in the remote past," 78–79
advancing, 188
aeon, 14
After Death (Miller), 241
afterlife, 236–37, 239–40
Alain, 7
alaya-consciousness, 232; working of the, 262–63
altruistic heart, 175
Amida Buddha, 32, 45–46
anger (*asura*), channeling the energy of, 126; peer pressure and, 140; world of, 106, 119–25, 129–30, 134, 138, 159
Angulimala, 41–42
animality, life space in, 111; world of 111–14, 172
Aniruddha, 42–43
annihilation, doctrine of, 241, 246
Annotations on "The Words and Phrases of the Lotus Sutra," 122
Antisthenes, 295
appreciation, 285
arhat, 44
Aristides, banishment of, 127–28
arrogance, 120; negative effects of, 142

Ashio Copper Mine Incident, 142
asogi, 13–14
Asvattha tree, 92
Athens, decline of, 128; practice of ostracism in, 127
Auschwitz, 181
authoritarianism, 220

Beethoven, Ludwig van, 245
"beginningless Buddhahood," 67–68
"beginningless nine worlds," 67–68
benefits, way to receive boundless, 209
"Benefits of the Teacher of the Law" chapter (Lotus Sutra), 103
Blake, William, 203
Bodh Gaya, 92; poems recited by Shakyamuni's during his spiritual struggle at, 95; Shakyamuni's spiritual struggle at, 93–94
bodhi tree, 91–93
bodhisattva, and all phenomena, 155; characteristics of, 172; spirit of the world of, 220; world of, 174–76, 181–84, 214

formlessness world, 153–54, 157
fortune, tapping into, 186
four noble worlds, 104
four sufferings, 146–48, 159
four teachings, 70
Frankl, Viktor, 182
friendship, 219
"fundamental mind," and chanting daimoku, 251
Fu Ta-Shih, 52

Gagarin, Yuri, 230
gaman (self-importance), different connotations of, 122–23
go (Japanese board game), 265
Goethe, Johann Wolfgang von, 129, 246
Gohonzon, 17, 209–10, 284, 292; benefits of chanting to, 51, 169; purpose of inscribing the, 51
gongyo (reciting the sutra), attitude toward, 286; practice of, 219;
good friends, importance of having, 105
Great Concentrations and Insight (T'ien-t'ai), 121

Hale-Bopp comet, 55
happiness, state of indestructible, 184–85
hard work, avoiding, 220–21
Hayakawa, Masami, 116
Hayashi, Tamiko, 114–17
heart, having lion's, 123; importance of the treasures of the, 286; treasures of the, 280
heaven (*deva*), Buddhist view of, 153; different kinds of, 153; life

space in the world of, 159; negative side of the world of, 107; people of the world of, 169; shortcomings of the world of, 162; world of, 145–46, 151–52, 154, 158–59, 162
hell (*naraka*), 97, 99, 104–08; bodhisattva world contained in the world of, 198; world of, 183
"Heritage of the Ultimate Law of Life" (Nichiren), 278
high priest, 193
Hilter, Adolf, 49
Himalaya, 262
Hinayana Buddhism, teachings of, 32, 43–44, 47, 291
Hiroshima, 210–11
ho (law), 288
L'homme et la mort (Man and Death) (Morin), 282
hope, 222, 246
human, becoming, 113
human being(s) (*manusya*), 136; means to become a, 140; significance of being born a, 141
human body, in Buddhism, 141
human existence, awakening to the true meaning of, 147
human revolution, 26, 284; effects of our, 146; original workings of the concept of, 262–64
human rights, Buddhist perspective on, 137
human world, Buddhahood present in the, 192
humanity, Buddhist practice and, 139; challenge of the world of, 139; condition of, 136; hell is

contained in the world of,
198; world of, 126, 135–38,
140–42, 159
hunger (*preta*), characteristics of
the world of, 172; and life
space, 109; world of, 108–110
Huxley, Aldous, 161
Huyghe, René, 258–59, 266

identical nature of cause and
effect, teachings of the, 74, 83
initial attainment, 78–80
Ikeda, Daisaku: characteristics of
people who betrayed, 125;
extending life, 297; spirit of,
114; as youth, 115–116
illusions, conquering, through
Buddhist practice, 157–58, 191
immortality, 298
India, ancient belief in, 152;
decline of Buddhism in, 31–
33, 44–45
individual(s), difference in, 269;
importance of an, 208; importance of encouraging an
unnoticed, 208
Indra (Indian god), 152
inner strength, 184

jigage. See verse section (of the
Lotus Sutra)
jealousy, 127–28, 130, 135; male,
106
Jung, Carl, 229; near death
encounter of, 229–31
Juryo, 295
justice, 186

Kant, Immanuel, 239
Kanzo Uchimura, 27

karma, 257–58; changing evil,
263; energy of, 259–62, 265
karmic retribution, lessening,
41–42
Katsura, Yuki, and extending her
life, 21–22
King, Sallie, 137
Kiryu, Yuyu, world of animality
and, 113
Kishimoto, Hideo, 162–63
Kobe earthquake, 231–32
kosen-rufu, 113, 175–76, 208,
219; benefit of thoroughly
exerting ourselves for, 134,
141, 183, 191, 222, 224, 273,
297–98; dedicated to, 23;
meaning of, 142; movement,
303; roles carried out to
advance, 214–15; strong sense
of responsibility for, 223
Kübler-Ross, Elisabeth, 5–6, 26,
234–36, 238–39
Kumarajiva, 302

leaders, and attitude of, 171;
human revolution and, 172
"Letter from Sado" (Nichiren),
113, 123
life, after death, 268, 272; Buddhist perspective of, 243; current, 270; eternity of, 27;
foundation of our own, 288–
89; inherent power of, 105;
leading vibrant, 222; quality
of, 230; true nature of, 18–19;
understanding the dignity of,
5–9; understanding the sanctity of, 107
life force, benefits of having
strong, based on faith, 272–73

state of life, 98; anecdote illustrating change in the, 114–16; benefits of revolutionizing one's, 114; function of one's, 141–42; way of transforming the, 117, 173, 210

study, Buddhist way of, 5

sufferings, causes of, 76; medicine to cure all, 11, 19

sutras, soul of all, 25

Tachikawa Culture center, 150

Taishaku, 152

Tamaki, Koshiro, 95

Tanaka, Shozo, 142

"temporary fusion of internal cause and relation," 154

"ten Dharma realms." *See* Dharma realms

ten factors, 61

Ten Worlds, 75–76, 98–99, 103–104, 197–98; existence of the, 108, 266–67; manifests, 204–05; studying the doctrine of the, 129; understanding the doctrine of the, 117

theoretical teachings, 35

"thirty four bodies," 216

three devotions, teaching of the, 136

three evil paths, 114, 119, 126

three fold world, 18

three good paths, 119

three poisons, 104, 109

three thousand realms in a single moment of life, actualizing the principle of, 223; core of, 62; "Life Span" chapter (Lotus Sutra), 24–25 and; principle of, 17–18, 29, 51, 58; of the

theoretical teachings, 60–62, 69–70; T'ien-t'ai and, 60

three truths, concept of, 206, 258

T'ien-t'ai: 15, 169; eternity of life, 25; truth of life and, 209; world of anger, 121; world of humanity, 137; world of hunger, 109

Toda, Josei: on absolute happiness, 80; Buddhahood, 185, 218; Buddhist practice of, 193; changing society, 114; on death, 22, 249; death of, 297; death of his daughter, 8–9; efforts for kosen-rufu, 298–99; encountering struggles and, 220–21; enlightenment of, 11, 17–18; "environmental effect," and, 260; faith, 10, 16–17, 280; Gohonzon and, 51; happiness and, 293; karma, 260–61; life, 267; life force effecting the deceased, 272–73; machine that sees the life of the dead, 268–69; Mystic Law and, 51; poem of, 288; power of daimoku, 272; premonition of death and, 299; remarks to a newspaper reporter, 48–49; respect for life, 107; Ten Worlds, 266; transition from death to life, 265–66; universe, 38; vow of, 273

Tolstoy, Leo, 91

transient Buddha, 34–35

true Buddha, 16, 34–35

true cause, 73

"True Aspect of All Phenomena, The" (Nichiren), 52

true entity of all phenomena,